Encounters with a Distant Land

Encounters with a Distant Land

Exploration and the Great Northwest

Edited by
Carlos A. Schwantes

With the Assistance of
Evelyne Stitt Pickett

University of Idaho Press
Moscow, Idaho
1994

Published by the University of Idaho Press, Moscow, Idaho 83844–1107

Printed in the United States of America

Design by Karla Fromm

98 97 96 95 94   5 4 3 2 1

Library of Congress Cataloging-in-Publication Data

Encounters with a distant land : exploration and the great Northwest /
edited by Carlos A. Schwantes ; with the assistance of Evelyne
Pickett.
p. cm.
Includes bibliographical references and index.
ISBN 0-89301-165-7
1. Northwest, Pacific—Discovery and exploration.   I. Schwantes,
Carlos A., 1945–   . II. Pickett, Evelyne.
F851.E48 1994
979.5—dc20
93-18483
CIP

Dedicated to William Kent Hackmann

Contents

     1778–1889 and After
     by Douglas Cole   149

11. A Taxonomy for Discovery
     by Martin Ridge   165

     Part II:
     Exploration History in Print and in the Field

12. Exploration History: A Publisher's Overview
     by Patricia Knapp   187

13. Keeping It in Perspective:
     Getting Exploration History into State and
     Local Journals
     by William L. Lang   194

14. On the Trail of Lewis and Clark Today
     by Robert Carriker   199

     Suggestions for Further Reading   207

     Contributors   217

     Index   219

Illustrations

Preface

Among various activities that the University of Idaho sponsored to celebrate its centennial year was a symposium devoted to "Exploration and the Great Northwest." The university's Centennial Committee generously supplied the funds necessary to bring to the Moscow campus a group of historians and editors who stood at the forefront of exploration history in North America. The Institute for Pacific Northwest Studies coordinated the three-day conference held August 3–5, 1988. From this congenial gathering came a heightened sense of camaraderie among the participants, new ideas for future research, and the essays that now constitute this volume. The University of Idaho Centennial Committee provided the financial support necessary to underwrite part of the cost of its publication.

It is appropriate that the University of Idaho should host a gathering that joined students of exploration history in a spirit of mutual inquiry and exchange. A primary reason for the territorial legislature's creation of the university in 1889 was to unite people by bridging the geographic and emotional chasm that then separated citizens living in northern and southern portions of Idaho. Few states have been as divided as Idaho, and the new university together with the new capitol building in Boise were seen as unifying symbols. The University of Idaho continues to serve the entire state, although its mission of bringing people together for scholarly inquiry today encompasses a much larger regional and national community, as the 1988 exploration symposium demonstrated.

The essays in this volume probe the topic of "Exploration and the Great Northwest" from a variety of perspectives. Some examine a single nation's involvement in exploration; others look at the role of Native Americans in the encounter experience, and at the artwork resulting from expeditions, and finally at the process of publishing exploration history. Much remains to be written about exploration of the Great Northwest, and it is my hope that the University of Idaho symposium and the publication of *Encounters with a Distant Land* will further that task.

In addition to those scholars who presented the papers included in this anthology, I wish to thank individual commentators and other formal participants in the conference: Susan Armitage, Judith Austin, Cort Conley, David Crowder, G. Thomas Edwards, William S. Greever, Keith Petersen, Jacqueline Peterson, William G. Robbins, Alfred Runte, Clark Spence, William R. Swagerty, and Thomas Vaughan. I am grateful to James Ronda for his helpful suggestions as I prepared the introductory essay. For the support they provided, I wish also to thank Roy Fluhrer, Centennial Coordinator; Thomas O. Bell, University of Idaho Provost; Richard Gibb, former president of the University of Idaho, and Elisabeth Zinser, the current president. I wish to note especially the role of Kent Hackmann, Chair of the Department of History, who has provided unflagging support for Pacific Northwest studies at the University of Idaho. It is fitting that this book should be dedicated to him.

Part I

The Exploration Experience

1. Exploring the Great Northwest: Personal Observations and an Overview

by Carlos A. Schwantes

I listened to the Columbia River. It spoke first in a whisper as water lapped steadily against the hull and then with a low steady hiss as the ship picked up speed after clearing the locks at John Day Dam. I rolled over in my bunk and stuffed an extra blanket between my back and the chilly outside wall of the cabin. Only two wool blankets and the ship's metal hull lay between me and the Great River of the West.

In this place the Columbia River forms the centerpiece of a stark landscape composed mainly of treeless hills and massive outcroppings of basalt. I knew that much without needing to leave the warmth of my bed and check outside through the skylight that doubled as a porthole. Since moving to the Pacific Northwest more than two decades ago, I had driven along both sides of the river many more times than I could remember and often captured the scenery on film. This time, in the pre-dawn hours of May 27, 1992, I wanted only to listen to the river. Suspended between deep sleep and full consciousness, I wanted to hear the soft splash of paddles dipped rhythmically by members of the Lewis and Clark expedition as they passed by in their dugout canoes. Would my imagination play a trick on me? I sincerely hoped so. I had been hired to give a nightly shipboard lecture about the expedition, and the more imagination I brought to my history, the better.

The previous evening I had stood on deck for an hour and watched as the lights of Umatilla, Oregon, drifted slowly past our port side and eventually disappeared astern. After clearing the locks at McNary Dam, Captain Don Johnson or one of his mates on the bridge eased the throttle forward slightly and the ship's twin diesels responded instantly to push us down river and steadily through the night. In the blackness and with no landmarks clearly visible, I easily imagined Lewis and Clark on these waters. Even if eight massive concrete and steel dams had now domesticated the once wild Columbia and Snake rivers on their journey from Lewiston to the sea, at least the stars overhead offered a timeless bridge across the nearly two centuries that separated our journeys. Was this the same night sky Lewis and Clark would have seen? I checked their journal entries. On this evening in May 1806 they were camped among the Nez Perce (near what is now Kamiah, Idaho) making final preparations for their return odyssey over the snow-covered Bitterroot Mountains. The two captains penned lengthy descriptions of their first encounter with a Columbian ground squirrel, but said nothing about the heavens. Perhaps to them the stars of a spring night were already a familiar presence.[1]

On my way to bed I noticed a small group of passengers huddled in the lounge to discuss the voyage or whatever else newcomers to the Columbia River deliberate around midnight. Some people find it hard to sleep their first night or two aboard ship. Many of the seventy passengers tonight are first-time visitors to the Pacific Northwest and have been attracted from homes as distant as Boston and Phoenix by the romance of spending a week following in the wake of Lewis and Clark. On

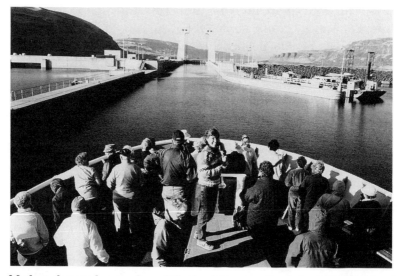

Modern-day explorers aboard the Sea Lion *approach the upriver side of John Day Dam in 1992. Sven-Olof Lindblad's Special Expeditions of New York City conducts several tours a year "In the Wake of Lewis and Clark" along the Columbia and Snake rivers. Author's collection.*

this particular voyage from Lewiston to the sea they would receive far more than had been advertised in their promotional brochures—in the waters near Astoria they would also rendezvous with memories of Robert Gray and George Vancouver, two captains who sailed this way exactly 200 years ago.

How much had the lower Columbia River changed since Vancouver dispatched Lieutenant William Broughton to explore and map its bays and estuaries in 1792? Like the paying passengers from distant regions, I wanted to answer such questions for myself. I knew from experience that the more conscientious of my fellow voyagers would study various maps to compare then and now, would ask many questions, and, upon encountering some prominent landmark, like Beacon Rock looming high in the mist near Bonneville Dam, would hurry to the ship's library to read what Lewis and Clark wrote about it in 1805 or 1806. I was the teacher, but I was also a student. Together we would explore Pacific Northwest history from a perspective that books alone could not provide.

Over the years I've grown fond of the hands-on approach to the past and would gladly describe myself as a field historian— one who pursues his craft with equal facility in archives or while tramping through the woods with a camera and notebook. I understand now why a high school vocational aptitude test predicted a career for me in forestry. Certainly I felt at ease in the woods on the morning of August 6, 1992, when, with camera in hand, I waited for dawn to backlight the crest of the Bitterroot divide between Idaho and Montana. That was the best time to see what Lewis and Clark saw without being distracted by the unsightly patches of clear-cut forest land below. Accompanying me on the ridge top, although most of them were still asleep in their tents, were two dozen students from the University of Idaho taking a week to retrace the footsteps of early explorers in the mountains above the Lochsa and Clearwater rivers. Perhaps as children some of these students had been intrigued by the brown and white signs posted along the federal highway below to mark the route of Lewis and Clark; perhaps some had been hooked by tales of discovery and exploration in the mandatory fourth-grade class in Idaho history. In much the same way, I hoped to use the study of Lewis and

Clark to interest them in new approaches to the larger history of the Pacific Northwest.

I myself did not grow up with exploration history. Most of what I recall from grade school history classes back in Indiana are tales of pioneers hacking homesteads out of the woods and building corduroy roads across a marshy landscape. In its own way it was fascinating history, but I liked best the high adventure of John Hunt Morgan's Confederate raiders slipping across the Ohio River in 1863 and dashing through the hill country of southern Indiana. My introduction to exploration history came later from Lewis and Clark interpretive signs posted along the roads of Montana and Idaho as I drove west for the first time in 1969. Could it be, I sometimes wonder, that exploration history for this region has the same romantic and enduring appeal that Civil War history has back east? Instead of following the armies of Blue and Gray, we retrace (if only in our minds) the wakes of George Vancouver or Robert Gray. Perhaps the experience of seeing for ourselves what Lewis and Clark encountered in the Pacific Northwest has the same popular appeal as studying battlefield tactics firsthand at Gettysburg or Vicksburg or Shiloh.

In the Pacific Northwest, many a locality recalls the importance of explorers, either by the names they gave a place or by the places later named for them. On Puget Sound are dozens of places named by Vancouver. He also named several prominent peaks in the Cascade Range: Mount Baker honors Lt. Joseph Baker, the first Englishman to sight the mountain, and Mount Rainier immortalizes British Admiral Peter Rainier. Probably no explorers are honored more than Lewis and Clark, from the city names of Lewiston, Idaho, and Clarkston, Washington, to several high schools, restaurants, and even used car lots.

For the Pacific Northwest, exploration history serves not only to affirm regional identity but was also long ago coined into a commercial commodity. The region's first world's fair was the Lewis and Clark Exposition held in Portland, Oregon, in 1905.[2] In the early twentieth century both the Northern Pacific and the Great Northern railroads lured tourists to the northern-tier states by inviting them to follow where famous explorers had gone before. As one railroad publicist phrased it in a mid-1920s promotional brochure:

To the California visitor in search of a new variety of scenery and a more interesting and diversified route for the return trip from the land of sunshine and flowers, we offer the 'Great Northern Way,' through America's real Adventure Land—on the world-famed highway of steel which James J. Hill constructed in regions where the bold Verendryes, the fearless David. Thompson and our own Immortals, Lewis and Clark, had explored but a few generations before.[3]

As recently as 1992 at least two separate companies offered exploration history cruises of the Columbia River at a cost of approximately $2,000 per person.

As important as exploration history is to the Pacific Northwest, it must be emphasized in any modern account of the subject that in the late 1700s and early 1800s the unknown land destined to become the Pacific Northwest was unknown only to Euro-American newcomers. Native Americans had long called the region home. As Robin Fisher emphasizes in his 1992 study of Vancouver's voyage, "In one sense the word 'discovery' was a misnomer, since the coast was not unknown to those who were already there. In another sense it was appropriate, because his would be a voyage of mutual discovery, as the coast became a line for the meeting of cultures."[4]

The story of discovery and exploration includes geographical and intellectual adventure as well as economic exploitation and empire building, and it remains a complex mix of human bravery, remarkable endurance, cultural chauvinism, and naiveté. Encounters that enriched the intellectual and economic life of one culture might simultaneously cause, if sometimes only unintentionally, the debasement of another. Even the names the newcomers gave to places they "discovered" were in a way acts of appropriation. What Vancouver called Mount Baker, some of the first inhabitants called Koma Kulshan, which for the Nooksaks meant white, steep mountain. Even when explorers attempted to preserve what they understood to be Native American names, they were not always successful. Lewis and Clark retained the Nez Perce name Kooskooske, but those who followed them later called it the Clearwater River.

Be forewarned that the Pacific Northwest is a slippery description for a region that has no commonly agreed upon boundaries. Most often the name is applied to the combined states of Oregon, Washington, and Idaho, as is the case here, and it is their exploration history that is the primary focus of *Encounters with a Distant Land.* However, because some of these essays also deal with Alaska and British Columbia, I have occasionally resorted to an even more elastic term, the Great Northwest. That designation was long popular with regional boosters, who usually emphasized the word Great in their spread-eagle style of oratory, but today it is also a convenient label for the quadrant of North America comprising Alaska, British Columbia, Alberta, Yukon Territory, Washington, Oregon, Idaho, and Montana. Together they encompass 1.8 million square miles, an area twice the size of the United States east of the Mississippi River. As large as it is, the Great Northwest long remained a mystery to Euro-Americans. For them it was a remote part of the globe that required more than a century and a half of discovery and systematic exploration to know in detail. In fact, the heart of Washington's Olympic Peninsula, enclosed by snow-capped mountains clearly visible from Seattle across Puget Sound, was not explored until 1890, some thirty years after David Livingstone had become the first Euro-American explorer to cross sub-Saharan Africa.[5]

Exploration of the Great Northwest involved several nations, but theirs was neither a coordinated nor a sustained effort. It involved both officially sanctioned military expeditions and accidental discoveries by merchant adventurers and mountain men in pursuit of fur wealth. Some explorers collected scientific data and published elaborate accounts of their activities, while the typical mountain man preserved in his head the results of firsthand encounters with the land or knowledge gleaned from Native American informants. In this way mountain men served as conduits of information for explorers who followed. Whether or not they were fully conscious of it, fur traders, and later the missionaries and overland trail pioneers, also contributed to discovery and exploration of the Great Northwest.

During some years the process was intense and highly competitive; at other times it was halfhearted and desultory. For the three states of the Pacific Northwest, discovery and exploration occurred mainly during three different eras: the maritime phase, which lasted from the 1770s until the early 1800s; the interior phase, which lasted from the 1790s through the 1820s; and finally what William Goetzmann has aptly labeled the Great Reconnaissance, from the 1840s through the 1860s.

During the maritime phase a generation of seafarers penetrated the fog of geographic ignorance and misconception that had previously shrouded the North Pacific Coast from outsiders. This was the world's last temperate zone coastline to yield its secrets to Euro-Americans. Their voyages provided cartographers with detailed information on the coasts of Oregon, Washington, British Columbia, the lower Columbia River, the Strait of Juan de Fuca, and Puget Sound. During these same years, seaborne traders from several nations developed a profitable commerce in the region's furs and skins.

The voyage of Captain James Cook to the Northwest coast offers a convenient promontory from which to survey the maritime phase of discovery and exploration. Only days after the rebellious colonists in America signed their Declaration of Independence in Philadelphia in July 1776, Cook set sail from England on a voyage that took him to the waters of the North Pacific two years later. Though he failed to find the fabled Northwest Passage, his official objective, Cook's expedition added new lands to the British Empire and new knowledge about the North Pacific coast. Cook lost his life in the Hawaiian Islands, but when the first account of his expedition was published in 1781 it gave the North Pacific region for the first time a clearly defined niche in European imperial and commercial systems. Cook's voyage initiated the first *sustained* contacts between Europe and the maritime regions of future Oregon, Washington, and British Columbia.

Cook, it must be emphasized, was not the first European explorer in the Great Northwest, but more than anything else it was news from his expedition that set in motion a rush to exploit the fur wealth of the North Pacific. The region would never be the same. Joining the race to learn more about and profit from the lands and waters of the North Pacific were Russia, Spain, France, and the newly formed United States. From Siberia and Alaska, Russians made their way south, even as Spaniards probed north from their base in Mexico.

In the search for furs, the Russians had established a modest presence in the far eastern reaches of Asia as early as the 1640s, but Russian interest intensified after Catherine I dispatched Vitus Bering on an elaborate and ambitious assignment to the North Pacific. The main body of his five-hundred-person expedition—soldiers, surveyors, interpreters, painters, and secretaries, in addition to a large library of scientific books—departed St. Petersburg in 1733 and made its way slowly across Siberia to the Pacific. After constructing two ships, the Russians explored along the coast of Alaska in 1741. Misfortune overtook Bering, marooning him on a cold, forbidding island where he and many crewmen perished. Aleksei Chirikov, commander of the expedition's other ship, fared better. He was among the survivors who straggled back to Saint Petersburg, the last of them arriving only in 1749, sixteen years after they first set out. Although many lives were lost, Bering's expedition established that it was possible to travel from Asia to North America by water and that the North Pacific region was rich in furs. A profitable commerce might be developed there.

During the next fifty years other Russians followed in the wake of Bering and Chirikov, expanding the trade in sea otter and other furs. Outstanding among them was Aleksandr Baranov, a businessman who headed the Russian-American Company, founded in 1799, and made it a major economic force in the North Pacific. His headquarters at New Archangel (Sitka) was among the first nonnative communities in the region. Under Baranov, the Russian company established a presence as far south as Fort Ross (short for Russia) near Cape Mendocino north of San Francisco.

Although Russian activity was shrouded in secrecy, including the extent of their fur trade, their expansion into the North Pacific did not go unnoticed in other capitals of Europe. When Russian explorers and traders started probing south through the seas off Siberia and Alaska, Spain cast a concerned look up the coast from her domain in Mexico. Spain undertook land and sea expeditions northward into California in 1769 and 1770 and established permanent settlements there. Juan Pérez led an expedition in 1774 that sailed slightly north of the Queen Charlotte Islands before scurvy forced it to turn back.

On the return voyage, the Spanish anchored in the vicinity of Vancouver Island's Nootka Sound, which Pérez called San Lorenzo. Twenty-one canoes carrying nearly 150 Nootka villagers made contact with the Spaniards and exchanged gifts. Some bolder Indians boarded the *Santiago* and took silver spoons, which Cook's expedition noted four years later. The Spaniards studied the natural setting and its inhabitants, but Pérez failed to make any charts or take formal possession of the region. The following year a Spanish expedition under the command of Juan Francisco de la Bodega y Quadra sailed up the Pacific coast and reached 58° north before scurvy forced it to retreat. An associate, Bruno de Hezeta (or Heceta), sighted the entrance to the Columbia River on his return voyage, but because he hesitated to cross the treacherous bar that blocked the Columbia's mouth, credit for the discovery goes to the American Robert Gray, who, in 1792, sailed a short distance upriver.

In 1776, the year that James Cook began his lengthy voyage to the North Pacific, the Spanish established the first permanent Euro-American settlement on San Francisco Bay. Another major Spanish expedition followed in 1779 under the command of Ignacio de Arteaga. It probed as far north as 59°52′, where Mount Saint Elias loomed in the distance. At this point, which Bering sighted from a different direction in 1741, the empires of Russia and Spain made tentative contact. Arteaga's ships continued slightly farther north before turning south, adding on paper a large area to the far-flung Spanish empire.

But as Russians pushed south and Spaniards north, the British under Cook wedged themselves between the two expanding empires at Nootka, creating the potential for a major international clash. The British intrusion intensified interest in profiting from the region's furs, or "soft gold" as some have labeled them. Cook's men understood that the Russians had turned a profit in furs, but they did not realize the full economic potential of the trade until they reached Canton, where they sold twenty worse-for-wear animal skins for an exorbitant price even by today's standards. And the Chinese besieged Cook's men for still more. The object of their attention was the lustrous pelt of the sea otter, a rich, jet-black fur with a glossy surface and shimmery silvery undertones.

Among the world's business enterprises in the early nineteenth century, few were more important than the fur trade. The hat-making industry alone used a hundred thousand beaver pelts each year to supply fine headgear to European aristocrats and a rising middle class. Fur was the commodity that pitted Euro-Americans against one another in a spirited commercial rivalry and motivated early discovery and exploration.

As seafarers exploited the natural resources of North Pacific waters in the 1780s and 1790s, they continued to explore its islands, bays, and inlets. Their voyages of discovery through the Strait of Juan de Fuca provide a vivid illustration of the process of knowledge accumulation. It is ironic that the man who gave his name to that body of water did so by a simple feat: telling what most authorities regard as a big lie. A Greek named Apostolos Valerianos, commonly called Juan de Fuca, claimed to have made a voyage for Spain in 1592 that took him north from Mexico along the Pacific coast to a point between forty-seven and forty-eight degrees latitude. In a region he described as being rich in gold, silver, and pearls, he discovered the Strait of Anian, the Spanish designation for the fabled Northwest Passage. For twenty days he sailed through the strait, he said; reached the North Atlantic; and then backtracked to Mexico. By the early 1600s the curious tale had found its way from the barrooms of Europe into histories and maps of the North Pacific.

On his northern voyage, James Cook looked in vain for de Fuca's fabled strait and acidly commented, "We saw nothing like it, nor is there the least possibility that ever any such thing existed."[6] In the fog, he missed seeing the body of water that separates Vancouver Island and the Olympic Peninsula, a twenty-mile wide strait opening remarkably near where de Fuca claimed to have crossed the continent. An Englishman, Captain Charles Barkley, made the first indisputable European discovery of the Strait of Juan de Fuca in 1787. He made no attempt to penetrate its hundred-mile length, but a year later John Meares sent in a company of explorers, who he later claimed took possession of its shores for Great Britain. Further British and Spanish explorations followed, until in 1792 Captain George Vancouver sailed through the strait and around the island that today bears his name. For two months his men also explored the great inland sea that Vancouver named after Peter Puget. To the principal bays, inlets, and other physical features, he assigned names that in many cases still identify them.

Often the exploratory activity of one nation spurred that of its rivals. When Alejandro Malaspina, a Spanish naval officer, sought imperial approval for a round-the-world scientific expedition, he cited the achievements of British and French explorers and urged Spain to do likewise. Receiving all necessary official assistance, the Malaspina expedition departed Spain for the New World in 1789 and after two years reached the waters off Alaska's Yakutat Bay. The Spaniards remained among the Tlingit for nine days, compiling extensive written and visual records and collecting artifacts. The expedition continued its scientific activities for two weeks at Nootka and then cruised south along the coasts of Washington and Oregon, carefully delineating various headlands.

Ethnographic records were vital to the scientific part of the expedition, but the Spaniards also made hydrographic and oceanic charts to aid commercial navigation in these remote waters, and they assessed the political intent of other nations in the North Pacific. The discovery of the fabled Strait of Anian, which persistent Spaniards believed might yet be found, and the strengthening of Spain's claim to exclusive sovereignty in the Pacific Northwest and the entire Pacific Ocean were two added objects of the Malaspina expedition. In that regard the mission failed, but it provided the world with a wealth of North Pacific Coast artifacts and observations of native lifestyles.

The last of the great eighteenth-century discoveries along the Pacific coast of Oregon and Washington was made by an American, Captain Robert Gray, whose ship, the *Columbia,* became the first United States vessel to circumnavigate the globe when it returned to Boston harbor in 1790. A swarm of American fur traders and whalers followed Gray's lead, making the long voyage from New England ports, rounding Cape Horn, and fanning out into all parts of the Pacific.

Gray was a trader who came late to the North Pacific. Like all latecomers to any frontier, he found the field of opportunity considerably narrowed. Undiscouraged, he returned to the North Pacific in 1791 to trade for pelts. In the process, Gray discovered the harbor on the coast of Washington that bears his name and, in May 1792, the majestic river he named for his ship: Columbia's River, a spelling soon modified to the more familiar form. Although Gray's men explored only thirty or thirty-five miles upstream, they laid the foundations for a later United States claim to the area.

The matter of conflicting imperial claims finally led to an international incident in 1789 known as the Nootka Sound Controversy. In that year the Russians were a well-established presence in the North Pacific; Spain laid claim to Nootka and the entire western coast of North America; Great Britain challenged that notion; and the United States, seeking new markets to replace those lost by the separation from Great Britain, showed increased interest in the Pacific fur trade. (A French scientific expedition under Jean de Galaup, Count La Pérouse, had also explored the area between 1786 and 1788, but that effort ended disastrously with only one man surviving. This tragedy, coupled with the outbreak of the French Revolution a short time later, discouraged follow-up voyages. In short, despite their vastness, the North Pacific waters had become too small to accommodate the territorial and economic ambitions of rival nations. Fortunately, Spain and Britain backed away from war over Nootka, and during the years from 1790 to 1825 the various national rivals resolved their differences peaceably through treaty negotiations.

The peak years of the maritime fur trade lasted from the 1790s through the 1820s, and during that time the Americans edged out the British. Over-trapping took such a toll on profits that, by the first decade of the nineteenth century, the future clearly belonged to fur empires spanning the continent by land. There would be no more surprise discoveries of major consequence on the North Pacific Coast after the 1790s, but the unknown lands of the interior were another matter. No Euro-American knew what lay east of the Cascade Mountains, nor did they know the course of the Columbia River. Here were more curiosities, more possibilities for commerce, and more lands to claim.

In 1793, shortly after Vancouver undertook to dispel the last wisps of mystery surrounding Juan de Fuca's Northwest Passage, Alexander Mackenzie and a party of fur traders from the opposite side of North America crossed the Continental Divide and approached the very waters Vancouver was mapping. Mackenzie's report on various exploratory expeditions for the North West Company of Montreal was published in 1801 and bolstered British claims to the region. This report and related maps in turn spurred the Americans Meriwether Lewis and William Clark, whose military expedition reached the Pacific coast in 1805 and added a new dimension to the geopolitical contest evolving in that far region. Well before they returned to the East, their first year's specimens and writings had spurred fur merchants to extend their reach into new corners of the far Northwest.

Among the fur traders and trappers exploring the Pacific Northwest about the same time as Lewis and Clark was David Thompson. Beginning in 1807 he undertook the first of several journeys that led him through the labyrinth of mountains and valleys of the upper reaches of the Columbia River system in British Columbia, Idaho, and Montana. A talented surveyor, mapmaker, and trader for the North West Company of Montreal, Thompson is remembered for his explorations and for the several important fur trading posts he established, including Kullyspell House in northern Idaho in 1809.

Even as Thompson and his fellow Nor'westers extended the reach of Montreal's fur merchants, and the British empire, the first American traders probed the Rocky Mountains from another direction. When Lewis and Clark neared the Mandan villages on their return journey to Saint Louis, they released Private John Colter to head west in search of beaver. His wanderings took him to the upper Yellowstone country and the Teton Valley of Idaho. Colter and another expedition member, George Drouillard, both eventually ended up as employees of the merchant and trader Manuel Lisa. Excited by information gathered by Lewis and Clark, Lisa dispatched parties of traders up the Missouri River to channel the fur wealth of the new land through his Saint Louis-based enterprise. After they broke camp in the spring of 1811 and fanned out through the Rocky Mountain country, one of the parties met another group of

American traders and trappers heading west. These were the Astorians.

John Jacob Astor was a German-born businessman who dreamed of making a fortune in the fur trade of the far Northwest. Encouraged by reports of the region's natural wealth, he laid plans for a vast new business empire. From a post he proposed to build near the mouth of the Columbia River, his traders and trappers would fan out across the Northwest to collect the furs they would ship to markets in China. To turn his dream into reality Astor dispatched two expeditions, one by land and another by sea, to the North Pacific Coast. Heading the overland party was Astor's field marshal, Wilson Price Hunt, a twenty-seven-year-old Saint Louis merchant woefully inexperienced for an undertaking of this complexity. Assisting him was Donald Mackenzie, formerly of the rival North West Company. The Hunt party departed Saint Louis in October 1810, a month after the seafaring Astorians left New York. Seeking to reconnoiter an overland route and locate sites for a string of trading posts extending from the Missouri to the Columbia rivers, members of the Hunt party—consisting of a small group of company officials and about fifty employees—were plagued by errors of judgment, troubled relations with Indians, and scheming rivals. The Astorians occasionally meandered needlessly and endured great hunger, thirst, sickness, and death crossing rugged and barren expanses of wilderness.

In the contest for survival in the Pacific Northwest, the Astorians waged a heroic but ultimately futile struggle. In October 1813, in the midst of the War of 1812, they sold out under duress to their Canadian rivals, the North West Company of Montreal. The Nor'westers were absorbed in turn in 1821 by the Hudson's Bay Company, an old and powerful British fur enterprise headquartered in London.

The Hudson's Bay Company had confined its operations mainly to north-central Canada until the merger, but it became a transcontinental giant when it acquired the seven Pacific Northwest posts of its erstwhile Montreal rival. Among these was Fort Nez Perce, located near the confluence of the Snake and Columbia rivers and a main jumping-off point for fur brigades into the Snake River country of southern Idaho since

1818. The Hudson's Bay Company continued the Snake brigades until the early 1830s and in the process learned more about the geography of the interior Northwest.

After acquiring the American and Canadian interests, the British had the resources of the Pacific Northwest pretty much to themselves until the 1830s. It was during that decade that Captain Benjamin Louis Eulalie de Bonneville, a French-born officer in the United States Army, took a leave of absence in 1831 ostensibly to enter the fur trade of the West. Granted a two-year separation, Bonneville actually spent the next five years probing the West. On one of these trips, he traced a route from western Missouri to Idaho's rugged Salmon River country, where he established winter quarters in 1832. The next spring the Bonneville party retreated to the annual fur traders' rendezvous at the Green River (in present Wyoming), then headed west again across the Snake River plain, eventually reaching Fort Walla Walla and the Columbia Valley in 1834. It was Bonneville who took the first wagons through South Pass, gateway to the West on the later Oregon Trail. Many historians now believe he was actually spying out the promised land, searching for a route across the Rocky Mountains to California, but the proof is elusive. Publication in 1837 of Washington Irving's *The Adventures of Captain Bonneville* played a major role in renewing American interest in the Pacific Northwest, and this in turn increased the influence of influential expansionists on Capitol Hill, like Senator Thomas Hart Benton of Missouri.

The United States government reentered the process in a more visible way in the late 1830s and early 1840s when it launched what were ostensibly the first official exploratory expeditions to the Northwest since Lewis and Clark. Soon a new generation of maps, descriptive documents, and artwork provided federal officials and a curious public with more precise images of the region than ever before. These were the years of the Great Reconnaissance. Federal exploration proceeded from two different directions: from the West, members of the United States Exploring Expedition led by Lieutenant Charles Wilkes made detailed surveys of both maritime and inland portions of Oregon and Washington in 1841. From the East came the Army engineers under the leadership of John C. Frémont.

Frémont was a new type of explorer—a member of the United States Army's Corps of Topographical Engineers, established in 1838. Most personnel in this elite unit (though not Frémont himself) were West Point graduates trained in such skills as engineering and map-making. They brought a new degree of sophistication to the exploration of the West. The Army commissioned Frémont to map and survey the trail to Oregon. He and thirty-nine men set out from Independence, Missouri, in May 1843 on a "secret" mission to Oregon. The party pushed past the British outpost of Fort Hall (near the present city of Pocatello, Idaho), across the Snake River plain, and west along the Columbia River.

Frémont was the first explorer to recognize and name the Great Basin that encompassed parts of southern Idaho, Utah, and Nevada. His cartographer, Charles Preuss, completed a detailed map of the Oregon Trail. The Preuss map was a veritable gold mine for would-be emigrants, giving precise distances and information on landmarks, river crossings, and Indian tribes. When Frémont presented his report to Congress it created a sensation and was widely printed and distributed. It helped that Frémont was married to Jessie Benton, daughter of the expansion-minded Senator Thomas Hart Benton.

Perhaps the most impressive army reconnaissance venture in the West was launched in 1853 when Congress approved funding for the Topographical Corps to conduct a series of explorations in search of the best route for a railroad to the Pacific Ocean. Leader of the northern survey was Isaac I. Stevens, the new governor of Washington Territory. Assisting him in the Cascade Range was George B. McClellan, the future Civil War general. The men of the Stevens' survey reconnoitered several possible railroad routes across the future northern tier states. John Mullan, a young topographical engineer from West Point and a member of the Stevens party, remained in the field to oversee the work of surveying and building a military road across the northern Rocky Mountains in the late 1850s and early 1860s. Concluding the major federal surveys that explored remote portions of the northern Rocky Mountain country were those of Clarence King along the 40th Parallel (1867–72) and Ferdinand V. Hayden's U.S. Geological Survey of the Territories (1869–79).

Heading up the Columbia River in the fall of 1992, modern-day explorers aboard the Sea Lion *follow the* Defiance *and two barges through the busy locks of historic Bonneville Dam. Author's collection.*

The Great Reconnaissance left a rich scientific and artistic legacy. Accompanying the Stevens survey were the artists Gustav Sohon and John Mix Stanley, who produced an outstanding series of two- and three-color chromolithographs. When the railroad surveys were completed, the resulting maps, descriptive observations, and artwork were compiled into thirteen volumes that represented the most comprehensive body of information about the West at that time. Accompanying the King survey was the pioneer photographer Timothy O'Sullivan, who made a side trip to Idaho's Shoshone Falls in 1868 and recorded an early film view of the natural wonder. Another pioneer photographer, William Henry Jackson, accompanied the Hayden survey and captured early images of the interior west.[7]

As would be expected, all of the official explorers came to the far Northwest from somewhere else. For them the experience was truly an encounter with a distant land. For readers today, exploration of the early Northwest is still an encounter with a distant land, although we are separated from it mainly by time and not geography. It is still possible to observe many of the same physical features that attracted the attention of explorers nearly two centuries ago, and by means of the essays that follow, we can also diminish the chronological distance that separates our past from present.

―――――

Much of the exploration history of the Great Northwest is preserved in diaries, journals, and official reports. Lewis and Clark were, in the words of the late Donald Jackson, the "writingest" of all explorers; and preparing a superb new edition of their voluminous records is Gary Moulton, who shares some of his insights in one of the following essays. Yet Lewis and Clark, unlike some of the other explorers, took no artist on their long odyssey, and that is history's loss. Artists who accompanied various maritime explorers left a rich visual legacy, and Iris Engstrand's essay provides several examples from Spanish archives. The legacy of the Pacific Railroad Survey of the 1850s is the massive multi-volume report to Congress (1854–59) which contains several outstanding chromolithographs by expedition

At the confluence of the Snake and Palouse rivers, near where Lewis and Clark camped in 1805, Special Expeditions tour members leave the Sea Lion *in rubber rafts to explore the scenic canyon below Washington's Palouse Falls in 1992. For the many modern voyageurs who come from outside the Pacific Northwest, the trip remains a truly wondrous encounter with a distant land. Author's collection.*

artists like Sohon and Stanley, both of whom accompanied the Stevens survey. Yet, as David Nicandri's portfolio reveals, not all of the art treasures from the expedition were published in the original volumes.

No contemporary historian has done more to define the field of western exploration scholarship, especially its relationship to intellectual history, than William Goetzmann, who served as keynote speaker for the "Exploration and the Great Northwest" conference. His essay in this volume provides an interpretive framework for this large subject. Also grappling with the "big picture" is Martin Ridge, who offers a typology of discovery.

A key purpose of the symposium was to highlight the rich variety of approaches that scholars are currently taking to western exploration history. Providing a superb example of the historiographical work currently being done is Stephen Haycox, whose essay focuses on Russian exploration in Alaska and

California. James Ronda uses the biography of Peter Pond to examine how Euro-Americans assembled the pieces of a geographical puzzle in the far Northwest. This essay forces readers to reexamine the background of Alexander Mackenzie's western explorations and later those of Lewis and Clark. Richard Maxwell Brown examines exploration and the Chinook Jargon, the hybrid language used by Native Americans of maritime Oregon and Washington to facilitate trade. Douglas Cole's approach to the subject combines history and anthropology, while Mary Lee Spence uses collective biography to provide a social portrait of the personnel associated with Frémont's five major expeditions. Her essay also highlights the continuing importance of French Canadians and Franco-Americans as a primary source of labor in the northern West during the first half of the nineteenth century.

Two essays deal with the task of publishing exploration history, a challenge that is far more difficult than it may first appear. Providing perspective from the desk of a journal editor is William Lang, former editor of *Montana, the Magazine of Western History,* one of two scholarly publications sponsored by the Western History Association. The difficulty of publishing a new edition of the Lewis and Clark journals is the subject of an essay by Patricia Knapp, former acquisitions editor of the University of Nebraska Press.

One modern application of exploration history is the subject of Robert Carriker's essay. A professor of history at Gonzaga University, he is also a field historian after my own heart, though he may not feel completely at ease with that term. In fact, I followed in Carriker's footsteps, and those of historian Stephen Dow Beckham of Portland's Lewis and Clark College, when I developed my own field-based Lewis and Clark course in the Bitterroot Mountains.

Encounters with a Distant Land concludes with a list of suggestions for further reading. The compilation is by no means exhaustive, yet for readers new to the subject it offers a convenient way to pursue numerous topics in greater detail. A primary goal of this anthology, after all, is to encourage various forms of personal exploration of the region's past.

Chapter 1 Notes

1. Gary E. Moulton, ed., *The Journals of the Lewis & Clark Expedition*, vol. 7 (Lincoln: University of Nebraska Press, 1991), 290–97.

2. Carl Abbott, *The Great Extravaganza: Portland and the Lewis and Clark Exposition* (Portland: Oregon Historical Society, 1981).

3. *From California through Adventure Land* (St. Paul: Great Northern Railway, ca. 1926).

4. Robin Fisher, *Vancouver's Voyage: Charting the Northwest Coast* (Seattle: University of Washington Press, 1992), 4

5. Richard A. Van Orman, *The Explorers: Nineteenth-Century Expeditions in Africa and the American West* (Albuquerque: University of New Mexico Press, 1984).

6. J. C. Beaglehole, *The Life of Captain James Cook* (Stanford: Stanford University Press, 1974), 582.

7. Portions of this overview are derived from Carlos A. Schwantes, *The Pacific Northwest: An Interpretive History* (Lincoln: University of Nebraska Press, 1989). Individual book and article titles are cited in Suggestions for Further Reading at the end of this volume. I am especially indebted to James P. Ronda's masterful new summary, *The Exploration of North America* (Washington, D.C.: American Historical Association, 1992).

2. Western Exploration and Its Impact*

by William H. Goetzmann

I. A "Moral Drama"

When we speak of exploration by Euro-Americans we must speak first in terms of a *moral drama*[1] that had begun to unfold since the days of Columbus and, a bit later, with the debates between Father Bartolomé de Las Casas and Juan Gines de Sepulveda at Valladolid, Spain, in 1550–51 over the human status of the Native American or "Indians," as they were mistakenly called. That sense of moral drama, with its overtones of forcible conquest of regions already settled by complex societies, has now become all too apparent to students of western, as well as American, history as a whole. Dr. Samuel Johnson perhaps put the question most succinctly. He declared, according to Boswell: "I do not much wish well to discovery [sic] for I am always afraid that they will end in conquest and robbery."[2]

Interestingly enough, he made that statement in the eighteenth century, the first of two centuries, the eighteenth and the nineteenth, that formed what I have elsewhere called "The Second Great Age of Discovery"[3]—the age in which the United States was born and spread over the North American continent on what it considered a divinely inspired mission to spread enlightened republican and Christian civilization around the globe, or "Manifest Destiny," as the Jacksonian editor J. L. O'Sullivan called it. And it *was* a religious mission in the eyes of the Euro-Americans. It spread the gospel of Christianity, the benefits of republican democracy, and those of modern science, which, as it revealed Nature, revealed the thoughts of the

---

* Parts of this essay are derived from my introductory essay in John Logan Allen, ed., *The Exploration of North America* (tentative title), to be published by the University of Nebraska Press. I am grateful for permission to use this material which actually originated as a lecture at the University of Idaho symposium "Exploration and the Great Northwest."

Creator.[4] Thus, globe-encircling scientific exploration could reveal very nearly the "mind of God." Some thought it was a "great pity" that the indigenous inhabitants of the places discovered, including the American West, did not understand these "Divine" blessings from western civilization.

As far as the United States and western America are concerned, historians and cultural critics from James Fenimore Cooper to Native American spokesmen like Vine Deloria have not only outlined the fact of discovery and exploration as Moral Drama, they have seen it as a continuing excursion into what Joseph Conrad called "the horror, the horror" in *Heart of Darkness*.[5] Alfred Crosby, in *The Columbian Exchange*, has seen it as not only human, but as biological imperialism, and he has wrestled with the question of who gave whom syphilis first—the Europeans to New World peoples or the New World peoples to the Europeans.[6] (The French explorer, Bougainville, blamed it on the fun-loving Tahitians, who cavorted with his sex-starved sailors in 1769![7]) Disease has ranked high as a horror in the history of exploration. Some suggest that as many as ten million Native Americans were killed by European diseases.[8] One commentator has even referred to the Euro-peopling of North America as a "Holocaust"[9] (a term that soon may be tragically debased by overuse). William Faulkner saw *both* Native and white Americans as guilty. Chief Doom (Issetibbeha) sold land that he did not and could not own to the white man, who also could not own it.[10] A more recent book has chronicled the *many* sins of *The Legacy of Conquest*—sins that are still with us and that desperately need to be expiated.[11] (Even Euro-American evacuation from the North American continent seems not out of the question as an option to the modern western historian.) Still another contemporary western historian has put the case of our national creation myth even more bluntly in an article entitled, "Explorers, Mountain Men and Other Varmints."[12]

George Catlin railed against "the juggernaut of civilization" plainly enough in his treatises on the American Indian, and in terms of today's "discourse" we cannot be quite sure that James Fenimore Cooper even *liked* his own archetypal creation, Leatherstocking.[13] Was Natty Bumppo really for Cooper a primitive, lower-class outcast roaming the wilds of nature (the

Devil's Den, it was once called),[14] or the harbinger of that evil
juggernaut of crude bourgeois civilization that Jefferson called
yeoman? The reason anybody in his or her right mind reads
Cooper today is *because* his Leatherstocking represents the
Euro-American dilemma vis-à-vis nature and nurture that lies
at the center of the history of the American civilization that followed on the paths of the explorers.[15]

John Gast, commissioned to make this illustration by George
A. Crofutt for his best-selling tourist guidebook, insouciantly
visualized the march of empire in his popular picture of 1872,
Westward Ho. Is this the sweet goddess of liberty and civilized
progress? Or is she the camp follower of ruthless conquest?
Note that the retreating parties are not exactly happy. This
conquest was made possible not only by disease, but also by science and technology and a belief in *imperialism* and *capitalism*
(forms of political and economic ownership), not to mention
aristocratic tourism that swept over the globe during the Second Great Age of Discovery. It was in this age that the American
colonies revolted from England, Captain Cook discovered and
took possession of South Seas paradises, Adam Smith published

John Gast, Westward Ho (American Progress), *1872. Courtesy Library
of Congress.*

that free-trade, capitalist bible *The Wealth of Nations*, and George A. Crofutt issued his guides for the tourist-explorer.

Having now outlined some of the negative legacies of exploration and discovery—or conquest—I should like to focus on what exploration and discovery did *to* and for *Euro-Americans*, rather than *to* Native American culture.

II. Cultures, Civilizations, and Exploration

First, let us begin with the somewhat novel concepts of *culture* and *civilization*. The one suffered continuing and massive dislocations, fractures, and turmoils during the Second Great Age of Discovery, while the other came to flower in the United States by the mid-twentieth century.

If one considers culture a construct of societal beliefs, rules, and accustomed ways of doing things, a social grid that *screens out* unwanted data (or habits) and only grudgingly admits new data that are deemed useful in traditional context, then one gets a picture of the *impact* of hundreds and hundreds of exploring expeditions and literally millions of bits of data bombarding existing Euro-American culture. Walter Webb called the result a "400-year boom."[16] Rather than just creating a dubious economic boom, both the First and Second Ages of Discovery *shattered* European, as well as Native American, philosophical structures erected to control cultural information. Continuous and relentless change in the perceptions of reality, values, and common utility resulted, culminating in the emergence of, among other things, modern science, an activity that sees reality merely as *process* and not as amenable to the erection of final or ultimate philosophical structures of order. This has made America a scientific civilization. As the product of the Second Great Age of Discovery when new lands, new men (and women), new oceans, new continents, new ecologies, new beauties, new wonders, and a whole restructuring of time as well as space resulted, and as this new data penetrated Euro-America and the United States, the new United States incorporated more of the new than any other culture in all history. The story of the exploration of the American West is merely a dramatic historic episode, or perhaps an *epistime* of this process.

If we are being asked today to evaluate this process by hindsight and today's self-referential values, we should at least be aware of and understand the meaning of moral, aesthetic, social, scientific, and institutional discourses of the past. Michel Foucault has called this "The Archeology of Knowledge,"[17] which we must understand much as we try to understand remote tribal totems and taboos, as anthropologists trying to understand ourselves before we judge the society or culture that we can only partially recover. We must, however, beware of *excessive* contemporary self-reference, which is an ultimate form of "ethnocentrism," i.e., "egocentrism."[18] It is important to note that doing history is as much an attempt to distance ourselves from our egos, prejudices, borrowed and often outmoded ideologies, and present-day journalistic fads as it is an attempt to recover the past. Lately we have been too quick to make American history a whipping boy for our favorite contemporary special interests as well as the ecstacies of fashionable guilt.

III. Exploration's Positive Impacts

Perhaps it is appropriate now, after due self-flagellation, to simply review or point out some of the ways in which exploration as a cultural process has had an impact on America, the American West, and Euro-American civilization.

1. It mapped and defined the West, including the North American continent. As a matter of fact, we have gone on from Lewis and Clark maps to the sophisticated United States Geological Survey satellite maps which explore not only space, but also planet Earth, taking us into a Third Age of Discovery, largely an age of prosthetic or nonhuman explorers and the far-flung space probes that make up big science.[19]

2. It discovered the natural resources of the West (and of the globe for that matter).

3. Explorers located the mountain passes, traversed the rivers, and laid out the trails, wagon routes, and railroads that would lead millions of settlers into the West, where, more often

than not, the poor, the weary, and the middle class could find opportunities for living. There they established their "dwellings" in the Heideggerian sense of the word.[20] They found true "homes"—stopping places where one could live with nature—and where one could always in theory return.

4. They established a network of commerce in the West (fur trading, mining, mustanging, the Santa Fe trade, agriculture, logging, even wine-making—and then, of course, much more, including appropriately the discovery of locations for shooting movies, the myth machine that helped make exploration heroes famous). For a long time, however, the West depended on federal aid and extractive industries that nonetheless required the pioneers to follow that Biblical directive to "earn thy bread by the sweat of thy brow." There were few "free lunches" in the early West and none for the explorers.

5. Western exploration, especially on the Great Plains and in California's valleys, eventually enabled the United States to assume a major role in feeding the world in the twentieth century.

6. It was explorers, too, who made the major contribution to the establishment of organized science in America. Much of this was the result of western exploration, but also global exploration as well. One need only recall the roll of governmental scientific expeditions: the 3,000-mile reconnaissance of Lewis and Clark; Major Stephen Long's expedition over the Great Plains to the Rockies; the many expeditions of the Topographical Engineers from 1840 to 1860, culminating in the Pacific Railroad Surveys of 1853–54; the great post-Civil War geological surveys, the work of hundreds of intrepid members of the U.S. Geological Survey; the U.S. Biological Survey; the Smithsonian-sponsored expeditions; the Bureau of Explorations and Surveys; the Coast and Geodetic Survey; and the many global seaborne ventures of the U.S. Navy, especially the Great United States Exploring Expedition of 1838–42, sometimes known as the "Wilkes Expedition," which proved Antarctica a continent and mapped the Northwest Coast of America pointing out the greater value of Puget Sound as a harbor, in comparison with the Columbia River.[21]

7. Western explorers, like John Wesley Powell, F. V. Hayden, N. P. Langford, and John Muir played an important role in

seeing the West as *a laboratory for social planning*. Water basin culture in the arid lands, national parks, and wilderness preservation, as well as land classification systems, were initially devised by these far-seeing statesmen of our richly varied landscape.

8. Explorers also, through geology, paleontology, and archeology, helped to rediscover time—three kinds of time: historical time, pre-historical human time, *and* the four- or five-billion-year history of the earth that replaced the Biblical count of six thousand years. This had a powerful effect on religion and on all other organized thought as well.

9. Explorers like O. C. Marsh, Joseph Leidy, and Charles Wright contributed the crucial proofs for Darwin's theory of evolution. Marsh and Leidy reconstructed the paleological proofs for the evolution of the horse, while Wright supplied the plant distribution data that enabled Asa Gray, an evolutionist, to vanquish the great Harvard zoologist-creationist Louis Agassiz.[22]

10. As part of the great global reconnaissance of the Second Age of Discovery, explorers mapped the oceans, the ocean floor, and the Arctic, and discovered and mapped a whole new continent—the Antarctic. They also, through the work of James Dwight Dana, made the first discoveries concerning plate tectonics in the Hawaiian Islands (today an extension of the American West).[23]

11. Also, of course, eighteenth-century Spanish, British, and American explorers mapped the West Coast of North America and proved that no Northwest Passage existed, including the mythical Straits of Anian and Juan de Fuca—while John C. Frémont and Charles Wilkes finally demolished the myth of the Rio Buenaventura, which was supposed to flow (according to that explorer manqué Baron Lahonton) from a great interior sea straight to the Pacific Ocean.[24]

12. Explorers including George Catlin, Karl Bodmer, Prince Maximilian of Wied-Neu-Wied, Horatio Hale, Captain John Gregory Bourke of the U.S. Army, John Wesley Powell, and dozens of anthropologists studied the Native Americans and helped to create not only a science of anthropology, but the world's first institution for the study of primitive men and women, the Bureau of American Ethnology, established by

Congress in 1879 with Powell as its first director. The B.A.E. was also one of the first government agencies to employ women as field explorers and archaeologists—Matilda Cox Stevenson and Alice Fletcher come to mind as two examples.

The study of Native Americans also advanced through the work of Horatio Hale, a philologist of the Wilkes Expedition who studied the cargo cult language of the Northwest Coast Indians. From his pioneering work came the concept of comparative linguistics and early cultural relativism (just a bit before a sailor, Herman Melville, articulated it in his novels of the 1840s and 1850s). Hale then passed on his idea of cultural relativism to young Franz Boas and thus began modern anthropology—an anthropology that already had enough data on American Indian tribes and South Seas natives to locate and call attention to alternate moral universes that began to cast light on, and even to serve as a critique of, Euro-American values.[25] Young men and women under the direction of the great Bronislaw Malinowski began to study remote cultures like the Trobriand Islanders so that they could better understand the Long Islanders.[26]

13. These alternate moral universes held by other people in other cultures also made clear that Euro-Americans believed that explorers were the heroic leaders of the *redemption*, rather than the *conquest*, of the continent—something Americans have been naïve enough, or perhaps proud enough, to adopt as our national creation myth. The explorers were considered our Odysseuses or, as Bernard De Voto once put it in typical overstatement, they were the "Odysseus Jed Smith" and the "Wing-Shod Fitzpatrick."[27] James Fenimore Cooper described Leatherstocking as no less than a *nature god* coming out of the sun! He wrote:

> The sun had fallen below the crest of the nearest wave of the prairie, leaving the usual rich and glowing train in its track. In the center of this flood of fiery light, a human form appeared, drawn against the gilded background, as distinctly, and seemingly as palpable, as though it would come within the grasp of any extended hand. The figure was *colossal*, the attitude musing and melancholy, and the situation directly in the route of the travellers. But embedded, as it was, in its setting of garish light, it was impossible to distinguish its just proportions or true character.

The effect of such a spectacle was instantaneous and powerful. The man in front of the emigrants came to a stand, and remained gazing at the mysterious object with a dull interest, that soon quickened into superstitious awe.[28]

14. And our explorers took us deeply into nature—its great "prairie oceans," its "American Zaharas [sic]" and "Death Valleys," its extraordinary mountain ranges (one marked by a great, shining, snowy cross), its lakes and rivers and pastoral paradises where flocks and herds abounded in a land of plenty—redeemed by explorers and settlers as the "instruments of the Almighty"—all this helping to create the American character, which Professor David Potter once called a "People of Plenty,"[29] and a country that Perry Miller described as "Nature's Nation."[30]

Dramatically, western explorers led us into very special sacred spaces in the West—Yosemite's silent valley, the titanic scientific drama of the Grand Canyon, and the wonders of Yellowstone. These became "sacred spaces"—the world's first wilderness parks, full of *meaning* as well as tourists.

15. And in all of this—a dramatic Second Age of Discovery—American explorers and their European counterparts played a significant role in the creation of an age of artistic, literary, and intellectual Romanticism on both sides of the Atlantic—a part that has not been sufficiently recognized by European scholars.

It is worthwhile to try briefly *visualizing* this romanticizing process that led beyond America to England and Europe. Hear the modern historian J. C. Beaglehole on Tahiti's influence on western civilization:

Wallis [when he discovered Tahiti] had not merely come to a convenient port of call. He had stumbled on a foundation stone of the Romantic Movement. Not as a continent, not as vast distances, was the ocean thought to be known. The unreal was to mingle with the real, the too dramatic with the undramatic; the shining light was to become a haze in which every island was the one island, and the one island a Tahitian dream.[31]

And in the context of the American West, a second quotation raises the cultural stakes even higher:

In *The Rocky Mountains*, Bierstadt became the orchestrator of a mighty, Wagnerian scene, which exaggerated the vertical thrust of the

Wind River range to achieve the monumental grandeur which Americans had come to expect from their continent. It is a synthesis, as Barbara Novak has pointed out in *Nature and Culture*, of a myriad of natural facts: from the snow-covered mountain summit and knife-edged peaks the like of which challenged the bravery of Clarence King as he cavorted in the Sierras to plunging waterfalls, natural meadows and peaceful Indians who are reminiscent of the Westphalian peasants in Bierstadt's European views. The artist dared, not merely a literal transcription of nature, but an act of creation itself, replete with all of the creatures which, as his friend Louis Agassiz, the Harvard naturalist, would suggest, were the outward manifestations of the mind of the Diety.[32]

Art historian Barbara Novak has also characterized the explorer artists of the American West, though in somewhat less exalted terms. Out in the vast plains and the complex, formidable Rocky Mountain barriers, "the artist became the hero of his own journey." She adds: "In this displacement of the heroic from the work of art to the persona of the artist lay, perhaps, part of the attraction of unexplored territory for the American artist at mid-century."[33]

Still, the artists and photographers who accompanied exploring expeditions into the American West in the nineteenth century often had a very special "capacity for wonder" that matched the Tahitian dream of eighteenth-century mariners in the Pacific. Geographical marvels like the sublime immensity of the Great Plains, which reached on to infinity, stunned their imaginations. And as they grew accustomed to the plains, the "Mountains of the Wind" deep in the West or the wonders of Yellowstone presented themselves, offering an unexpected paradise of cerulean paint pots, sky-high geysers, or a grand canyon comparable to that in far-off Arizona. And these were only the beginning of the wonders of the American West. With its strange tribes of noble savages and rugged fur trappers, heroic cowboys and cavalrymen, the West became a domain for the world's imagination, far transcending the proprietary claims of Americans who happened to live on the same continent, or who inhabited that hallowed region.

The American West, with its many explorers, red men of old, Hispanic gold seekers, and intrepid white scouts in the vanguard of a relentlessly growing modern civilization, was finally a vast temptation to adventure as much as to thoughtless exploitation. Rudyard Kipling knew the feeling well when he wrote in 1898:

"There's no sense in going further—it's the edge of cultivation,"
    So they said, and I believed it—broke my land and sowed my
        crop—
Built my barns and strung my fences in the little border station
    Tucked away below the foothills where the trails run out and
        stop.

Till a voice, as bad as Conscience, rang interminable changes
    On one everlasting Whisper day and night repeated—so:
"Something hidden. Go and find it. Go and look behind the Ranges—
    "Something lost behind the Ranges. Lost and waiting for you.
        Go!"

So I went, worn out of patience; never told my nearest neighbours—
. . . .

I remember lighting fires; I remember sitting by them;
    I remember seeing faces, hearing voices through the smoke;
I remember they were fancy—for I threw a stone to try 'em.
    "Something lost behind the Ranges" was the only word they
        spoke.

I remember going crazy. I remember that I knew it
    When I heard myself hallooing to the funny folk I saw.
Very full of dreams that desert: but my two legs took me through it . . .
    And I used to watch 'em moving with the toes all black and raw.

But at last the country altered—White Man's country past disputing—
    Rolling grass and open timber, with a hint of hills behind—
There I found me food and water, and I lay a week recruiting,
    Got my strength and lost my nightmares. Then I entered on my
        find.
. . . .

Well I know who'll take the credit—all the clever chaps that followed—
    Came, a dozen men together—never knew my desert fears;
Tracked me by the camps I'd quitted, used the water-holes I'd
    hollowed.
        They'll go back and do the talking. *They'll* be called the Pioneers!

. . . .

Yes, your "Never-never country"—yes, your "edge of cultivation"
      And "no sense in going further"—till I crossed the range to see.
God forgive me! No, *I* didn't. It's God's present to our nation.
      Anybody might have found it but—His Whisper came to Me![34]
                                    (Rudyard Kipling, "The Explorer")

Chapter 2 Notes

1. Stephen Pyne, "A Third Great Age of Discovery," in Carl Sagan and Stephen Pyne, eds., *The Scientific and Historical Rationales for Solar System Exploration*, Space Policy Institute, Elliott School of International Affairs, The George Washington University, SPI 81–1 (July, 1988), 36–46.

2. Quoted in Richard A. Van Orman, *The Explorers: Nineteenth Century Expeditions in Africa and the American West* (Albuquerque: University of New Mexico Press, 1984), 71.

3. See especially William H. Goetzmann, *New Lands, New Men, America and the Second Great Age of Discovery* (New York: Viking Penguin, 1986), 1–15.

4. See Herbert Hovenkamp, *Science and Religion in America, 1800–1860* (Philadelphia: University of Pennsylvania Press, 1978).

5. Quoted in Pyne, "A Third Great Age of Discovery," 42.

6. See Alfred W. Crosby, *The Columbian Exchange: Biological and Cultural Consequences of 1492* (Westport, Conn.: Greenwood Press, 1972), 122–60. Also see Crosby, *Ecological Imperialism: The Biological Expansion of Europe 900–1900* (Cambridge: Cambridge Press, 1986).

7. See Louis Antoine de Bougainville, *A Voyage Round the World*, trans. J. R. Forster (London: Printed for J. Norse, 1772). Wilbur Jacobs, *Dispossessing the American Indian: Indians and Whites on the Colonial Frontier* (New York: Charles Scribner's Sons, 1972).

8. See Francis Jennings, *The Invasion of America: Indians, Colonialism, and the Cant of Conquest* (Chapel Hill: University of North Carolina Press, 1975).

9. Ibid.

10. William Faulkner, "The Bear," in *Go Down Moses and Other Stories* (New York: The Modern Library published by Random House, 1942).

11. See Patricia Nelson Limerick, *The Legacy of Conquest: The Unbroken Past of the American West* (New York: W. W. Norton & Co., 1987).

12. Wilbur Jacobs, "Frontiersmen, Fur Traders and Other Varmints," *American Historical Association Newsletter*, 1970–71.

13. See James Fenimore Cooper, The Leatherstocking Tales, esp. *The Prairie* (1823) and the *Pioneers* (1826).

14. It was so termed in Michael Wigglesworth, *The Day of Doom* (1662).

15. See Henry Nash Smith, *Virgin Land: The American West as Symbol and Myth* (Cambridge, Mass.: Harvard University Press, 1950).

16. Walter P. Webb, *The Great Frontier* (Austin: The University of Texas Press, 1951), 21–28, 413 ff.

17. See Michel Foucault, *The Archaeology of Knowledge and the Discourse on Language*, trans. A. M. Sheridan Smith (New York: Harper Colophon Books, 1972). Also see Foucault, *The Order of Things: An Archeology of the Human Sciences (Les Mots Et Les Choses)* (New York: Vintage Books, 1973).

18. See Limerick, *Legacy of Conquest*, n. 11.

19. See Pyne, "A Third Great Age of Discovery," n. 1. However, expeditions in the Third Great Age of Discovery need not be prosthetic and non-human. It is important to consider that the current projections for a manned trip to Mars are between eight months and eighteen months, depending on the route. This makes a Mars trip, even a manned expedition, easily comparable in terms of time frames with the voyages of the Second Great Age of Discovery.

20. Martin Heidegger, *Basic Writings* (New York: Harper & Row, 1977), 319–40.

21. Goetzmann, *New Lands, New Men*, 265–97.

22. Ibid., 357–58.

23. Ibid., 293. Also see Herman Viola and Caroline Margolies, eds., *Magnificent Voyagers: The United States Exploring Expedition, 1838–1842* (Washington, D.C.: Smithsonian Press, 1985).

24. Goetzmann, *Exploration and Empire: The Explorer and the Scientist in the Winning of the American West, 1800–1900* (New York: Alfred A. Knopf, Inc., 1966), 246–47. See Goetzmann, *New Lands, New Men*, 68, for Baron de Lahonton's map showing the "Morte or River Longue," i.e., the Buenaventura.

25. See Lee Clark Mitchell, *Witness to a Vanishing America: The Nineteenth-Century Response* (Princeton, N.J.: Princeton University Press, 1981), ch. 7 and 8, pp. 189–251.

26. Professor Norman Holmes Pearson to Professor Bronislaw Malinowski, story related to William Goetzmann, 1954, Yale University.

27. Bernard De Voto, "Introduction," *The Life and Adventures of James P. Beckwourth*, T. D. Bonner, ed. (New York: Alfred Knopf, 1931), xxvii.

28. James Fenimore Cooper, *The Prairie* (New York: Rinehart Edition, 1950), 8.

29. David Potter, *People of Plenty: Economic Abundance and the American Character* (Chicago: University of Chicago Press, 1954).

30. Perry Miller, *Nature's Nation* (Cambridge, Mass.: Belnap Press of Harvard University Press, 1967).

31. J. C. Beaglehole, *Cook's Journals*, I, XCIV–XCV.

32. William H. Goetzmann and William N. Goetzmann, *The West of the Imagination* (New York: W. W. Norton & Co., 1986), 155.

33. Barbara Novak, *Nature and Culture, American Landscape Painting, 1825–1875* (New York: Oxford University Press, 1980), 137.

34. Rudyard Kipling, "The Explorer", in *Collected Verse of Rudyard Kipling* (Garden City, N.Y.: Doubleday, Page and Company, 1980), 19–22.

3. In Search of the Great Bear: A Historiography of Russian Exploration in Alaska and California*

by Stephen Haycox

Historians of the exploration and development of the American West overlook the role of the Russians and the Russian American colony in generating and synthesizing geographic and scientific data from northwest North America and California and determining the extent and nature of the North Pacific Ocean and its eastern shores.[1] Yet Russian contributions added materially to the steady accumulation of knowledge in the eighteenth and nineteenth centuries, which made the American West first an object of diplomatic and commercial rivalry, and then a destination for settlement. The Russians not only mapped the western and eastern sides of the Pacific, but accomplished navigation of the Bering Strait between Asia and America in 1648.

By the end of the eighteenth century they had identified and charted all of the Aleutian Island groups. They had compiled a general knowledge of the coastal geography of northwest North America from Dixon Entrance (54°40' north latitude) northward along the American coast to the Arctic and along the coast of Siberia and Amuria to the Sea of Japan. This alone ranks Russian achievements alongside English, Spanish, and American exploration in the seas and along the Northwest Coast. The Russians also made significant contributions to natural history and to the ethnographical and ethnological understanding of North America, a body of knowledge that added significantly to European and American appreciation of the resources of the American West.

Although some non-Soviet scholars are aware of the record of Russian navigators, *promyshlenniki* (Russian fur trappers), and

* A version of this paper was published in the *Pacific Historical Review* 59 (May 1990): 231–52. I am grateful to the University of Idaho for supporting its initial publication there.

overland explorers, much of the historiography of Russian developments in the Northwest is not well known to North American historians.[2] This is partly because the history of Russian America itself is not well known. In western history texts and courses, Russian America is generally mentioned only briefly, usually in the context of the Pacific maritime fur trade in the last decade of the eighteenth century and the first several decades of the following century.[3] Much of what is commonly understood rests on the work of two historians, Frank Golder, who wrote near the beginning of the present century, and Hubert Howe Bancroft, who published a history of Alaska in 1886.[4] Modern scholarship demonstrates that Golder misunderstood important aspects of Russian exploration and expansion, and Bancroft's view of the Russian presence in North America was often negative and uninformed.[5] There has been, however, an extraordinary volume of scholarly work on the history of Russian America published in the last twenty years, much of which has contributed to a substantive alteration in traditional ways of understanding that history, and which suggests a much more significant role for Russian navigators and scientists—and contemporary historians—than has been appreciated.

Initially, Russian exploration in North America was part of the expansion of European Russia into Siberia and part of the persistent search by Europeans for a sea passage above Asia and North America which would facilitate trade between Europe and Asia and which would also satisfy geographers.[6] Later the principal motivation for Russian exploration was the search for Pacific trading partners and a desire to establish sovereignty over some of the Pacific Coast. The history of Russian exploration of North America can be divided into five phases: (1) the voyage of Semen Dezhnev in 1648; (2) the voyages of Vitus Bering in 1728 and 1741; (3) the voyages of promyshlenniki and Cossacks to the Aleutian Islands and the Alaska Peninsula after 1743; (4) the maritime exploration of the North American coast from 1762 to 1800, and beyond to 1826; and (5) the overland expeditions into the interior of southwest Alaska from 1829 to 1851.

I

Less than forty years after the death of Henry Hudson in 1611 during a voyage of discovery in Hudson Bay, Semen Dezhnev, an aggressive Cossack, completed the first navigation between the Arctic and Pacific oceans with a daring sea voyage of 1,450 miles around the far eastern tip of Asia. He traveled from the mouth of the Kolyma River, which empties into the Arctic Ocean, to a point south of the mouth of the Anadyr River, which drains into the Pacific. Dezhnev's voyage was a remarkable and early journey; it was over a century later that the Spanish dispatched their first tentative voyage of discovery to the North Pacific in 1774. James Cook's epic third voyage, which took him along the American and Siberian coasts, came in 1778.[7] He gave the name East Cape to the farthest eastern tip of Asia, but the Russians have preferred the name Cape Dezhnev, and well they might, for Dezhnev was there long before anyone else. Like Columbus, however, he did not know exactly where he had been; though he knew he had rounded Asia, he did not know just where the American mainland was.[8]

Dezhnev's epic voyage was not the only remarkable Russian geographical accomplishment in the north. The two voyages of Vitus Bering in 1728 and 1741 were also highly significant, coming well before those of Spain or Britain and contributing to the understanding of northern geography.[9] Following Bering, numerous promyshlenniki and one government expedition mapped large portions of the Aleutian Islands and the Alaska Peninsula and discovered the seal-rich Pribylov Islands, all prior to George Vancouver's charting voyages of 1793 and 1794.[10]

Russian maritime exploration of the North Pacific and the Arctic continued sporadically into the nineteenth century. With the basic coastline mapped by 1800, overland expeditions became the principal focus of activity. The Russians did not penetrate much of the interior of what is now Alaska, but considering the vast distances involved, the inhospitable character of the terrain, and the severe climatic conditions, the contribution they did make was substantial, especially considering the small number of personnel assigned to the colony and to exploration and the difficult supply problems. Much of the area of south-west Alaska was mapped, as were the Yukon and Kuskokwim River deltas. The work of Il'ia Voznesenskii, Ivan Vasiliev, Andrei Glazunov, and Lt. Laurenti Zagoskin resulted in major additions to the geographic and ethnological knowledge of northwest North America, as well as to its flora and fauna.[11]

II

The work of recording and interpreting the exploratory expeditions and observations of the North Pacific and northwest America by Russians began almost contemporaneously with the expeditions themselves, and its subsequent history can be divided into several distinct phases: the first, involving near contemporaries, lasted into the first half of the nineteenth century, and includes writers such as Gerhard Muller (called by Raymond Fisher the father of Siberian historiography) and Vasiliy Berkh; the second consists of the official history of the Russian American Company written by P. Tikhmenev and Bancroft's *History of Alaska*; Professor F. A. Golder represents the third phase; and the fourth includes a host of contemporary historians in both the Soviet Union and in North America who have been writing since the end of World War II. The contemporary group includes particularly Semen Okun, who published a Marxist history of the Russian American Company in Leningrad in 1939; James Gibson of York University, Ontario; Svetlana Fedorova of the Institute of Ethnography in Leningrad; the Soviet historians Raisa Makarova and Boris Polevoi; and, most notably, Raymond Fisher of the University of California at Los Angeles, who has revolutionized Russian historiography for English-reading scholars with recent works on the voyages of Dezhnev and Bering. Also of great importance is James Gibson's work in historical geography which addressed initially the problem of supply and more recently the conditions of trade in Russian America, including substantial information on the relationship between American and British private traders and the Russian American Company. I will be concerned here principally with the contemporary historians since they represent what is new in the field. The works of these scholars are widely, though not completely, available in English, but unfortunately they seem not to be generally well known and utilized by contemporary western historians.[12]

First, however, it is important to acknowledge the contribution of Richard A. Pierce, formerly of Queen's University, Kingston, Ontario, and now of the University of Alaska, Fairbanks campus. Since 1972 Pierce has undertaken to translate and publish significant primary and secondary materials dealing with the history of Russian America. To date, thirty-five volumes have been published by his Limestone Press. Primary sources include Davydov's account of his naval voyages for the Russian American Company in the North Pacific from 1802 to 1807, Wrangell's statistical and ethnographical survey of Russian America in the 1830s, the journals of the Aleut Orthodox priest Iakov Netsvetov, the account of Grigorii Shelikhov, founder of the first permanent European settlement in Russian America in 1784, and M. D. Teben'kov's voyage to Northwest America in 1827.[13] Secondary accounts include not only those close in time to the developments they describe and interpret, such as K. T. Khlebnikov's 1835 biography of Baranov and Berkh's 1823 chronological history of the discovery of the Aleutian Islands, but also such modern works as Svetlana Fedorova's survey of the Russian population of Alaska and California and Raisa Makarova's history of Russian occupation in North America from Bering's discovery to the formation of the Russian American Company in 1799.[14] Translation of these and other works under Pierce's series title, Alaska History Series, has greatly advanced the accessibility of critical sources for students of Alaska and western history and constitutes an immeasurable contribution to the field.

Particularly helpful also have been three conferences of Soviet and North American scholars held in Sitka in 1979 and 1987, the first sponsored by the Kennan Institute for Advanced Russian Studies, the second by the University of Alaska, among others, and the third by the Anchorage Museum of History and Art in association with the museum exhibit, "Russian America: The Forgotten Frontier."[15] Publication of papers presented at these conferences brought to readers of English the work of

important new Soviet scholars, including Polevoi, Nikolai Bolkhovitinov, and Elena Okladnikova, among others.[16] Papers from
the first conference include an extensive review of published
sources on Russian America by Patricia Polansky of the University of Hawaii, and a review of archival and bibliographic materials outside the U.S.S.R. by Pierce. Another significant contribution has been made by Pierce with the publication of *Russian
America: A Biographical Dictionary*, containing the biographies
of 675 individuals "who influenced developments in Alaska in
[the Russian period]."[17] This monumental study will remain a
basic reference tool for decades to come. Still another contribution is a comprehensive collection of documents on relations
between the United States and Russia, compiled by a Joint
Soviet-American Editorial Board and published in 1980 under the auspices of the U.S. State Department, the National Archives, the Kennan Institute, the U.S.S.R. Ministry of Foreign Affairs, the Academy of Sciences, and the U.S.S.R. Main Archival
Administration: *The United States and Russia: A Beginning of Relations, 1765–1815.*[18]

III

To convey the present state of historiography of Russian America, it is useful to review in broad outlines recent interpretations
of some principal problems in the Russian exploration of North
America. The voyage of Semen Dezhnev around the northeast
tip of Siberia in 1648 did not become known in European Russia
until many years after the event. Dezhnev was on a trading mission, not one of exploration, and neither he nor his immediate
superiors fully appreciated the implications of his navigational
feat.[19] One of the first to do so was probably Vitus Bering, who
led the government expedition to Kamchatka between 1725 to
1730 and then northward along the Siberian coast and through
the strait now named for him.[20] When he returned to St.
Petersburg, Bering brought with him stories of Dezhnev's voyage. Another who understood its significance was Gerhard
Friedrich Muller, head of the academic contingent of the Second Kamchatka Expedition (Bering's second voyage) which dis-

covered North America from the west.[21] Muller published several summaries of the exploration of Siberia, one of which has recently appeared in a Historical Translation Series published by the University of Alaska.[22]

Some eighteenth-century writers doubted reports of Dezhnev's sea voyage from the Kolyma to the Anadyr principally on the grounds that attempts to duplicate it were unsuccessful.[23] In fact, Dezhnev's feat was not duplicated until the Swede Adolph E. Nordenskiold did it in 1878–79 during a circumnavigation of Eurasia.[24] One doubter was Gavriil Sarychev, who headed a northern section of an expedition sent from Russia in 1785 under Joseph Billings with the object of surveying the whole of the North Pacific region.[25] Sarychev attempted to sail eastward along the coast from the Kolyma River, but only went a short distance because of ice conditions.

Nonetheless, Muller's acceptance of the Dezhnev voyage remained the dominant interpretation of the beginning of northern Pacific exploration throughout the nineteenth century.[26] Bancroft accepted it in his *History of Alaska*.[27] Challenge to the Dezhnev voyage was revived by Frank A. Golder, a professor first at Washington State University and then at Stanford. In an article in *The Geographical Journal* in 1910 and four years later in a book, *Russian Expansion on the Pacific, 1641–1850*, Golder rejected the idea of the 1648 voyage,[28] arguing that Dezhnev's description of the cape named for him was inaccurate, that the distance was too great for the time taken by the voyage, that ice conditions would have prevented it, and that the frailty of the craft used and ignorance of ocean navigation made such a trip unbelievable.[29] Several Soviet historians contested Golder's refutation, particularly after 1945 when there was a sudden burst of Soviet scholarship regarding Siberia and Russian America.[30] But for North American historians unable to read Russian, Golder's became the standard interpretation for much of the twentieth century.[31]

In 1956 Professor Raymond H. Fisher of the University of California, Los Angeles, published an article in the *Pacific Historical Review*, "Semen Dezhnev and Professor Golder," in which he challenged Golder's refutation.[32] Pointing to gaps in Golder's research and to conclusions based on faulty translations of critical portions of Dezhnev's accounts and Muller's histories, Fisher convincingly discredited Golder's work.[33] In 1981 Fisher returned to Dezhnev and to Golder in his publication with the Hakluyt Society, *The Voyage of Semen Dezhnev in 1648: Bering's Precursor, with Selected Documents.*[34] Fisher demonstrated that while Dezhnev's descriptions were sometimes vague, they were more than adequate, particularly when clarified by later explorers. Golder had argued that an ignorant Cossack could not have produced the documents ascribed to Dezhnev, a conclusion which Fisher thought was a vague and even haughty condemnation.[35] Golder had erred in his computation of the distance covered on the voyage; he had been ignorant of some types of vessels used on the north Siberian coast and travel times recorded for them. Fisher's exhaustive review of the historiography and his close study of the documentation convincingly erased any lingering suggestion that Golder's interpretation might be tenable.[36]

At the time of his work on Semen Dezhnev, Fisher had already revised the standard interpretation of the motivation for and the significance of the two voyages of Vitus Bering in a book published in 1977 entitled *Bering's Voyages: Whither and Why?*[37] Fisher had challenged Golder's conclusions in that work as well, along with those of other writers including Robert Kerner of the University of California and Hubert Howe Bancroft in his much earlier *History of Alaska.*[38] Bancroft's Alaska history had already been largely discredited by other writers, among them Pierce and Morgan Sherwood of the University of California, Davis.[39] Bancroft's writer for much of the Alaska volume was Ivan Petrov, a man usually thought to have been a Russian but whose origins actually are obscure, and whom Pierce has concluded was a habitual liar.[40] Bancroft's Alaska history must be read with the character of its principal author in mind, as critical analysis has shown.

Bancroft's volume owed a major debt to the work of P. A. Tikhmenev, whose official history of the Russian American Company, published between 1861 and 1863, has been called unsurpassed as a comprehensive survey.[41] It has been translated into English by Pierce and Alton S. Donnelly and by Dmitri Krenov.[42]

Bancroft echoed the traditional interpretations of Bering's voyages. It had long been accepted that the main objective of the 1728 voyage was to determine whether Asia and America were connected and that the principal—perhaps the only— motive for the expedition was scientific.[43] Fisher convincingly revised this thesis. Through a detailed history of the knowledge of Siberian geography and cartography in the seventeenth and eighteenth centuries, as well as meticulous reading of imperial instructions, he concluded that Tsar Peter had accepted the assertion of geographers that a major subcontinent or peninsula, called Gamaland, lay in the North Pacific along an east-west axis between America and Asia.[44] Fisher concluded further that Peter had wanted Bering to sail along the shore of Gamaland to see if it was connected to America and to determine what its resources might be. He was then to go on to the nearest European port on the American mainland to attempt to establish trade relations.[45] However, upon reaching the Pacific, Bering had learned there was no Gamaland, at least not that anyone in Siberia knew of, and thus instead of sailing east he headed north through the strait now named for him, and through which Dezhnev had navigated eighty years earlier.[46]

In regard to Bering's second voyage, the traditional view held, once again, that science—geography, ethnography, and natural history—was the principal objective.[47] Certainly the objects of science were well served. Not only did Bering and his subordinate, Aleksei Chirikov, mark the location of the North American coast between 60° and 56° north latitude, but Georg Steller, the chief scientist on the expedition, made significant comparative observations on Kayak Island, Bering's landfall, and on islands off the Alaska Peninsula.[48] Fisher, however, argued persuasively that the future extension of Russian sovereignty into the Pacific was a concomitant objective, a conclusion now widely accepted among both Soviet and North American scholars partly because it has been corroborated by work done in Soviet archives.[49] Fisher also disputed Kerner's hypothesis that Bering had a secret mission to recover land along the north side of the Amur River, which Russians had been forced to cede to the Chinese by treaty in 1649. Some of Kerner's work was based on translations of Russian documents made by

Golder on a trip to the Soviet Union in the 1920s.[50] Kerner was led astray, Fisher determined, by errors in Golder's translations and had misread some of his own evidence, erroneously concluding that secret instructions sent to Bering contained statements about the Amur region not included in the public instructions.[51]

Among recent works which place Bering's voyages in broad perspective are L. N. Neatby's *Discovery in Russian and Siberian Waters* and particularly J. Arthur Lower's *Ocean of Destiny: A Concise History of the North Pacific, 1500–1978*, which seeks to survey Russian America in the context of European discoveries, the fur trade, and 400 years of trans-Pacific contacts.[52]

Subsequent phases of Russian exploration of North America have yet to undergo thorough treatment by modern historians. Important work, however, has been done on the discovery of the various Aleutian Islands, the Prybilov Islands, and the Alaska Peninsula by Cossacks, promyshlenniki, and government operatives. The translation of Vasilii Berkh's 1823 history, Grigorii Shelikhov's account of his founding of the first permanent European settlement in northwest North America on Kodiak Island in 1784, and especially the translation of Raisa Makarova's 1968 study of Russian expansion into the Pacific from 1743 to 1799 all constitute major contributions to an understanding of the Russian mapping of lands and population of the North Pacific. Shelikhov was a principal player in Russian expansion into North America, and Berkh's history, which has the freshness of a firsthand record, is nearly a contemporary account and is based in part on materials not available to modern historians.[53]

Berkh's work was preceded fifty years earlier by an account by the Russian academician Petr Pallas.[54] James Masterson and Helen Brower published a translation of Pallas' work in the *Pacific Northwest Quarterly* in January and April 1947 and later in book form with the title *Bering's Successors*.[55]

Raisa Makarova's study, published by Pierce with the title *Russians on the Pacific, 1743–1799*, is one of the most important works on Russian exploration in North America to have been published in recent years. In addition to providing the most complete and detailed list of voyages by the profit-seeking promyshlenniki before 1799, Makarova recounts the government expeditions by Krenitsyn to Unalaska and the Alaska Peninsula in 1768, and by Billings and Sarychev in 1790 and 1791.[56] The latter expedition surveyed the Aleutians, Kodiak Island, Cook's Prince William Sound, and the adjacent coast, as well as Bristol Bay and the newly discovered Pribylov Islands in the Bering Sea and the east coast of Siberia from Cape Dezhnev to the Anadyr River.[57] Maps prepared by the expedition were still in use in 1940.[58] The ethnographical data collected on the coast of North America were particularly significant. Makarova concludes that the numerous finds by the Russian voyagers rank with the most important geographic discoveries in world history.[59] Certainly when the information collected on the Russian voyages was added to that collected by Cook and Vancouver, it produced for the first time a comprehensive picture of the North American continent, far eastern Asia, and the islands and peninsulas between them.[60]

There were a number of Russian government expeditions in the early geographic history of North America. Many were important in terms of ethnography, ethnology, and natural history. For example, Iiurii Lisianskii, who with Ivan Kruzenstern pioneered a sea route from Kronstadt to Russian America in 1803–5, produced one of the most comprehensive works ever written on life and culture in Russian America.[61] A member of this expedition, G. H. von Langsdorff, published one of the most important primary sources on the ethnography of North American Indians.[62] Langsdorff sailed on a Russian vessel to California from Sitka in 1806, and along the way he was able to make a brief reconnaissance of Gray's Harbor, in the present state of Washington.[63]

In 1816–18, O. E. Kotzebue continued Russian explorations in the Bering Strait region, and in 1818 one of the most renowned geographical expeditions of the nineteenth century was undertaken by M. N. Vasil'ev, who explored the Arctic above North America, surveyed the Aleutian Islands, and made detailed notes on the natural resources and populace of the far north. Expedition members also visited California and one member, Rydalev, produced sailing directions for San Francisco Bay.[64] There were other important Russian voyages, but no one has yet written a comprehensive history of their tasks or achievements, though a number of writers have listed them, including Sherwood, and, most recently, Elena Okladnikova.[65]

The final phase of Russian contributions to North American geography concerns overland exploration in Russian America. Again, no comprehensive review of these efforts, of which there were several, has yet been undertaken, though Sherwood, Okladnikova, and Svetlana Fedorova, among others, include brief descriptions of the principal expeditions in their works.[66] In 1818 Petr Korsakovskii made an important journey from Lake Clark to the source of the Mulchatna River, and Eremei Rodionov explored the course of the middle Kuskokwim.[67] This was followed in 1819 by a second expedition which included both a land and sea contingent. Several sections of the coast were charted by an Aleut, Andrei Ustiugov, who named several important land features. In 1829 Ivan Ia. Vasil'ev explored the lower Kuskokwim and other streams lying northwest of Bristol Bay, including the Nushagak.[68] In 1833 M. D. Teben'kov established a settlement on St. Michael Island, sixty miles from the mouth of the Yukon. In 1835 the creole Andrei Glazunov explored the lower Yukon (called by the Russians the Kvikhpak and not yet known by Northwest Canadian Indians to be the same as their Yuk'ana, or Yukon), and in 1839 the creole Petr Malakhov established a post at Nulato, 500 miles up the Kvikhpak from its mouth.[69] These and other expeditions are reviewed in Fedorova's population study. In addition to information on expeditions, Fedorova includes extensive data on population and social conditions in the colony. Of considerable significance, for example, is her thoroughly documented finding that the greatest number of Russians ever in the North American colony at one time was 823 in 1839. This is an astonishing figure when one remembers that the Russian American Company's jurisdiction extended nearly three thousand miles from the Kurile Islands south of Kamchatka, across the Aleutians to the Alaska Peninsula and Cook Inlet, and southward to New Archangel in the Alexander Archipelago, and that the Company's tenure in Alaska lasted from 1799 to 1867.[70]

Virtually all writers accessible in English who have reviewed Russian overland expeditions single out two for special comment, however, that of Il'ia Voznesenskii after 1839 and that of L. A. Zagoskin between 1842 and 1844.[71] Okladnikova calls Voznesenskii's work a landmark of the period in ethnographic and biological studies of northwest America and California.[72] Sherwood noted that Voznesenskii must be considered one of the most important figures in the history of science in Russian America.[73] Outfitted by the Academy of Sciences for an extended trip in Asia, Alaska, and the Pacific, he spent a decade on the shores of the North Pacific from California to Kotzebue Sound. He collected tens of thousands of specimens and made meticulous notes on native culture.[74] In 1967 Sherwood reported that Voznesenskii's zoological, botanical, and mineralogical specimens were still being used for study in the U.S.S.R.[75]

According to Okladnikova, however, the most significant expedition to the Alaskan interior was Zagoskin's.[76] While his purpose was to survey the relationship between the Kvikhpak and Kuskokwim rivers, Zagoskin also discovered a then unknown world of Indian and Eskimo peoples whose lives and habits he recorded faithfully.[77] He became the first Russian specialist in the field of American Eskimo spiritual culture, ritual, and shamanism. He established the tribal continuity of various Athapaskan groups and compiled extensive linguistic notes.[78] His materials are on exhibit in Leningrad and Moscow today.[79] Again, no comprehensive history of the Russian overland expeditions has been published, though Fedorova and Okladnikova both have discussed them in other contexts.[80]

IV

This brief review should suggest, then, that the history of Russian America is a rich and vital part of the broader history of the Northwest, and that Russian exploration in this area had an integral relationship with Northwest development. The discovery of the Pacific Ocean from the west and of a sea channel around the tip of Asia led ultimately to the probing of North Pacific waters from the Russian side and to the discovery of the North American mainland in the area north of 54°40' north latitude.[81] Continuing investigation led to the discovery of the Aleutian

Islands and the Alaska Peninsula and to the charting of the North Pacific coast above sixty degrees, as well as to the collection of significant seminal information on the ethnography, ethnology, biology, geology, and other natural history of northwest North America. Several important expeditions included information about the coast below 54°40', particularly California. A growing corpus of both primary and secondary materials is now readily and widely accessible to English-reading researchers, most especially through the various publications in Richard Pierce's Alaska History Series and the proceedings of the Kennan Institute conference at Sitka in 1979, edited by S. Frederick Starr, which includes a comprehensive review of archival and published sources. It is to be hoped that historians will take advantage of these resources to learn more about the relationship between Alaska and the discovery and development of the American West and the North Pacific.

Finally, it might be useful to note how close in the past Alaska and the American West have sometimes come to more direct and continuing communication. In March 1806, seeking to obtain badly needed food supplies for Sitka and hoping to open trade negotiations with the Spanish, Nikolai Rezanov, an official of the Russian government and a representative of the directors of the Russian American Company, sailed for San Francisco on the ship *Juno*, captained by Lt. Nikolai Khvostov.[82] It was this ship that had carried Georg von Langsdorff to Gray's Harbor.[83] Rezanov had hoped to construct a Russian post at the mouth of the Columbia River, and on March 31 and April 1, the *Juno* lay off Cape Disappointment, waiting for a good wind to enter the river,[84] but the winds continued to be unfavorable. When a strong north breeze came up, Khvostov used it to hasten on toward San Francisco.[85] Remarkably, Lewis and Clark had left their encampment at Ft. Clatsop at the mouth of the Columbia on March twenty-third, just a few days earlier.[86] As the *Juno* lay off Cape Disappointment near the Columbia estuary on the thirty-first, Lewis and Clark were camped near the present site of old Ft. Vancouver, and on the first of April they were camped across from the mouth of the Sandy River.[87] It is entirely conceivable that had Rezanov's ship made it past the Columbia River bar, Indian runners would have been sent after Lewis and Clark since they had already delayed their departure from Ft. Clatsop partly in hopes they might make contact with an American or English trading vessel sailing along the coast.[88]

What would these agents of their respective governments have discussed if they had met, and what might have eventuated in terms of a Russian presence on the Columbia and in the Pacific Northwest? We can only speculate, of course, but this remarkable "non-incident" serves as a notable reminder that Alaska and western American history have come close together in the past, and it is to be hoped that in the future their union may be more complete and fully enduring.

Chapter 3 Notes

1. Ray Allen Billington and Martin Ridge, *Westward Expansion: A History of the American Frontier*, 5th ed. (New York: Macmillan Publishing Co., 1982), 381–82, 451, 493, and Frederick Merk, *History of the Westward Movement* (New York: Alfred A. Knopf, 1978), pp. 310–11, are representative. Typical of regional histories is *Empire of the Columbia: A History of the Pacific Northwest* (New York: Harper & Row, Publisher, 1957), 26–67.

2. Raymond H. Fisher, *The Voyage of Semen Dezhnev in 1648: Bering's Precursor, with Selected Documents* (London: The Hakluyt Society, 1981), xii. As examples see Michael P. Malone and Rodman Paul, eds., *Historians and the American West* (Lincoln: University of Nebraska Press, 1983) and Edwin R. Bingham and Glen A. Love, eds., *Northwest Perspectives: Essays on the Culture of the Pacific Northwest* (Seattle: University of Washington Press, 1979).

3. See nn 1 and 2. Some recent reviews fail to mention Russian America in the context of the fur trade, e.g., Gordon B. Dodds, "The Fur Trade and Expansion," in Malone and Paul, *Historians*, 57–74. The view that the history of Russian America is neglected by western historians is confirmed by a review of recent programs of the Pacific Northwest History Conference, an annual regional meeting of professional historians, and of the recent annual meetings of the Pacific Coast Branch of the American Historical Association, where few papers are found which deal with Russian America. A 1980s review of college catalogues in western universities shows an American-period Alaska history course offered only at the University of Washington (Prof. Robert Burke) and at the University of California, Davis (Prof. Morgan Sherwood), and no course on the history of Russian America. On the other hand, both *Pacific Northwest Quarterly* and the *Pacific Historical Review* have published several articles on the history of Russian America.

4. F. A. Golder, *Russian Expansion on the Pacific, 1641–1850: An Account of the Earliest and Later Expeditions made by the Russians along the Pacific Coast of Asia and North America, including some related Expeditions to the Arctic Regions* (Cleveland: The Arthur H. Clark Company, 1914); Hubert Howe Bancroft,

History of Alaska (San Francisco: A. L. Bancroft & Company, 1886). For recent scholarship see Raymond H. Fisher, *Bering's Voyages: Whither and Why?* (Seattle: University of Washington Press, 1977), 18; R. H. Fisher, *The Voyage of Semen Dezhnev*, 276; Richard A. Pierce, "Archival and Bibliographic Materials on Russian America outside the USSR," in S. Frederick Starr, ed., *Russia's American Colony* (Durham: Duke University Press, 1987), 355–56.

5. R. H. Fisher, *Bering's Voyages*, 67–68, 92–93, 115–16; *The Voyage of Semen Dezhnev*, pp. 77–289; Bancroft, *History*, 674–75, 704, 706–7; Pierce, "Materials on Russian America," 355–56.

6. Golder, *Russian Expansion*, 13–14; George V. Lantzeff and Richard A. Pierce, *Eastward to Empire: Exploration and Conquest on the Russian Open Frontier, to 1750* (Montreal: McGill-Queen's University Press, 1973), 226–27; Patricia Polansky, "Published Sources on Russian America," in Starr, ed., *Russia's American Colony*, 333–34; R. H. Fisher, *Bering's Voyages*, 9, 25, 35–36. A summary which does not take advantage of much new research is Oleks Rudenko, "Russia in the Pacific Basin," *Journal of the West* 15 (April 1976): 49–64.

7. Jeannette Mirsky, *To The Arctic: The Story of Northern Exploration from Earliest Times to the Present* (Chicago: University of Chicago Press, 1970), 62–64; R. H. Fisher, *The Voyage of Semen Dezhnev*, 1; Stuart Ramsay Tompkins, *Alaska: Promyshlennik and Sourdough* (Norman: University of Oklahoma Press, 1945), 57–70.

8. R. H. Fisher, *The Voyage of Semen Dezhnev*, 8, 273–74.

9. Raisa V. Makarova, *Russians on the Pacific, 1743–1799*, trans. and ed. Richard A. Pierce and Alton S. Donnelly (Kingston, Ontario: The Limestone Press, 1975), 36; Tompkins, *Alaska*, 44.

10. Makarova, *Russians*, 167.

11. Morgan Sherwood, "Science in Russian America, 1741–1865," *Pacific Northwest Quarterly* (January 1967): 33, 35–36, 37–38; E. A. Okladnikova, "Science and Education in Russian America," in Starr, ed., *Russia's American Colony*, 224–26, 230–32; for population figures for Russians in the North American colony, see n. 69.

12. Gerhard Friedrich Muller, *Bering's Voyages: The Reports from Russia*, trans. with commentary by Carol Urness (Fairbanks: University of Alaska Press, 1986), the Rasmuson Library Historical Translation Series, Vol. 3, ed. Martin W. Falk; R. H. Fisher, *The Voyage of Semen Dezhnev*, 3; V. N. Berkh, *A Chronological History of the Discovery of the Aleutian Islands*, trans. Richard A. Pierce (Kingston, Ontario: The Limestone Press, 1974); P. A. Tikhmenev, *A History of the Russian-American Company*, trans. and ed. Richard A. Pierce and Alton S. Donnelly (Seattle: University of Washington Press, 1978); *A History of the Russian American Company*, Vol. 2, trans. Dmitri Krenov, ed. Richard A. Pierce and Alton S. Donnelly (Kingston, Ontario: The Limestone Press, 1979); S. B. Okun, *The Russian-American Company*, ed. B. D. Grekov, trans. Carl Ginsburg (Cambridge: Harvard University Press, 1951); James Gibson, *Imperial Russia in Frontier America: The Changing Geography of Supply of Russian America, 1784–1867* (New York: Oxford University Press, 1976); Svetlana G. Fedorova, *The Russian Population in Alaska and California: Late 18th Century-1867*, trans. and ed. Richard A. Pierce and Alton S. Donnelly (Kingston, Ontario: The Limestone Press, 1973); B. P. Polevoi, "The Discovery of Russian America," in Starr, ed., *Russia's American Colony*, 13–31; about Raymond H. Fisher see Polansky, "Published Sources," in Starr, ed., *Russia's American Colony*, 334–35.

13. G. I. Davydov, *Two Voyages to Russian America, 1802–1807;* trans. Colin

Bearne, ed. Richard A. Pierce (Kingston, Ontario: The Limestone Press, 1977); F. P. Wrangell, *Russian America: Statistical and Ethnographic Information*, trans. Mary Sadouski, ed. Richard A. Pierce (Kingston, Ontario: The Limestone Press, 1980); *The Journals of Iakov Netsvetov: The Atkha Years, 1828–1844*, trans. from the Russian manuscript, with introduction and supplemental historical and ethnographical material by Lydia Black (Kingston, Ontario: The Limestone Press, 1980); Grigorii I. Shelikhov, *A Voyage to America, 1783–1786*, trans. Marina Ramsay, ed. Richard A. Pierce (Kingston, Ontario: The Limestone Press, 1981); M. D. Teben'kov, *Atlas of the Northwest Coasts of America* (Kingston, Ontario: The Limestone Press, 1981). Teben'kov's atlas and hydrographic notes are based on his own and other explorers' expeditions.

14. K. T. Khlebnikov, *Baranov: Chief Manager of the Russian Colonies in America*, trans. Richard A. Pierce (Kingston, Ontario: The Limestone Press, 1973). Information can be obtained from The Limestone Press, c/o Prof. Richard A. Pierce, History Department, University of Alaska, Fairbanks, Alaska, 99775.

15. Starr, ed., *Russia's American Colony*; additional sponsors of the conference included the National Park Service, the University of Alaska Foundation, and the Alaska Humanities Forum; director of the steering committee for the conference was Prof. Lydia Black of the Anthropology Department, University of Alaska, Fairbanks; see Pierce, ed., *Russia in North America: Proceedings of the 2nd International Conference on Russian America* (Kingston: Limestone Press, 1990). "Russian America: The Forgotten Frontier," curator Barbara Sweetland Smith, was financed in part by the National Endowment for the Humanities, and was assembled in cooperation with the Washington State Historical Society; see Smith and Redmond J. Barnett, *Russian America: The Forgotten Frontier* (Tacoma: Washington State Historical Society, 1990); see also *Pacifica: A Journal of Pacific and Asian Studies* 2, no. 2 (November 1990), ed. Robert Craig, in which additional papers are published from the "Forgotten Frontier" conference (publication sponsored by the Cook Inlet Historical Society).

16. N. N. Bolkhovitinov, "Russian America and the International Relations"; E. A. Okladnikova, "Science and Education in Russian America"; R. G. Liapunova, "Relations with the Natives of Russian America," in Starr, ed., *Russia's American Colony*.

17. Richard A. Pierce, *Russian America: A Biographical Dictionary* (Kingston: Limestone Press, 1990).

18. *The United States and Russia: A Beginning of Relations, 1765–1815* (Washington, D.C.: U.S. Government Printing Office, 1980). U.S. historians involved in this masterful collection include David F. Trask, Milton O. Gustafson, S. Frederick Starr, and William Z. Slany; Soviets include Sergei L. Tikhvinskii, Nikolai Bolkhovitinov, and Lionid I. Panin.

19. R. H. Fisher, *The Voyage of Semen Dezhnev*, 23, 127–45.

20. Ibid., 1–3.

21. R. H. Fisher, *Bering's Voyages*, 14–16; *The Voyage of Semen Dezhnev*, 3–6.

22. See n. 12.

23. R. H. Fisher, *The Voyage of Semen Dezhnev*, 11–15.

24. Ibid., 180, 215, 217. Professor Lydia Black reports that a collection of seventeenth-century documents assembled by the historian A. V. Efimov of the Academy of Sciences of Russia shows several voyages around Cape Dezhnev to the Anadyr River. Unfortunately, Black reports, this material has not yet been utilized by any North American historian: personal communication with this author, July 8, 1988.

25. Ibid., 10, 12.

26. Ibid., 15–16, 18.

27. Bancroft, *History*, 22–24.

28. R. H. Fisher, *The Voyage of Semen Dezhnev*, 17–18; Golder, "Some Reasons for Doubting Dezhnev's Voyage," *The Geographical Journal*, no. 1 (1910): 81–83; *Russian Expansion*, 77–95; Golder spent three years in Alaska as a school teacher before the beginning of his academic career.

29. Golder, *Russian Expansion*, 78, 81, 87 (description); 78, 86 (distance, time); 96 (ice conditions, frailty of craft).

30. R. H. Fisher, *The Voyage of Semen Dezhnev*, 18–22, 273.

31. Ibid., 18; R. H. Fisher, *Bering's Voyages*, 18–19.

32. R. H. Fisher, "Semen Dezhnev and Professor Golder," *Pacific Historical Review* (August 1956): 281–92.

33. See also R. H. Fisher, *The Voyage of Semen Dezhnev*, 92–93, 67–68.

34. R. H. Fisher, *The Voyage of Semen Dezhnev*.

35. Ibid., 279–80.

36. Ibid., 277–89.

37. R. H. Fisher, *Bering's Voyages*; cp. F. A. Golder, *Bering's Voyages: An Account of the Efforts of the Russians to Determine the Relation of Asia to America*, 2 vols. (New York: American Geographical Society of New York, 1922, 1925; repr., 2 vols., New York: Octagon Books, 1968).

38. Robert J. Kerner, "Russian Expansion to America: Its Bibliographical Foundations," in *Papers of the Bibliographical Society of America* (New York: Bibliographical Society of America, 1931), pp. 111–29; R. H. Fisher, *Bering's Voyages*, 18.

39. Morgan B. Sherwood, *Exploration of Alaska, 1865–1900* (New Haven: Yale University Press, 1965), pp. 57–69; Richard A. Pierce, "New Light on Ivan Petroff, Historian of Alaska," *Pacific Northwest Quarterly* (January 1968): 1–10.

40. Pierce, "Archival and Bibliographic Materials," 356.

41. Fedorova, *Russian Population*, 8; Makarova, *Russians*, 15.

42. Tikhmenev, *A History of the Russian-American Company*.

43. Bancroft, *History*, 35–98; R. H. Fisher, *Bering's Voyages*, 3–21.

44. R. H. Fisher, *Bering's Voyages*, 53–55, 67–69, 139–40, and passim; Polevoi, "The Discovery of Russian America," 21

45. R. H. Fisher, *Bering's Voyages*, p. 23; Polevoi, "The Discovery of Russian America," pp. 20–21.

46. R. H. Fisher, *Bering's Voyages*, pp. 78, 103–7.

47. Bancroft, *History*, 44–46; Golder, *Russian Expansion*, 165–71; R. H. Fisher, *Bering's Voyages*, 108–19.

48. Okladnikova, "Science and Education," 220–21.

49. R. H. Fisher, *Bering's Voyages*, 152–79; Polansky, "Published Sources," 334–35; Polevoi, "The Discovery of Russian America," 19–23.

50. Kerner, "Russian Expansion;" R. H. Fisher, *Bering's Voyages*, 175–76.

51. R. H. Fisher, *Bering's Voyages*, 176–79.

52. Leslie H. Neatby, *Discovery in Russian and Siberian Waters* (Athens: University of Ohio Press, 1973); J. Arthur Lower, *Ocean of Destiny: A Concise History of the North Pacific, 1500–1978* (Vancouver: University of British Columbia Press, 1978).

53. See n. 11, n. 12; Makarova, *Russians*, 123, and passim (on Shelikhov), 13–14 (on Berkh).

54. Makarova, *Russians*, 10–12.

55. James R. Masterson and Helen Brower, *Bering's Successors, 1745–1780* (Seattle: University of Washington Press, 1948). Pallas printed a map with his account, which was published first in 1781 and included the information collected by the third Cook expedition. It showed the North American continent above 48° in general outline, northeast Asia and Kamchatka with reasonable accuracy, and the Aleutian Island groups in considerable detail.

56. Makarova, *Russians*, 3–14, 143–49 (Krenitsyn), 23–29, 54–168 (Billings/Sarychev); cp. Polevoi, "The Discovery of Russian America," pp. 23–31, Mary E. Wheeler, "The Russian American Company and the Imperial Government: Early Phase," in Starr, ed., *The Russia's American Colony*, 48–50, 58. Makarova lists over one hundred separate promyshlennik voyages between 1743 and 1778.

57. Makarova, *Russians*, 158–61.

58. Ibid., 160.

59. Ibid., 167.

60. Neatby, *Discovery in Russian and Siberian Waters*, 88–99; Lower, *Ocean of Destiny*, 24–33.

61. Okladnikova, "Science and Education," 224–25.

62. Ibid.; Fedorova, *Russian Population*, 18.

63. George H. Von Langsdorff, *Voyages and Travels in Various Parts of the World*, Vol. 2 Bibliotheca Australiana #41 (1814; repr. New York: DaCapo Press, 1968), 140–44.

64. Okladnikova, "Science and Education," 225–26; see also Dorothy Jean Ray, *Ethnohistory of the Arctic: The Bering Strait Eskimo* (Kingston, Ontario: The Limestone Press, 1982).

65. Okladnikova, "Science and Education," 224–29; Sherwood, "Science," 33–34; Fedorova, *Russian Population*, 70–75, 256–60.

66. Sherwood, "Science," 34–35; Okladnikova, "Science and Education," 226–30; Fedorova, *Russian Population*, 259–61.

67. Fedorova, *Russian Population*, pp. 66–67, 308–10; James VanStone of the Field Museum in Chicago will soon publish an edition of Petr. Korsakovskii's travel journey for the 1818 expedition in English translation; VanStone also will soon publish an edition of one of Ivan Ia. Vasil'ev's expeditions in English translation.

68. Ibid., 253–56.

69. Ibid., 139–42. In 1852 an "Atlas of the Northwest Coasts of North America" was published by Teben'kov, together with hydrographic notes, the whole covering much more than his own 1827 voyage. Editions of the charts were engraved and printed at Sitka (Sherwood, "Science," 34). Fedorova calls the atlas "a high form of hydrographic science" (*Russian Population*, 260), a judgment shared by other scholars (Okladnikova, "Science and Education,"

233–34); see M. D. Teben'kov, *Atlas of the Northwest Coasts of America from Bering Strait to Cape Corrientes, and the Aleutian Islands, with Several Sheets on the Northeast Coast of Asia* (Kingston, Ontario: The Limestone Press, 1981).

70. Fedorova's book is a detailed and insightful study of the historical, ethnographic, geographic, and social characteristics of Russian settlement in Alaska and California and the relations of the Russians with the native populations. Polansky ("Published Sources," 345) says "it represents Soviet scholarship at its best"; the population figures are summarized on 275–80 (Table 8) of Fedorova's *Russian Population*.

71. Okladnikova, "Science and Education," 230–31; Sherwood, "Science," 35, 37–38; see also A. I. Alekseev, *The Odyssey of a Russian Scientist: I. G. Voznesenskii in Alaska, California and Siberia, 1839–1849*, trans. Wilma C. Follette, ed., Richard A. Pierce (Kingston, Ontario: The Limestone Press, 1987).

72. Okladnikova, "Science and Education," 230.

73. Sherwood, "Science," 35.

74. Okladnikova, "Science and Education," 231.

75. Sherwood, "Science," 35.

76. Okladnikova, "Science and Education," 231.

77. Ibid., 231.

78. Ibid., 232.

79. Ibid..

80. *Lieutenant Zagoskin's Travels in Russian America, 1842–1844: The First Ethnographic and Geographic Investigations in the Yukon and Kuskokwim Valleys of Alaska*, ed. Henry N. Michael (Toronto: University of Toronto Press for the Arctic Institute of North America, 1967); Fedorova, *Russian Population*, 223, 226, 256, and passim; Okladnikova, "Science and Education," 230–32.

81. R. H. Fisher, *The Voyage of Semen Dezhnev*, 76, 240–42; Polevoi, "The Discovery of Russian America," 14–23; Rudenko, "Russian in the Pacific," 49–51; Neatby, *Discovery*, 87; Lower, *Ocean of Destiny*, 26.

82. Tompkins, *Alaska*, 122.

83. Okladnikova, "Science and Education," 225; Langsdorff, *Voyages*, 137.

84. Langsdorff, *Voyages*, 144–46. The dates given in Langsdorff's account have been adjusted here from old style to new style; Langsdorff gives the dates in both styles at the beginning of the chapter which includes the account of the voyage. Cape Disappointment is on the north shore of the mouth of the Columbia River; Ft. Clatsop, Lewis and Clark's winter quarters in 1805–6, was on the south shore of the river mouth.

85. Ibid., 146 ff; Rezanov included a full description of the attempt to enter the river in a report to Count Nikolai P. Rumiantsev of the Russian imperial court: June 17/29, 1806, from New Archangel (Sitka), *The United States and Russia* (see n. 18), 443–44.

86. *Original Journals of the Lewis and Clark Expedition, 1804–1806*, vol. 4 (New York: Antiquarian Press, 1959; originally published, 1904–5), 196–98.

87. Ibid., 219–21, 227–42.

88. Ibid., 180–81.

4. Images of Reality:
Early Spanish Artists on the Pacific Coast

by Iris H. W. Engstrand

Macuina, chief of Nootka. Charcoal sketch by Tomás de Suría. Courtesy of the Museo Naval, Madrid.

The first brief European contact with the Pacific Northwest Coast was made in 1774 by the Spaniard Juan Pérez, commander of an expedition instructed to explore to sixty degrees north latitude and take possession of those lands for Spain. Pérez sailed northward to approximately 54°40' before fog, the crew's illness, and contrary currents forced him to turn southward short of his goal.[1] The Spaniards sailed along the western shores of Queen Charlotte and Vancouver islands, anchoring in a bay later called Friendly Cove at Nootka Sound by Captain James Cook. Pérez did not go ashore at Nootka, but entertained several natives on board and took part in a courteous exchange of gifts. The Indians nevertheless pilfered some silver spoons that were found in their possession by Cook's men four years later. This confirmed the earlier arrival of the Spaniards.[2]

The subsequent activities of Cook's expedition, especially with regard to profits made in the fur trade, soon brought the Pacific Northwest Coast to the attention of England, other European countries, and the fledgling United States. Spain, which at that time claimed possession of the entire Pacific Coast from the tip of South America to Alaska, sent an expedition to Nootka in 1789 to discourage foreign encroachment by establishing a military outpost and planning for the arrival of missionaries. These preparations, however, did not curb the activities of international trader-adventurers, and Nootka Sound became a prime target for official investigation by the Spanish navy. The first Spanish artists reached the Northwest Coast as a part of this military reconnaissance.[3]

Another and equally important objective of the Spanish government in sending artists to the Pacific Northwest arose from the Crown's keen interest in scientific investigation. Although the projects of Carlos III, the reigning Bourbon monarch from 1759 to 1788, were many and varied, those involving extensive surveys of American lands easily received the king's patronage.[4] Carlos III also decreed, as a part of the first major expedition, the establishment of a royal institute of botany in Mexico City to study, classify, and produce sketches of the plants collected during field excursions throughout New Spain.[5]

Other factors influencing scientific activity during the late eighteenth century ranged from philosophic challenges to the

Woman of Nootka by Tomás de Suría. Courtesy of the Museo Naval, Madrid.

concept of naturalism and the questioning of ancient authority, to the practical desire of discovering new lands and classifying all new (and old) fauna and flora according to the Linnean system of nomenclature.[6] Forests valuable for naval stores and revenue producing mines were, of course, not to be ignored. The spirit of competition with the voyages of Captain Cook and the French Count of La Pérouse also encouraged the Spanish monarch to send out major expeditions into the Pacific.

The second scientific enterprise organized in Spain, and certainly one of the most ambitious, was conceived and led by Alejandro Malaspina, a distinguished Spanish naval officer born in Italy in 1754.[7] Malaspina had circumnavigated the globe in 1786–88 as captain of the vessel *La Astrea* and, with fellow officer José Bustamante y Guerra, had submitted a "Plan of a Scientific and Political Voyage Around the World" to the Minister of Marine, Antonio Valdés y Bazán, on September 10, 1788.[8] Both men were familiar with the voyages of Cook and La Pérouse and were eager to extend Spain's knowledge of navigation and natural history. For this reason, the expedition was staffed with personnel handpicked for their skills in cartography, astronomy, botany, zoology, and artistic reproduction. They also hoped to find the elusive Strait of Ferrer Maldonado, or Northwest Passage, opening into the Pacific from the Atlantic at approximately 59°30′ north latitude.[9] Another objective of the Malaspina expedition involved the Spanish claim to Nootka Sound, where the seizure of British ships in 1789 had touched off a five-year controversy with England over territorial rights.[10]

One of the two official artists on the journey to the Northwest Coast was José Cardero, a native of the Andalusian town of Ecija, who sailed with Malaspina from Cádiz as a twenty-one-year-old cabinboy in 1789. He was promoted to first boatswain and began producing volunteer sketches along the coast of South America. By the time the expedition reached Alaska, "Pepe," as he was called, had drawn a series of zoological illustrations, a number of general views, coastal profiles, and portraits of natives. He continued his productivity at Nootka Sound and Monterey, where he carefully depicted Indian features, dress, and activities. Upon his return to Acapulco, Cardero was assigned to a more specialized expedition returning to

View of Indian dwellings at the Port of Mulgrave (now Yakutat Bay) by José Cardero. Courtesy of the Museo de América, Madrid.

Indian fortification in the Strait of Juan de Fuca by José Cardero. Courtesy of the Museo de América, Madrid.

Nootka Sound and Vancouver Island under Captains Dionísio Alcalá Galiano and Cayetano Valdés in 1792.[11]

Tomás de Suría, the second Spanish artist to accompany Malaspina, was born in 1761 and studied at the Royal Art Academy of San Fernando in Madrid under Jerónimo Antonio Gil. He accompanied Gil to Mexico when his mentor was named director of the Mexican Art Academy of San Carlos. Suría was working as an engraver in the Mexican mint when Malaspina needed another artist to go to the Northwest Coast in 1791.[12] The young man was excited by the opportunity to travel and kept a diary of his experiences. Even though the sailing was rough at times, Suría was not disappointed. He thought the Tlingit Indians were "strange and marvelous subjects" and kept busy sketching portraits and general scenes. At Nootka Sound he produced a drawing entitled *A Dance on the Beach at Friendly Cove* and a portrait of Chief Maquinna. After returning to Mexico City, Suría worked for eight months on his drawings and then resumed work at the mint.[13] The majority of Suría's artwork can be found in the archives of the Museo Naval in Madrid.

The Royal Scientific Expedition to New Spain had been created by royal decree of Carlos III on October 27, 1786, under the direction of Dr. Martín de Sessé, a physician born in Aragón. Sessé and several other Spaniards, including the naturalist José Longinos Martínez, had reached Mexico in 1787 and set up the botanical garden and institute as specified by the king. Longinos preferred the study of birds and other fauna rather than plants and set up a small museum of natural history. Because of personal problems with Sessé, Longinos requested permission to travel on his own to San Blas and the Californias. The naturalist, who described and classified many of the birds along the way, completed his overland trek from Cabo San Lucas to Monterey in 1791 and 1792. His accompanying journal was probably completed somewhat later. Longinos eventually went to Guatemala to pursue a career as a naturalist in Guatemala City.[14]

By the time Malaspina's scientists arrived in Mexico in 1791, Sessé was able to show the visitors tangible results of his efforts. His plant collections were extensive and the institute's primary

Red-shafted flicker (Colaptes cafer) *by José Cardero. Courtesy of the Museo Naval, Madrid.*

illustrator, Atanásio Echeverría y Godoy, and several others from the San Carlos Academy, had produced hundreds of full-color illustrations. Echeverría, born in Mexico, was extremely talented and created such perfect reproductions of insects and butterflies that they looked like "they could escape from the page."[15] Because of his expertise, Echeverría was later chosen to accompany the expedition of Juan Francisco de la Bodega y Quadra to Nootka Sound in 1792. There he made drawings of Friendly Cove in addition to numerous portraits of Indians, sketches of native customs, and illustrations of botanical and zoological specimens.

Also accompanying Bodega y Quadra was José Mariano Moziño, a Mexican-born graduate of the botanical institute with previous formal training in theology and medicine. He soon became a hard-working member of the scientific group and a favorite of Sessé, but did not receive official full-time status until appointed to Bodega y Quadra's staff. Moziño spent six months

Fumaria cuculata, *fulmitory, based on a sketch by Atanásio Echeverría by Francisco Lindo. Courtesy of the Ministerio de Asuntos Exteriores, Madrid.*

at Nootka Sound and prepared a complete ethnographical account of the natives entitled *Noticias de Nutka*.[16] Echeverría's sketches, which illustrate this account, are today housed in the archives of the Ministerio de Asuntos Exteriores in Madrid.[17]

A final extension of both the efforts of Malaspina and Bodega y Quadra was the further exploration of the Northwest Coast by Alcalá Galiano and Valdés. Two small, shallow-draft schooners, the *Sutil* and *Mexicana* were built especially for entry into the islands and channels forming the inland passage behind Vancouver Island. José Cardero, finally given the title of "official artist," sailed aboard the *Mexicana* and also took over duties as scribe, cartographer, pilot, and journalist. The expedition visited Nuñez Gaona (Neah Bay) where Cardero sketched Chief Tetacu and other natives. The Spaniards then joined the English ships as they circumnavigated Vancouver Island.[18] The *Sutil* and *Mexicana* returned to Nootka Sound, where Bodega y Quadra was still in command, and immediately departed for Acapulco. Cardero's numerous drawings of general scenes, Indians, native customs, artifacts, and coastal profiles are today preserved in the archives of the Museo Naval and the Museo de America in Madrid.

Bodega y Quadra met with Vancouver for a short time to discuss settlement of the Nootka Sound controversy. Despite a most cordial relationship, the two commissioners could only agree to refer the matter to Madrid and London.[19] Bodega y Quadra departed from Nootka on September 22, 1792, and Vancouver set sail three weeks later. Moziño and Echeverría returned to Mexico City early in 1793 to resume work with the Royal Scientific Expedition in New Spain and Guatemala. Echeverría was instructed to turn over his sketches to artists at the Academy of San Carlos for completion.[20]

The Malaspina venture, completing its sixty-two-month exploration of the Americas, the Pacific Islands, Australia, and New Zealand, reached Cádiz in 1794. Malaspina was praised for his success, but his fame was short lived. A court intrigue involving Queen María Luisa of Parma, wife of Carlos IV, resulted in Malaspina's eight-year exile. Hundreds of volumes of documents, charts, coastal profiles, and illustrations, together with artifacts and other materials, were gathered together by Felipe Bauzá Canas, chief of charts and maps of the expedition, and

Scomber? mahvinos (species unknown) based on a sketch by Atanásio Echeverría by José María Montés de Oca. Courtesy of the Ministerio de Asuntos Exteriores, Madrid.

A chief from the north end of Vancouver Island in present-day Kwagiulth
territory by José Cardero. Courtesy of the Museo de América, Madrid.

preserved in the Depósito Hidrográfico, which later became the Museo Naval of Madrid.[21] Other materials retained by the Bauzá family were eventually deposited in the Museo de América in Madrid. Most of the botanical sketches were preserved in the archives of the Royal Botanical Garden of Madrid.

The Royal Scientific Expedition received an extension of its original six-year contract and continued in Mexico until 1803. In that year Martín Sessé and José Moziño returned to Madrid. Like Malaspina, although for different reasons, Sessé was unable to publish the results of his work; he died in mid-1808. Most of the descriptions and drawings of the expedition were placed in the archives of the Royal Botanical Garden and Museum of Natural History. In the fall of 1808, when Napoleon's forces took Madrid and placed Joseph Bonaparte on the throne, Moziño was appointed director of the Natural History Museum and given an opportunity to work on the flora and fauna of New Spain. The position proved to be the Mexican scientist's downfall. When the French withdrew from Madrid in 1812, Moziño was looked upon with disfavor by Spanish patriots and forced to flee with his manuscripts, some 2,000 drawings, and herbaria to Montpellier and Geneva.[22]

Echeverría, who had served in Cuba before returning to Madrid in 1802, took his family to Seville. As a result, the expedition's work was never completed. Today, however, some of the drawings remain in Geneva while the majority that Moziño had with him, including Echeverría's Nootka sketches, are presently housed in the Hunt Institute for Botanical Documentation at Carnegie Mellon University in Pittsburgh.[23]

Because of a new generation of scholars both in Spain and the United States, led primarily by the work and guidance of Donald C. Cutter, the early Spanish artists, scientists, and explorers of the Pacific Northwest Coast are receiving the recognition their contributions merit. As their fine watercolors, black and white washes, and pencil sketches become known, these official illustrators can take their place alongside their better-known English counterparts. The bicentennial celebrations of the 1790s in Spain and the Pacific Northwest have publicized the names of José Cardero, Tomás de Suría, and Atanásio Echeverría, and have awarded these artists some well-deserved acclaim.[24]

Chapter 4 Notes

1. Viaje de la Navegación hecha por el Alferez Graduado D. Juan Pérez...a la altura de los 55 grados, San Blas 3 de noviembre de 1774, Ms. Historia 62, Archivo General de la Nación, Mexico, D.F. The Spanish claim to 54° 40' north latitude was ceded to the United States by Spain in the Adams-Onís Treaty of 1819.

2. James Cook entered Nootka in 1778 and called the inlet King George's Sound; he later changed it to what he believed to be the native name of Nootka. See José Mariano Moziño, *Noticias de Nutka: An Account of Nootka Sound*, trans. and ed. by Iris H. Wilson Engstrand (Seattle: University of Washington Press, 1970; rev. ed., 1991), xxviii–xxix.

3. See Donald C. Cutter, "Malaspina's Grand Expedition," in *The Malaspina Expedition* (Santa Fe: Museum of New Mexico Press, 1977) 28–41;and Warren L. Cook, *Flood Tide of Empire: Spain and the Pacific Northwest, 1543–1819* (New Haven and London: Yale University Press, 1973).

4. At home, Carlos III centralized the administration of government, increased revenues, improved agriculture, reorganized the military, and in general gained a new prestige for Spain in Europe. As a patron of science, he founded the Royal Botanical Garden, the Museum of Natural Science, the Astronomical Observatory, and the Royal Academy of Medicine in Madrid. See Iris H. Wilson (Engstrand), "Spanish Scientists in the Pacific Northwest, 1790–1792," in John A. Carroll, ed., *Reflections of Western Historians* (Tucson: University of Arizona Press, 1969), 31–47.

5. Real Cedula del 27 de octubre de 1786, Flora Española—Año 1786, archives of the Museo Nacional de Ciencias Naturales, Madrid.

6. The major works of nomenclature developed by Swedish botanist Carolus Linnaeus (1707–78) were well known throughout the European scientific community by the late eighteenth century. His *Systema naturae* (1735), *Genera Plantarum* (1737), and *Species Plantarum* (1753) were used extensively as guides in the New World.

7. See Pedro de Novo y Colson, ed., *La Vuelta al Mundo por las corbetas Descubierta y Atrevida al Mando del Capitan de Navio D. Alejandro Malaspina desde 1789 a 1794* (Madrid: Depósito Hidrográfico, 1885). See also Donald C. Cutter, *Malaspina in California* (San Francisco: John Howell, 1960).

8. Plan de un Viaje Científico y Político a el Rededor del Mundo Remitido a el Exmo. Sr. Bailio Fray Antonio Valdés de Madrid en 10 Sept. de 1788, MS 316, archives of the Museo Naval, Madrid.

9. Donald C. Cutter, "Spanish Scientific Exploration along the Pacific Coast," in *The American West: An Appraisal*, ed. by Robert G. Ferris (Santa Fe: Museum of New Mexico Press, 1963), 153.

10. See William R. Manning, "The Nootka Sound Controversy," *American Historical Association Annual Report of 1904* (Washington, D.C.: U.S. Government Printing Office, 1905), 279–478; see also Derek Pethick, *The Nootka Connection: Europe and the Northwest Coast, 1790–1795* (Douglas & McIntyre Ltds., 1980).

11. Donald C. Cutter and Mercedes Palau de Iglesias, "Malaspina's Artists," *The Malaspina Expedition* (Santa Fe: Museum of New Mexico Press, 1977), 19–27.

12. Iris H. W. Engstrand, *Spanish Scientists in the New World: The Eighteenth-Century Expeditions* (Seattle: University of Washington Press, 1981), 52–53.

13. See Henry Raup Wagner, "Journal of Tomás de Suría of his Voyage with Malaspina to the Northwest Coast of America in 1791," *Pacific Historical Review* 5 (1936), 234–76. Rev. and newly ed. by Donald C. Cutter, Fairfield, Washington: Ye Galleon Press, 1980, 154–55. See also John Frazier Henry, *Early Maritime Artists of the Pacific Northwest Coast, 1741–1841* (Seattle: University of Washington Press, 1984).

14. See Engstrand, *Spanish Scientists in the New World*, 129–42. A manuscript copy of Longinos's journal is located in the Huntington Library, San Marino, California; see also Lesley Byrd Simpson, ed. and trans., *Journal of José Longinos Martínez* (San Francisco: John Howell, 1961).

15. Engstrand, *Spanish Scientists in the New World*, 25.

16. The translated title of Moziño's manuscript is "An account of Nootka Sound, of its discovery, location, and natural products; about the customs of its inhabitants, government, rites, chronology, language, music, poetry, fishing, hunting, fur trade: with an account of the voyages made by Europeans, particularly Spaniards, and of the agreement made between them and the English." Copies are located in the archives of the Museo Naval in Madrid and the Beinecke Library at Yale University, New Haven. A Spanish version edited by Alberto Carreño was published in Mexico in 1913. See Moziño, *Noticias de Nutka*, trans. and ed. by Engstrand, introduction.

17. Viaje a la Costa N. O. de la América Septentrional por Don Juan Francisco de la Bodega y Quadra . . . en el año de 1792, MS 145. A second set of drawings, a part of the privately owned Revilla Gigedo Collection, has been purchased by the Canadian government.

18. José Espinosa y Tello, ed., *Relación del viaje hecho por las goletas Sutil y Mexicana en el año 1792* (Madrid: Imprenta Real, 1802; repr. in Colección Chimalistac, Madrid: José Porrua Turanzas, 1958) and as edited by María Dolores Higueras and María Louisa Martin-Merás (Madrid: Museo Naval, 1991). See also Donald C. Cutter, *Malaspina and Galiano* (Seattle: University of Washington Press, 1991).

19. See Pethick, *The Nootka Connection*, ch. 7.

20. Engstrand, *Spanish Scientists in the New World*, 126.

21. See Thomas Vaughan, E. A. P. Crownhart-Vaughan, and Mercedes Palau de Iglesias, *Voyages of Enlightenment: Malaspina on the Northwest Coast 1791/1792* (Portland: Oregon Historical Society, 1977).

22. Engstrand, *Spanish Scientists in the New World*, pp. 173–85.

23. Engstrand, "The Unopened Gift: Spain's Contributions to Science during the Age of Enlightenment," *Terra* 22 (July/August 1984): 12–18.

24. Recent Spanish publications include a reprint of Novo y Colson's 1885 edition of Malaspina's *La Vuelta al Mundo por las corbetas Descubierta y Atrevida . . .* (Madrid: Museo Universal, 1984); Carmen Sotos Serrano, *Los Pintores de la Expedición de Alejandro Malaspina*, 2 vols. (Madrid: Real Académia de Historia, 1982); Mercedes Palau de Iglesias, *Catálogo de los Dibujos Aguadas y Acuarelas de la Expedición Malaspina* (Madrid: Ministerio de Cultura, 1980); Juan Felix Pimentel Igea, *Malaspina y La Ilustracion* (Madrid: Instituto de Historia y Cultura Naval, Ministerio de Defensa, 1989); *El Ojo del Totem: Arte y Cultura de los Indios del Noreste de América* (Madrid: Comisión Nacional Quinto Centenario, 1988); Belen Sánchez, ed., *La Botánica en la Expedición Malaspina, 1789–1794* (Madrid: Real Jardín Botánico, 1989); María Dolores Higueras, *Iconographic Album of the Malaspina Expedition to the Northwest Coast of America* (Madrid: Museo Naval, Ministerio de Marina, 1991).

5. Peter Pond and the Exploration of the Greater Northwest

by James P. Ronda

Henry Hamilton, governor of Lower Canada, had a quick eye when it came to sizing up others. His letters sparkle with sharp comments and astute judgments. When the governor met Peter Pond in the spring of 1785 he soon caught Pond's true temper. The trader, so Hamilton reported, had "a passion for making discoveries."[1] And the crown officer was right. Pond was no ordinary trader, busy exchanging hardware and cloth for pelts. In the years between 1776 and 1788 he was the foremost explorer of west-central Canada, what are today the provinces of Manitoba, Saskatchewan, and Alberta. But Pond was more than an explorer. He proved to be the era's keenest student of fur trade expansion and imperial geo-politics. Pond understood that the Northwest would be the final battleground for American empires. In that confrontation Pond's ideas would spark the imaginations of everyone from Alexander Mackenzie and Thomas Jefferson to George Vancouver and John Astor.

Governor Hamilton saw passion in Pond's heart and mind, and throughout Pond's life there was an excess of that passion. That drive had its dark side. Pond was implicated in the violent deaths of two, or perhaps three, fellow trappers. Such quick fury has prompted at least one scholar to write a brief essay with the telling title, "Was Peter Pond a Murderer?"[2] The answer is yes, but that violent streak was not the essential Pond. He was what Hamilton called him—a man in search of discovery.

That restless quest began early in life. Born in Milford, Connecticut, in 1740, Pond came from a family he once described as five generations "all waryers [warriors] Ither by Sea or Land."[3] Apprenticed to a cobbler, Pond soon broke the laces of bench and awl. The Seven Years War promised escape and adventure. "So strong was the Propensatey for the arme," he recalled later, "that I could not with Stand its Temtatons."[4] At sixteen, charmed by drums and uniforms, Peter Pond enlisted in the Seventh

Company of the First Connecticut Regiment. From 1756 until 1761 Pond pursued a military career, serving four enlistments in various militia outfits.

With the war against France winding down and Canada already in Anglo-American hands, the soldier's life promised less excitement and fewer rewards. His appetite for travel not yet satisfied, Pond turned to the sea. A merchant voyage to the West Indies showed him a world far removed from eastern lakes and woodlands. Upon returning to Milford, Pond found that his father had gone off on a three-year trading journey to Detroit. The three years young Pond stayed in Milford taking care of the family were by his own admission the longest time he had spent in one place since the age of sixteen.[5]

The elder Pond's trading venture to Detroit points to a fundamental shift in Western realities after 1760. In the years before the English conquest of New France, French traders and their native partners had forged a trade empire that stretched from Montreal through the Great Lakes and on to the very shadow of the Rockies. With the exception of posts held by the Hudson's Bay Company, English traders found the French monopoly a tough nut to crack. But by 1760, in the wake of French military defeats, that monopoly began to crumble. In the mid-1760s a tidal wave of Anglo-Americans washed through the Great Lakes and headed to the *pays d'en haut*. One of those eager young men was Peter Pond.[6]

Pond began his western trade career working out of Detroit. There he entered into a partnership with Felix Graham, a Montreal supply merchant. Pond quickly became part of the Great Lakes fur trade world. From Mackinac to Prairie du Chien he and his companions exchanged European goods for those of Indian manufacture. But the lure of thicker pelts and richer profits steadily drew Pond and the other "pedlars from Quebec" west and north into the Canadian provinces. By the mid-1770s men like Pond, Alexander Henry the elder, and Joseph Frobisher were doing business with Indians well beyond Lake Winnipeg.

Those dealings involved more than passing goods around a circle of Indian and European hands. Information—news about trails, passes, lakes, and rivers—also changed hands. In the summer of 1776 Henry and Frobisher set up trading shop among the Athabasca Indians at the mouth of Isle-à-la-Crosse Lake in present-day Saskatchewan. In the course of trade Henry began to hear about a lake and river system that might provide a quick connection to the Pacific. "They informed us," so Henry wrote later, "that there was, at the further end of that lake [Lake Athabasca], a river called Peace River, which descended from the Stony or Rocky Mountains, and from which mountains the distance to the salt lake, meaning the Pacific Ocean, was not great."[7] Here was the sought-after, the ever-elusive passage to India. By a lake and river system and an easy portage over the Rockies the Pacific could be reached at last. It was an intriguing idea not to be forgotten. It was also the sovereign idea that drove western exploration for the next two generations.

1778 was a year of extraordinary coincidences. There were parallels in time that year that would eventually shape the destiny of the greater Northwest. In the spring of 1778 Peter Pond led three canoes up the Churchill River, across La Loche River, and met a ridge of land called the Methye Portage. "As far as fur traders were concerned," writes historian Daniel Francis, "Methye was the top of the world."[8] Pond and his men crossed that height of land and entered the fur-rich Athabasca country. The Athabasca had not only brown gold but rivers that trended north and west. On the Athabasca River Pond built a post and virtually traded the clothes off his back. By July his party had collected some 140 packs of prime pelts.

But that trading brought more than rich fur. Alexander Henry had shared his geographic notions with Pond before heading to a well-deserved Montreal retirement. Pond then began to fashion his own vision of Northwestern realities. As he listened to native people talk about their world, the trader formulated a set of persuasive theories to explain what he heard. Vast lakes and swift rivers dominated the landscape. Might these somehow, just as Henry thought, be a plain path to the Pacific? In firelight and shadow, hope and illusion danced with reality. But for now Pond could give such dreams only scant attention. Business, and a growing relationship with the new North West Company, demanded all his time.

At the same moment as Pond and his men were struggling

over Methye Portage, another group of weary explorers was assaulting the Northwest from the opposite direction. More than a thousand miles west of Methye Captain James Cook pressed his search for the Northwest Passage. In late May his ships *Resolution* and *Discovery*, sailing along the Alaska coast, entered an opening north of the Kenai Peninsula. The shape of the bay and the presumed river beyond it seemed to fit prevailing notions about the passage. After several days of probing, Captain Charles Clerke of the *Discovery* characterized the waterway as "a fine spacious river . . . but a cursed unfortunate one for us." Cook agreed that the river (a river they had not really seen) was probably not *the* passage, but like Clerke he thought it stretched deep into the interior and would someday serve as "a very extensive inland communication."[9] It was not until 1794—fifteen years after Cook's death—that Captain George Vancouver found Cook's River to be a dead end now properly known as Cook's Inlet. But throughout the 1780s published accounts of the final Cook voyage kept the illusion alive.[10] Speculation about the course and use of the river intensified with the rapid growth of the fur trade between the Northwest Coast and China. Cook's mysterious river and the immense profits to be made selling sea otter pelts in Canton tantalized Pond and his entire generation.

The year 1778 also marked the publication of a book destined to extend Pond's ideas in ways he never imagined. The names Robert Rogers and Jonathan Carver are now only faint ink on history's pages. Rogers, a daring eighteenth-century soldier, is now associated with the style of partisan warfare his Rangers waged against Indians in northern New England. Jonathan Carver is almost wholly forgotten. But in the 1760s Rogers and Carver were in the advance guard of those exploring the Northwest and seeking the fabled passage to India.

In the mid-1760s Rogers began to think in a comprehensive way about the river systems of western North America. His mental geography pictured the continent divided north to south by a single height of land, a ridge that separated eastern waters from western ones. As Rogers imagined it, an exploring party need only follow the Mississippi to its headwaters, cross the divide, and come upon the source of a great river bound for the Pacific. Following the river Rogers named the Ouragon the hardy explorers would easily make their way to the riches of India and China.

Pleas for financial support from the British government fell on deaf ears and by 1766 Rogers was back in Massachusetts. There he laid plans for his own transcontinental passage to India. Recently appointed commander of the garrison at Michilimackinac, Rogers hoped to use that post as a base for his expedition. His chosen explorers were James Tute, a former officer in the Rangers, and Jonathan Carver, lately mustered out of the Massachusetts provincial militia. Carver's travels on the upper Mississippi in 1768 did not produce an easy portage to Pacific waters. What they did yield was a widely-read book and a much-consulted map based on his journals. In 1778, ten years after Carver's ill-fated search for the Ouragon, London booksellers offered a volume entitled *Travels through the Interior Parts of North America*. The first printing of the book contained a map depicting the headwaters of the Ouragon somewhere within present-day Minnesota or North Dakota. In subsequent editions Carver expanded his cartographic vision. The 1781 printing, appearing the year after his death, held a second map landmark. Here was the phrase "River of the West," located approximately where today's Columbia runs. The Ouragon had become the River of the West. Cook's River and a waterway Pond came to call the Naberkistagon were about to run in the same channel.[11]

Sometime after 1781 Pond took up the Cook's River challenge, and by extension the challenge that had obsessed Rogers and Carver. Just how Pond learned about the river remains unclear. He may have read an early account of the Cook voyage. More likely he heard about the waterway from Alexander Henry, just back from a visit to London and a meeting with the illustrious Sir Joseph Banks.[12] However that knowledge came to him, Pond was now convinced that one of the great rivers of the Athabasca country was in fact Cook's River. Wintering at Athabasca in 1784, Pond began to put his notions down in cartographic form. That earliest sketch is now lost, but a map he drafted the next year contains all its essential features. In fact, all the Pond maps express the same optimistic vision—that Lake Athabasca and the Great Slave Lake form a giant water hub for the entire Northwest. Pond imagined several rivers reaching out like spokes in a wheel toward the north and west. He was partially right. The Mackenzie, Peace, and Athabasca rivers do indeed point north and west from the lakes, but none is the navigable highway Pond eagerly sought. His 1785 map shows Cook's River striking inland from the Pacific while several Athabasca streams flow west to join it. In the early 1780s Pond was uncertain about connections between the lakes and the Pacific. He easily confused Cook's River with the Mackenzie, a simple error like the later one that made the Columbia and the Fraser one river. Pond's last map shows that by 1789 all his wishful thinking had hardened into conviction. Cook's River appears as a direct water link between Great Slave Lake and the Pacific.[13]

Pond's notions were expressed in more than maps. In October 1784 Montreal merchants and sometime Pond associates Benjamin and Joseph Frobisher declared their readiness to test his theories by sending out a formal exploring party. Most of the Frobisher petition to Governor-General Frederick Haldimand dealt with the need to find a new route from Lake Superior to Winnipeg now that Grand Portage was in American hands. But Pond's stamp was plain when the Frobishers claimed to have "in view another discovery of greater magnitude." The discovery they alluded to was the Cook's River passage to the sea. The Montreal merchants were willing to venture the passage if the crown would grant a ten-year trade monopoly west of Lake Superior. Here was the first sign that North West Company partners were prepared to strike west for the Pacific. Here were the origins of what became the Columbian Enterprise.[14]

In the spring of 1785 Pond launched his own campaign to win government financing for a western journey—and which government mattered little. Early in March he presented a now-lost petition to the Continental Congress then in session at New York. What has survived is a remarkably detailed map of the Northwest. This map is in two sections, the northern portion differing little from earlier Pond charts. The map shows a direct water connection from the western sea by way of Lakes Athabasca and Great Slave. There are also unnamed rivers piercing the Rockies to join the Pacific. Sensitive to his Amer-

ican audience, Pond conveniently repackaged his earlier proposals, shifting east-west river systems farther south. The
southern portion of the map contains elements that were fix-
tures in western cartography until after Lewis and Clark. In
territory that would someday become part of the United States,
Pond drew a Missouri River heading toward an easily portaged
Rocky Mountain continental divide. Once over the divide,
travelers were sure to find the great river "Naberkistagon,"
Pond's own version of the Great River of the West. Not wanting
any in Congress to miss his message, Pond noted that the distance from Pittsburgh to the confluence of the Ohio and Mississippi rivers was a mere 351 leagues. The cartography had been
tailored for new customers but the fabric of the dream remained the same. Pittsburgh to the Pacific, like Montreal to
Canton, was no fantastic voyage. Exploring distant rivers and
building posts to the western sea promised the wealth of the
Orient and a mighty western domain—surely prizes enough to
tempt the young Republic. But a Congress struggling to secure
independence so soon after a costly war had no time for such visionary schemes.[15]

Rebuffed by the Americans, Pond headed back to Montreal
and a meeting with Lt. Governor Henry Hamilton. During that
interview, and in a subsequent petition, Pond stressed the economic and imperial implications of his proposals. He warned
that time was moving against British interests. "Positive information" from Indians had confirmed a growing Russian presence on the Northwest Coast. Certain New England sources
were reporting Boston merchants busily preparing two vessels
for the coastal fur trade and the China market. Pond's intelligence was indeed accurate. Russian traders, led by Grigorii
Shelikhov, were eager to expand their influence south from
Kodiac. In less than fifteen years, Shelikhov and his rivals would
join forces to create the powerful, semi-official Russian American Company. The Yankees were equally aggressive. The ships
Columbia and *Lady Washington* were just the first in a growing
fleet headed from Boston to Pacific waters. That maritime
thrust, combined with newly-drawn Great Lakes borders, stood
to give the Americans a decided edge in any struggle for the
Northwest. Never mind that just a month before Pond was ready

to aid and abet that American advance. What he now proposed was an audacious plan to steal a march on both the Americans and the Russians. The North West Company, backed by crown sanction and funds, would explore the Cook's River route, construct a chain of posts from Atlantic to Pacific waters, and seize a western empire for Britain. From these posts the English could dominate the fur trade, strengthen Indian alliances, and defeat any imperial rival. Here was an ideal means to recover the national honor and economic initiative lost in the recent colonial rebellion. As Pond, or some more literate North West Company amanuensis put it, the plan "will be productive of Great National Advantages." Forceful as ever, Pond kept insisting that without royal support his passage to India might "very soon fall a prey to the enterprizes of other Nations."[16]

Hamilton proved a sympathetic audience. He plainly valued Pond's experience and quickly recognized the imperial rewards for exploration. "Mr. Pond's discoveries," he wrote, "may prove of infinite utility to this country." The explosive Nootka Sound Controversy was several years away but English ships were already challenging Spain's claims to the distant coast. It seemed to Hamilton that the same intense rivalries that had shaped the destiny of eastern North America now shifted to the Northwest. Britain could have a western kingdom but the price would be conflict with Russian, Spanish, and American pretenders. Hamilton believed that "the prosecution of [Pond's discoveries] may lead to establishments, at this period (considering the active and encroaching spirit of our neighbors) particularly necessary. The pre-occupying certain advantageous stations may be highly expedient." The governor was enthusiastic but the same could not be said of official London. What seemed urgent at Athabasca and Quebec was less pressing on the other side of the Atlantic.[17]

Pond's conjectures may not have found ready favor in government circles but there were always his friends and partners in the North West Company. During the summer of 1787 he was again in the North, this time exploring Great Slave Lake. Pond was especially attracted to what is today the Mackenzie River. Pondering the Mackenzie and its course, Pond became persuaded that Cook's River joined the Mackenzie. Here was the

Pacific highway. The map Pond drew that summer illustrates his expectations. Immediately above Cook's River he wrote the following:

Capt. Cook found the water on this coast to be much fresher [hole in ms.] Salt or Sea water: also a quantity of drift wood no doubt carried thither by the Rivers Araubaska, Peace, & Mountain as they commonly overflow their banks in the months of May and August the former owing to the breaking up of the ice and the latter to the great quantity of snow upon the mountains melting about that time and at each of these periods there arrives down a vast quantity of large wood such as is not to be meet with to the Northward of the abovementioned Rivers.[18]

Pond now had someone to instruct in these geographic notions. His wintering partner at Athabasca was the young and eager Alexander Mackenzie. The old trader—Pond was now a ripe forty-seven—became Mackenzie's tutor in geography and discovery. Mackenzie's future ventures to the Arctic and Pacific oceans were all predicated on Pond's theoretical geography. While some Nor'westers were not impressed by such speculations, ridiculing them as "extravagant ideas," Mackenzie and at least some partners were won over. When Pond quit Athabasca for the last time in May 1788 he left behind a potent legacy.[19]

It was not until 1789 that Pond's imperial geography got its first real test. Sometime in the spring, North West Company partners decided to send a small party to the Pacific by way of the presumed Mackenzie River–Cook's River passage. Pond's unsavory reputation made him an unlikely candidate to head the expedition. Instead, leadership fell to Mackenzie, who wrote years later, "I went on this expedition in hopes of getting into Cook's River."[20]

While Mackenzie was spending most of the summer pressing up the river that now bears his name, Pond was in the East still promoting his western program. He did not yet know that his protégé would eventually find not the Pacific but the ice-choked Arctic. In June Pond may have been in Philadelphia. Spanish ambassador Diego Maria de Gardoqui noted the presence of "one of the many enthusiastic Englishmen who roam these western countries inhabited only by Indians." Whoever this much-traveled adventurer was, he claimed to have gone as far as the Continental Divide. More telling, and further suggesting a Pond identification, the trader asserted that "the furthest nation he reached assured him that about 100 miles from that place was a river which empties into the Pacific Ocean." Like Pond, this explorer had a map of the far countries—a map that has evidently not survived.[21]

By early November 1789 Pond was most certainly in Quebec. It was there that he gave last and fullest expression to the project that had dominated his life for nearly a decade. In the first week of November he had talks with Isaac Ogden, a prominent Quebec merchant. As he had played mentor to Mackenzie, so now Pond sought to instruct Ogden. Using his 1787 map he began by giving a quick tour of the familiar Great Lakes and the trading routes to Great Slave Lake. At Great Slave Pond's geography slipped from reality to illusion. He confidently reported that a surging river ran out of the lake, striking southwest toward the Pacific. Pond was equally confident and mistaken about the character and extent of the Rocky Mountains. He claimed that the narrow chain ended abruptly south of his great river, allowing it to freely join Cook's River. Here was an inland, ice-free Northwest Passage bound to revive all the dreams of Jacques Cartier and Samuel de Champlain. Goods from Canton might yet find places in Lachine's warehouses.

The discussions with Isaac Ogden were more than mere classroom exercises. Pond always intended his discoveries to have both commercial and national applications. He certainly believed the Pacific route would bring wealth and power to any who ventured it. Such a water passage might easily shape the destiny of the entire Northwest. For Ogden's benefit Pond conjured up an empire peopled by more than fur merchants and their native partners. This West, so he claimed, had a rich agricultural future. Pelts, grain, tea, and silk—all would flow through a West linked to Montreal on the one hand and China on the other. All these economic wonders would be under the protection of an expanding British empire. Pond ended this lesson in the geography of imagination on a tantalizing note. He told Ogden that Alexander Mackenzie was already exploring the Cook's River region and would soon be in London by way of Russia. Still unaware of Mackenzie's unhappy discovery, Pond dreamed with all the confidence of any visionary.[22]

Isaac Ogden was not the first to fall under Pond's spell. The merchant described the wily trader as a "Gentleman of observation and Science" and carefully recorded their conversations in a long letter to his father in London. Enclosed in that letter was a redrawing of the 1787 map. Both the letter and map were published in the March 1790 issue of London's popular *Gentleman's Magazine*.[23] And as fortune would have it, Pond's thoughts caught the attention of government officials planning Captain George Vancouver's expedition to the Northwest Coast. Despite news of Mackenzie's initial failure—news already current in London—Pond's optimistic geography carried the day. Vancouver was instructed to seek out Cook's River and evaluate its economic and imperial potential.[24]

Odgen was not the only Quebecer taken with Pond's rough charm and appealing ideas. The trader caught the attention of Dr. John Mervin Nooth. Nooth was a respected physician with an abiding interest in natural history. The doctor regularly corresponded with Sir Joseph Banks. Banks had been deeply involved in the Cook voyages and eagerly collected any scrap of information about possible Northwest passages. Nooth was certain Banks would want to hear about that "very singular Person of the name of Pond" just come to Quebec. Pond repeated the now-familiar Cook's River tale, adding for Nooth some vague stories about new animals and unusual fossils to be found in the Northwest. Pond had no specimens for Nooth's natural history cabinet but there was his map, probably the same one he displayed for Ogden. The talk and the map were enough for Nooth. He was persuaded that exploring the Cook's River country would yield a rich scientific harvest.[25]

Pond's influence was much in evidence in September 1794 when Mackenzie was returning from his second and successful effort to reach the Pacific. Meeting with Lt. Governor John Graves Simcoe at Niagara, the explorer presented a grand program aimed at "the entire command of the fur trade of North America." If Pond had outlined the grand strategy, it was Mackenzie who filled in the tactical details. Like his teacher, Mackenzie knew the plan meant playing a high stakes imperial game. Both agreed that Britain had to field a single, government-funded company to meet Russian and American

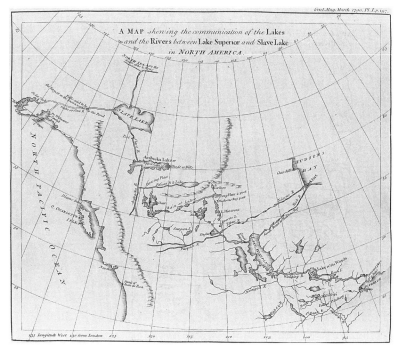

Peter Pond, map of northwestern America, Gentleman's Magazine,
March 1790. Author's collection.

competition. Pond had thought in terms of monies channeled
directly to the North West Company. Mackenzie now advanced
a bolder scheme—the kind of enterprise that would have ap-
pealed to the daring side of John Jacob Astor's character. He
proposed a merger, wedding the North West Company to the
Hudson's Bay Company. As Mackenzie saw it, the union would
be blessed with abundant capital and unrivaled power. Furs
from the Northwest would move swiftly to Pacific coast ports
along an efficient transport system based at Hudson Bay. Posts
operated by the joint company would dot the entire West, holding back the Yankees and keeping the Russians at bay. Commerce and sovereignty, the dual preoccupations of the eighteenth century, would now march in company to give Britain
domain from the Arctic to the Columbia.[26]

Water connections to the Pacific, dreams of China, trading
houses stretching across the continent, and money from a na-

tional treasury—these were the fundamentals of Peter Pond's imperial vision. Tracing exploration bloodlines can be a chancy business. It is plain that Mackenzie's ideas came directly from Pond. Those ideas became the conceptual core for what the North West Company called its Columbian Enterprise. Bringing that enterprise to life occupied the energies and intellects of men like Simon Fraser and David Thompson. If one Pond line has a Canadian course, another flows south to Monticello. Pond's notions, carried in Mackenzie's book *Voyages from Montreal*, had a profound effect on Jefferson and the planning of the Lewis and Clark expedition. As Donald Jackson has observed, when Jefferson read the conclusion of *Voyages from Montreal* with its lines about British commercial and imperial domination in the West, the president was "jolted back into thinking in terms of hemispheric geography."[27] A third Pond line runs to John Astor and the Astorians. Astoria, or more properly the Pacific Fur Company, was principally an imperial undertaking. Astor's notions of empire did not come from Lewis and Clark. Instead, they came from Pond by way of Astor's business partner and mentor in things western, Alexander Henry the elder.[28]

The genealogy of Northwest exploration is full of twists and surprises. Whatever its turns and switchbacks, part of its main line runs through the life and thought of Peter Pond. He never saw the Snake, the Columbia, or the Pacific, but his ideas were in the baggage of virtually every expedition that rode the region's rivers and threaded its passes. It was his passion for discovery, his remarkable grasp of imperial geography, that put him on the main stem. His passion informed and enlivened the schemes and journeys of others. Mackenzie, Fraser, Thompson, Vancouver, Jefferson, Lewis and Clark, Astor and the Astorians—all bore the imprint of Peter Pond, a Connecticut Yankee gone West.

Chapter 5 Notes

1. Hamilton to Colonial Office, Quebec, April 9, 1785, CO 2/47/667–668, Public Record Office, London.

2. W. Stewart Wallace, *The Pedlars from Quebec* (Toronto: Ryerson Press, 1954), 19–26. Additional details on Pond's life can be found in Barry M. Gough, *The Northwest Coast: British Navigation, Trade, and Discoveries to 1812* (Vancouver: University of British Columbia Press, 1992), 172–80; Harold A. Innis, *Peter Pond Fur Trader and Adventurer* (Toronto: Irwin and Gordon, 1930); Henry R. Wagner, *Peter Pond Fur Trader and Explorer* (New Haven: Yale University Library, 1955).

3. Pond, "Narrative, 1740–1776," in Charles M. Gates, ed., *Five Fur Traders of the Northwest* (St. Paul: Minnesota Historical Society, 1965), 18.

4. Ibid.

5. Ibid., p. 19.

6. Daniel Francis, *Battle for the West: Fur Traders and the Birth of Western Canada* (Edmonton: Hurtig Publishers, 1982), 42–47; E. E. Rich, *The Fur Trade and the Northwest to 1857* (Toronto: McClelland and Stewart, 1967), ch. 8.

7. Alexander Henry, *Travels and Adventures in Canada and the Indian Territories Between the Years 1760 and 1776* (1809; repr., Rutland, Vermont: Charles E. Tuttle, 1969), 331.

8. Francis, *Battle for the West*, 44.

9. J. C. Beaglehole, ed., *The Journals of Captain James Cook. The Voyage of the Resolution and Discovery 1776–1780* (Cambridge: Hakluyt Society, 1967), pt. 1, cxxviii, 367. See also Glyndwr Williams, "Myth and Reality: James Cook and the Theoretical Geography of North America," in Robin Fisher and Hugh Johnston, eds., *Captain James Cook and His Times* (Seattle: University of Washington Press, 1979), 59–80.

10. John Ledyard, *A Journal of Captain Cook's Last Voyage to the Pacific Ocean and in Quest of a Northwest Passage, between Asia and America*, ed. James K. Munford (1783; repr., Corvallis: Oregon State University Press, 1963), 80–81; John Rickman, *Journal of Captain Cook's Last-Voyage to the Pacific Ocean* (London: E. Newbery, 1781), 253. See also Barry M. Gough, "James Cook and the Origins of the Maritime Fur Trade," *American Neptune* 38 (1978): 217–24.

11. Jonathan Carver, *Travels through the Interior Parts of North America* (1778; repr. Minneapolis: Ross and Haines, 1956); John Parker, ed., *The Journals of Jonathan Carver and Related Documents 1766–1770* (St. Paul: Minnesota Historical Society, 1976).

12. Henry to Banks, Gravesend, March 25, 1781, Banks Papers, Sutro Library, San Francisco, California.

13. Reproductions of Pond's maps are in Wagner, *Pond*, map portfolio.

14. North West Company to Haldimand, Montreal, October 4, 1784, MG 11, Q Ser., vol. 24–2, pp. 405–8, National Archives of Canada, Ottawa.

15. Pond, "A Map Presented to Congress, New York, March 1, 1785," Wagner, *Pond*, map 1. A thorough search of congressional records for this period has failed to turn up Pond's petition.

16. Hamilton to Colonial Office, Quebec, April 9, 1785. CO 42/47/667–668, PRO-London; North West Company to Hamilton, Quebec, April 18, 1785, CO 42/47/649–651, PRO-London.

17. Hamilton to Colonial Office, Quebec, April 9, 1785, CO 42/47/667–668, PRO-London; Hamilton to Sidney, Quebec, June 6, 1785, MG 11, Q Ser., vol. 24–2, pp. 403–4, NAC-Ottawa.

18.. Wagner, *Pond*, map 3.

19. Patrick Small to Simon McTavish, Montreal, February 24, 1788, MG 19, Masson Collection, NAC-Ottawa.

20. Mackenzie, undated note, W. Kaye Lamb, ed., *The Journals and Letters of Sir Alexander Mackenzie* (Cambridge: Hakluyt Society, 1970), p. 19.

21. Diego Maria de Gardoqui to Conde de Floridablanca, Philadelphia, June 25, 1789, A. P. Nasatir, ed., *Before Lewis and Clark: Documents Illustrating the History of the Missouri, 1785–1804*, 2 vols. (St. Louis: St. Louis Historical Documents Foundation, 1952) 1: 130–31.

22. Isaac Ogden to David Ogden, Quebec, November 7, 1789, MG 11, Q Ser., vol. 49, pp. 357–59, NAC-Ottawa.

23. *Gentleman's Magazine*, March 1790, pp. 197–99.

24. Instructions to Captain George Vancouver, March 8, 1791, George Vancouver, *A Voyage of Discovery to the North Pacific Ocean and Round the World*, 4 vols., ed. W. Kaye Lamb (London: Hakluyt Society, 1984), 1: 284.

25.. Nooth to Banks, Quebec, November 4, 1789, Banks Papers, Sutro Library, San Francisco.

26. Mackenzie to Simcoe, York, September 10, 1794, Lamb, ed., *Journals and Letters of Mackenzie*, 455–56. See also Simcoe to Privy Council, York, early September 1794, E. A. Cruikshank, ed., *The Correspondence of Lt. Governor John Graves Simcoe, with Allied Documents*, 5 vols. (Toronto: Ontario Historical Society, 1923–1931), 3: 68–69.

27. Donald Jackson, *Thomas Jefferson and the Stony Mountains* (Urbana: University of Illinois Press, 1981), 121.

28. James P. Ronda, *Astoria and Empire* (Lincoln: University of Nebraska Press, 1990), ch. 1.

6. Language and Exploration: The Role of the Chinook Jargon*

by Richard Maxwell Brown

Chinook Jargon played a significant but largely overlooked role in the Pacific Northwest phase of what William H. Goetzmann terms the worldwide "Second Great Age of Discovery."[1] Goetzmann sees science as a key to the Second Great Age of Discovery with its emphasis on native peoples and on rocks, minerals, and plants as well as on mapping terrestrial space. Naturalists and artists vividly portrayed a remote world that was almost intoxicating in its variety and vitality, and in the age as a whole there was a strong tincture of romanticism.[2] All of these interpretive motifs are relevant to Chinook Jargon, for the latter fits into this broad paradigm of discovery as both a cause and a consequence of the exploration of the Pacific Northwest from the late eighteenth to the early twentieth century: as a *cause* in that Chinook Jargon was a crucial aid to the exploration of the Northwest from Oregon to Alaska through the early 1900s, and as a *consequence* in that the rapid spread of Chinook Jargon through the Northwest in the early nineteenth century was a result of the Euro-American exploration of the region's coast

For exploration, Chinook Jargon was, above all, a solution to the interpreter problem. Historians have not much emphasized the Indians who, from the time of the earliest European explorers of North America, almost invariably accompanied, supported, and guided the white discoverers. A notable exception to this neglect is James P. Ronda's 1984 book[3] which shows that what we call the Lewis and Clark expedition was really a joint white and Indian undertaking. Meriwether Lewis and William Clark were beset with a problem that plagued many a European- or Canadian- or American-led exploration: the multipli-

---

* This paper is based on a longer version (about forty pages of text) of July 23, 1988; it has the same title and is cited, below, as "long version."

city of Indian languages which hampered communication with the native inhabitants.

Several memorable passages in Ronda's book depict the "interpreter chain" which arose as a laborious, cumbersome, time-consuming, and not-very-satisfactory solution to the interpreter problem. On one typical occasion Lewis and Clark were able to carry on a critical conversation with Salish-speaking Indians only by means of an awkward, irritating interpreter chain of Salish to Shoshoni to Hidatsa to French to English.[4] As the Pacific Northwest's lingua franca consisted mainly of Chinook, Nootka, Chehalis, English, and French words, Chinook Jargon was spoken by upwards of 250,000 Indians and whites in the period from about 1810 to 1890.[5] It largely did away with the unwieldy, frustrating interpreter chain. Firsthand accounts of discovery in the Pacific Northwest almost always show that the guiding and support activity of Indians was a necessity. As time passed, these Indians usually knew Chinook Jargon, and on the white side of the expedition there was likely to be, also, a speaker of Chinook Jargon. In addition to providing much-needed geographical knowledge to white explorers, the Chinook Jargon-speaking Indian guides were an invaluable liaison to the Indians encountered along the way.

In this paper I will deal with Chinook Jargon in regard to four salient aspects of the exploration of the Pacific Northwest in the Second Great Age of Discovery: first, territorial exploration; second, scientific exploration; third, ethnographic exploration; and fourth, artistic exploration. Under each of these four rubrics, examples will be given of the role of Chinook Jargon. Chinook Jargon became a factor in the exploration of Alaska, but I will focus on Oregon, Washington, and British Columbia here.[6]

Territorial Exploration

Among the greatest epics of exploration in western North America were those conducted in the United States and Canada from the 1850s to the 1880s in search of railway routes to the Pacific.[7] During the 1870s, Sandford Fleming, Chief Engineer of the Canadian Pacific Railroad (CPR), directed a far-flung and remarkable exploratory enterprise.[8] Catching the imagination of Canadians in 1872, much as Frémont had caught the imagination of Americans at an earlier time, was Fleming's famous ocean-to-ocean expedition spearheading a transcontinental route for the CPR.[9] Playing a key role in the process of exploration led by Fleming was a heroic journey of discovery undertaken by Charles Horetzky.

A former employee of the Hudson's Bay Company, Horetzky was a strapping, black-bearded giant whom Fleming had taken aboard his ocean-to-ocean team of explorers and surveyors in mid-1872. Horetzky was a controversial figure who, however, had a remarkable talent for wilderness survival and exploration, which he demonstrated in the fall and winter of 1872–73 when, at Fleming's behest, he explored a possible Peace River route through the Rocky Mountains and into western British Columbia and on through the Skeena and Nass river country to the Pacific. Horetzky went through some of the grandly wild back country that, a century later, Edward Hoagland described in his own 1966 journal of British Columbia.[10] For Horetzky it was a journey of nearly 900 miles and, although underrated ever since, was one of the leading explorations of far western Canada.[11] As a result of it, Horetzky was one of the first to extol the mild climate and agricultural potential of the Peace River country,[12] and his exploration of the Skeena-Nass country provided the background for the early twentieth-century construction of the railway to Prince Rupert that flourishes today.[13]

By January 4, 1878, Horetzky was traveling without any white companions. He had reached the critical final stage of his intrepid exploration, which would take him from the infant frontier hamlet of Hazelton at the Forks of the Skeena to the sea. Of this last stretch, the decisive segment was from Hazelton along the Skeena and then northwest through rugged country to the Nass River and down it to its mouth. Skillful Indian guiding and support got Horetzky down to tidewater.

Horetzky's four Indian guides and carriers spoke no English, but they were, said Horetzky, "masters of the Chinook Jargon, a vocabulary of which . . . I carried with me, and by its aid I was soon upon a good understanding with my companions."[14] As he explored the Skeena-Nass country, Horetzky could not have known that he was traveling through an area that has been down to our own time—one of the stress points of Indian-white conflict in British Columbia. The Nass River was (and is) in the country of the Nisga'a (Tsimshian) Indians whose century-long land claim has lately been an explosive one in British Columbia.[15]

The first major stop of the Horetzky party was at Kitwancool, a village of Gitskan (also Tsimshian) Indians, which would soon assume its long status as one of the most conservative and militant Indian communities of British Columbia.[16] But this was in the future, and, although the arrival of Horetzky created a sensation, he was only surrounded but not harmed by curious, noisy villagers. Horetzky was both attracted to and repelled by what he saw at Kitwancool. He was dazzled by the Kitwancool totem poles. "My attention," he later wrote, "was caught by several tall and stately spars, beautifully carved into the most hideous and fantastic forms of creatures impossible to designate. One of recent construction, and measuring, I should think, four feet at the butt, had just been erected." This was the finest totem pole Horetzky had ever seen, and he thought it "worthy of a place in the British Museum."[17]

Horetzky's attention was riveted, also, by the house carvings of Kitwancool.[18] His aesthetic judgment was sound, for this was the place whose totem poles and buildings would fascinate Emily Carr fifty-five years later. Horetzky's mixture of attraction and repulsion in regard to Indian culture was elicited again one rainy night at Kitwanshelt on the Nass River where he witnessed a spectacular display by fifty masked Nisga'a dancers.[19] Horetzky's exploration of this wild, mountainous terrain was entirely successful, but it never would have been, he readily admitted, had it not been for the skill of the four Indian guides and carriers with whom he communicated in Chinook Jargon. One of them, known as "Doctor," Horetzky deemed the wisest of all, as he learned the first night on the trail when Doctor identified a campsite which to Horetzky looked impossible. Seeing the doubtful expression on the explorer's face, Doctor addressed him in Chinook Jargon, "Cloosh spose nisika sleep," which meant, said Horetzky, "that if I did not follow his advice we might go further and fare worse."[20] Horetzky took Doctor's advice as he did at future moments along the way.[21]

Scientific Exploration

Few if any explorers of the Pacific Northwest saw more of it than botanist David Douglas, whose mission was to describe the region's flora and collect botanical specimens to be sent back to England. Douglas's richly detailed journal of his travels of over 7,000 miles and his scientific achievements reveal that his mastery of Chinook Jargon was crucial to his botanical exploration of the Northwest between 1825 and 1827.[22] Douglas encountered Chinook Jargon as soon as he landed near the mouth of the Columbia, and he quickly began learning it. After less than a year in Oregon Country, Douglas proved his frontier mettle when, at the Dalles with a Hudson's Bay Company brigade, he was the only one present who knew Chinook Jargon well enough to calm down nearly 500 Indians who were in a "troublesome mood."[23] Douglas gained the respect of the Indians with whom he was in almost constant contact, and to them he became something of a legend. Bemused by his incessant collecting of flora, they termed him the "Man of Grass."[24]

This young Scottish botanist scientifically described the giant conifer which bears his name, but Douglas felt his greatest achievement was his discovery of another distinctive towering tree of the Pacific Northwest, the sugar pine, the search for which forms the thematic high point of Douglas's Northwest journal.[25] Having learned from the Indians of the tree and its location in the middle Umpqua country of southern Oregon, Douglas joined a Hudson's Bay Company headed in that direction in the early fall of 1826. Douglas's expert knowledge of Chinook Jargon was to be a key to his successful quest. By October thirteenth, Douglas and his HBC companions were approaching the Umpqua and the pivotal stage of his mission when they met two Indians upon whom Douglas would depend for valuable guidance. In his journal, Douglas happily recorded that both of the Indians spoke Chinook Jargon "fluently, in which I make myself well understood."[26] Douglas's journal then becomes a tale of wilderness survival in the challenging, hazardous, dripping-wet landscape. On October seventeenth, Douglas struck out accompanied only by an eighteen-year-old Indian guide with whom he had "no difficulty" conversing in Chinook Jargon.[27]

More Indian encounters and more conversations in Chinook Jargon ensued until, at last, on October 26, 1826, Douglas found the sugar pine at a place in the mountains west of present Roseburg, Oregon—a site to which he had been directed by a local Indian. One can sense Douglas's excitement that night as, by the light of a resinous brand of wood—which he called his "Columbia candle," he inscribed in his journal his "great impressions" of the "most beautiful and immense" sugar pine whose girth at the ground was nearly 80 feet and whose "remarkably straight" trunk was crowned 215 feet above him by "pendulous" branches with "the cones hanging from their points like small sugar-loaves in a grocer's shop."[28]

Ethnographic Exploration

In the ethnographic exploration of the Pacific Northwest, Chinook Jargon had a vital role as both object and agent of scholarly study. Among ethnographic explorers of the Pacific Northwest who were involved one way or another with Chinook Jargon, two, in particular, stand out for the originality and importance of their work. Each is an imposing figure in the history of anthropological scholarship in North America: Horatio Hale and, even more eminent, Franz Boas.[29]

As a member of the renowned, globe-girdling Wilkes Expedition of 1838–42, Horatio Hale was the first scholar to do sustained research and writing on Chinook Jargon. The official philologist of the expedition, Hale made his scholarly reputation by writing *Ethnology and Philology* (1848).[30] In this impressive and influential sixth volume of the expedition's publications was a significant fifteen-page treatment of Chinook Jargon that included a vocabulary.[31] Chinook Jargon vocabularies had been compiled and published before by Joel Palmer and others, but they were brief and amateurish.[32] Hale's was by far the most complete and the first to be done on scholarly principles. It was also the first to classify Chinook Jargon words by specific origin in an Indian or European language.

Hale composed his vocabulary at Fort Vancouver in 1841 during the visit of the Wilkes Expedition to that citadel of Northwest fur trading and exploration. Behind the post headquarters of Fort Vancouver was the so-called Kanaka Village of the *voyageurs* (some of whom were Kanaka, hence the village name) and other rank-and-file HBC employees and their families. Hale published a brief but striking description of Kanaka Village in which he emphasized its ethnic and racial pluralism and the major role of Chinook Jargon as a medium of speech within it. Among the 500 men, women, and children in the village were, said Hale, speakers of English, Canadian French, Hawaiian, and the Chinook and Cree languages. Yet many other tongues were in daily use by Indians visiting the fort for trade: Chehalis, Walla Walla, Calapooya, Nisqually, and other Indian languages were all to be heard.[33] Among such a medley of Indian and European languages, "the general communication" in the village was "maintained," Hale explained, "chiefly by means of the [Chinook] Jargon, which may be said to be the prevailing idiom."[34] The prevalence of Chinook Jargon at Kanaka Village is significant,[35] for the village was the social base of the HBC *voyageurs* who were vital to so many exploring and trading expeditions in the Northwest.[36]

Upon Hale's death in 1896, Franz Boas saluted him as one who "contributed more to our knowledge of the human race than perhaps any other single student."[37] Hale had maintained a life-long interest in Chinook Jargon. One of his last publications was an 1890 monograph on the language. Appearing forty-nine years after he first encountered Chinook Jargon, it was Horatio Hale's scholarly valedictory on the subject.[38] Also undertaken in the last decade of his life was Hale's supervision of a brilliant young ethnographer, Franz Boas, whose early years of British Columbia fieldwork were directed by Hale under what was, in effect, a long-term research grant to Boas for study of the Indians of the province.[39]

Indeed, Franz Boas's tremendous intellectual impact as an

anthropologist rested heavily upon his fieldwork (and that of his researchers) among Pacific Northwest Indians from 1886 to 1930[40]—a Herculean scholarly enterprise that resulted in nearly a score of books and book-length monographs. Boas did not hide his dependence upon Chinook Jargon as a principal means of contact with Indian informants.[41] On his first trip to the Northwest, Boas arrived at Victoria on September 18, 1886. Eleven days later he wrote to his parents in Germany that Chinook Jargon was the means of intertribal communication in the neighboring Indian village where, on the basis of his contacts among the Bella Coola, he was "gradually learning to understand" Chinook Jargon "quite well."[42] Much later, in 1933, when he was seventy-five years old and nearing the end of his career, Boas reminisced in the scholarly journal, *Language*: "I learned Chinook [Jargon] in 1885 [it was actually 1886, as I just indicated] from a number of Bella Coola and have used it with speakers of Tillamook, Clatsop, Chinook proper, Lower Chehalis, Songish, Kwakiutl, Bella Bella, Tsimshian, [and] Haida. . . ."[43]

One of the great moments in the span of Boas's nearly half century of fieldwork in the Northwest came when, against almost all hope, he discovered in 1890 that the last two native speakers of Chinook proper were residing on Willapa Bay on the Washington coast. These were a brother and a sister who lived in the town of Bay Center to which Boas eagerly made his way.[44] The contact with the sister, Catherine, was not productive, but the brother, Charles Cultee, proved to be a gold mine of Chinook language and lore. As Boas noted of his relationship with Charles Cultee in the introduction to the resulting important book, *Chinook Texts* (1894), "we conversed only by means of the Chinook Jargon."[45]

Artistic Exploration through Painting and Literature

Paul Kane's self-described mastery of Chinook Jargon[46] facilitated the travel and contacts that eventuated in his remarkable Indian portraits and paintings of Pacific Northwest scenes. Yet, in the quality of the artistic exploration of the Pacific Northwest, no one has exceeded Emily Carr of British Columbia, whose paintings of Indian villages, totem poles, tribal houses, and coastal forests have universal appeal.

Chinook Jargon was of value to Emily Carr in penetrating the Indian world, which was the ground of so much of her best art. Born in 1871, Carr grew to maturity in British Columbia at a time when the use of Chinook Jargon in the province was at its peak. Her immersion in the Indian world of British Columbia began in the summer of 1898 which she spent among missionaries to the Nootka band of Ucluelet Bay on the northwest coast of Vancouver Island. The twenty-six-year-old Emily was amazed to hear missionary E. May Armstrong deliver three sermons in Chinook Jargon to the Indians every Sunday. Emily and the Nootka took to each other.[47] Meanwhile, she envied May Armstrong's skill with Chinook Jargon, and, as the years passed, Carr gradually learned it herself and used it, along with English, to converse with her Squamish Indian friend, Sophie Frank, with whom she had one of the strongest bonds of her life.[48]

Just as David Douglas and Franz Boas, among others, had emotional high points in their exploration of the Pacific Northwest, Emily Carr had hers. A notable one was in 1928 when she visited the aforementioned Gitskan (Tsimshian) village of Kitwancool in the Skeena River country. Attracted by the fame of its carvings, which Charles Horetzky had probably been the first to mention, Carr overcame her fear of the well-known anti-white hostility of Kitwancool (which went back to the killing by whites of one "Kitwancool Jim" in 1888) to spend time in the village. As an inspiration for art, the village was all that Carr hoped it would be, and the Indians, aloof at first, warmed into friendship. The result included two of her greatest paintings, *Corner of Kitwancool Village* and *Totem Mother*.[49]

A part of the ambiance of her own time in British Columbia, Chinook Jargon was for Emily Carr a tool which, on occasion, she could use to speak to and be spoken to by Indians encountered in her artistic odyssey. For her, Chinook Jargon had no aesthetic significance, but it did for Theodore Winthrop, who put the lingua franca at the center of his artistic exploration of the Pacific Northwest. Winthrop's contribution, *The Canoe and the Saddle* (1863),[50]—despite its flaws of outlook and attitude—

was a classic book of regional description. About as anti-Indian as Emily Carr was pro-Indian, Winthrop, a patrician New England visitor to Washington Territory in 1853, tells the story of his sea and land journey from Port Townsend to The Dalles—a hegira in which he was guided and assisted by a succession of Indians with whom he conversed in Chinook Jargon.

With frequent quotations of dialogue in Chinook Jargon, *The Canoe and the Saddle* is one of the best accounts of just how Chinook Jargon replaced the interpreter chain and played a vital role in the practical function of Indian guiding in Pacific Northwest exploration, but Winthrop saw much more than utility in Chinook Jargon. *The Canoe and the Saddle* exemplifies the romanticism of the Second Great Age of Discovery, and Winthrop viewed Chinook Jargon in romantic terms. It is the passages in Chinook Jargon which give the book its distinctive flavor and spirit. Despite his disdain for most Indians, Winthrop loved Chinook Jargon but worried that its "beauties" would "be lost to literature."[51] To make sure that they were not was one reason that he wrote his book.

Social Significance: The Discovery of "The Character and Life" of Late Nineteenth-Century Urban Indians through Songs in Chinook Jargon

"The Chinook Jargon," announced Theodore Winthrop in *The Canoe and the Saddle*, "still expects"—meaning, awaits—"its poet."[52] A quarter of a century after those words were published, Chinook Jargon found its poet or, rather, its poets in the anonymous Indian authors of thirty-eight songs in Chinook Jargon transcribed and published by Franz Boas in 1888.[53] Noting that few were aware that "the Jargon is even used by native poets," Boas went on to state that the Indians of British Columbia

are at present in the habit of living part of the year in Victoria, Vancouver, or New Westminster, working in various trades: in saw-mills and canneries, on wharves, as sailors, etc. . . . At these places members of numerous tribes gather, who use Chinook [Jargon] as a means of communication. They have their own quarter in every city. The Indian is very hospitable, and particularly anxious to make a display of his wealth to visitors. Thus it happens that their little shanties are frequently places of merriment and joy; invitations are sent out, a great table is spread, and whiskey helps to stimulate the humor.... It is at such feasts that songs [in Chinook Jargon] frequently originate. If they happen to strike the fancy of the listening crowd they are taken up and, after a lapse of a few years, known all over the country.[54]

Boas printed the words of the thirty-eight songs in both Chinook Jargon and English. Only two to six lines long, these songs are, indeed, poetry of affecting emotion and appeal. Most of the songs, declared Boas, were composed by women. A number of them told of the parting or absence of friends or lovers. Here is one of those (in this and other songs below, the English version is given first, reversing Boas's order; in the Chinook Jargon version, Boas underscored words in English, and here they appear in italics):[55]

I cry always.	Ka'nowe *sun* naika kelai'!
Far away is my country now.	Saia e'eli naika mitlait alta.

The following song speaks for itself:

What is Billy doing now?	Ikta mamuk Billy* alta?
He is going to the beerhouse.	Yeke tlatowa *beerhouse*.
The American says: Get out of the way!	Boston wawa: *Get out o' way*!
	Yeke tlatowa. Haiu kelai.
He goes and cries aloud.	
	*Boas did not underscore this word.

Most touching in their pathos and with their own simple beauty are many songs to be found among those which, said Boas, composed the great majority of all: "songs of love and jealousy, such as are made by Indian women living in the cities, or by rejected lovers."[56] Here are some examples:

Good-bye, oh my dear Charlie!	*Good-bye, oh my dear Charlie*!
When you take a wife,	Spos maika iskum tlotchman,
Don't forget me.	Wek mainka ts'epe naika.

The author of this one was stricken but defiant:

I don't care	Kaltas kopa naika.
If you desert me.	Spos maika mash naika.

Many pretty boys are in the town.	Haiu puty *boys* kuli kopa *town.*
Soon I shall take another one.	Atlki weqt naika iskum.
That is not hard for me!	Wel k'al kopa naika.

Not all of the songs reflect the woman's viewpoint. Witness the following:

A white man is now your husband, Mary.	*White man* alta kopa maika *man, Mary.*
Ha, cast me off thus!	Dja! Tlos ka'koa maika mash naika.
I do not care now.	Kalta kopa naika alta.
Ya aya aya.	Ya aya aya.

Boas published the music for three of the songs.[57] This is the music for one of them:

And these are its words:

Ah, you my dear!	*Ah, you my dear*!
Where have you been all day?	*Where have you been all day?*
Thus Billy said to me.	Kakoa Billy wawa naika.

Of these brief, seemingly insignificant Chinook Jargon songs, Boas rightly concluded that they "convey a better idea of the character and life of the Indians living in the cities of British Columbia than a long description could do."[58]

Chapter 6 Notes

1. William H. Goetzmann, *New Lands, New Men: America and the Second Great Age of Discovery* (New York: Viking, 1986), 1.

2. Ibid., 1–11.

3. James P. Ronda, *Lewis and Clark among the Indians* (Lincoln: University of Nebraska Press, 1984).

4. Ibid., 116–17, 147, 156, 221, and passim. On p. 258, Ronda emphasizes Sacagawea's crucial importance to the expedition not as a guide but as a translator and key member of the interpreter chain.

5. Edwin Harper Thomas, *Chinook: A History and Dictionary of the Northwest Coast Trade Jargon* (Portland: Metropolitan Press, 1935), 4.

6. In addition to the activities of exploration and discovery by Charles Horetzky and others discussed below, additional cases of the role of Chinook Jargon in Alaska, British Columbia, Washington, and Oregon are discussed and cited in the long version.

7. In regard to the Pacific Northwest (American side of the border) dimension of these great railway surveys, Chinook Jargon was a significant aid to the explorers and surveyors under the direction of Isaac I. Stevens in 1853. This is discussed in the long version.

8. Sandford Fleming, *Canadian Pacific Railway: Report of Explorations and Surveys up to January, 1874* (1874). George M. Grant, *Ocean to Ocean: Sandford Fleming's Expedition through Canada in 1872...* (1873). Pierre Berton, *The Impossible Railway: The Building of the Canadian Pacific* (New York: Alfred A. Knopf, 1972), ch. 1–6.

9. Grant, *Ocean to Ocean*.

10. On Horetzky see Berton, *The Impossible Railway*, xvi, 32, 33–34, 94, 107, 112, 127, 161. Horetzky's brief official report of his 1872–73 exploration is appendix B, pp. 45–55, of Fleming, *Canadian Pacific Railway*. This Horetzky expanded into his book, *Canada on the Pacific: Being an Account of a Journey from Edmonton to the Pacific by the Peace River Valley...* (1874). In addition to his role as explorer, Horetzky was the official photographer for Fleming's 1872 expedition. During Horetzky's own 1872–73 exploration he was accompanied from Edmonton to Fort Saint James, B. C., by botanist John Macoun. Edward Hoagland's book is *Notes from the Century Before: A Journal of British Columbia* (New York: Random House, 1969).

11. For Horetzky's exploration in comparison to others in western Canada, see the map of Canada, "Exploratory Route Surveys, 1758 to 1905," *The National Atlas of Canada*, 4th ed., rev. (Toronto: Macmillan, 1974), 78.

12. Horetzky, *Canada on the Pacific*, 204–6. Bruce Ramsey, *PGE: Railway to the North* (Vancouver, B.C.: Mitchell Press, 1962), 193.

13. R. G. Large, *The Skeena: River of Destiny* (Vancouver, B.C.: Mitchell Press, 1957), 120. G. R. Stevens, *Canadian National Railways* (1962), vol. 2, ch. 8. Frederick A. Talbot, *The Making of a Great Canadian Railway...* (London: Seeley, Service, & Co., 1912), treats the building of the Grand Trunk Pacific Railway (later absorbed by the Canadian National) down the Skeena to its Prince Rupert terminus, a line that was completed in 1913. A key railway line advocated by Horetzky—one from the Peace River country and down into lower British Columbia via Pine Pass—was completed, at last, in 1957 with the opening of the Peace River extension (Prince George to Fort Saint John) of the Pacific Great Eastern Railway, which had already linked Vancouver with Prince George. Ramsey, *PGE*, ch. 8, 10. Thus, after an elapse of eighty-four years, explorer Horetzky's vision of the railway development of northern British Columbia was fully realized.

14. Horetzky, *Canada on the Pacific*, 114–16.

15. Robin Fisher, *Contact and Conflict: Indian-European Relations in British-Columbia, 1774–1890* (Vancouver, B.C.: University of British Columbia Press,

1977), 204–5, 208. Telephone interview with Glenn Bohn, reporter, *Vancouver Sun*, July 29, 1988.

16. Fisher, *Contact,* 208. Large, *Skeena,* 95–96.

17. Horetzky, *Canada on the Pacific,* 120–21.

18. Ibid.

19. Ibid., 130–32.

20. Ibid., 116.

21. Ibid., 117–33.

22. David Douglas, *Journal Kept by David Douglas during His Travels in North America, 1823–1827,* ed. W. Wilks (1914; repr. New York: Antiquarian Press, 1959). See also Athelstan George Harvey, *Douglas of the Fir . . .* (Cambridge: Harvard University Press, 1947).

23. Douglas, *Journal,* 107, 137–38, 142–43, 147, 149, 158.

24. Ibid., 199.

25. Ibid., 213–39. See, also, Harvey, *Douglas,* ch. 9.

26. Douglas, *Journal,* 221.

27. Ibid., 224.

28. Ibid., 229–31. Harvey, *Douglas,* 102.

29. On Hale see Walter Hough, "Hale, Horatio Emmons," *DAB* 8: 104–5. Goetzmann, *New Lands,* 293–95. On Boas see George W. Stocking, Jr., "Boas, Franz," *DAB,* suppl. III, pp. 81–86. Another significant ethnographic explorer of the Pacific Northwest was George Gibbs whose *Dictionary of the Chinook Jargon,* published in 1863 by the Smithsonian Institution, superceded Horatio Hale's 1846 vocabulary of the Chinook Jargon (see below) as the best scholarly treatment of the language. Gibbs is discussed in the long version. The most comprehensive treatment of Gibbs is Stephen Dow Beckham, "George Gibbs, 1815–1873: Historian and Ethnologist" (Ph.D. diss., University of California, Los Angeles, 1969), a perceptive study.

30. Horatio Hale, *Ethnology and Philology* (1846).

31. Ibid., 635–50.

32. Joel Palmer, *Journal of Travels over the Rocky Mountains, to the Mouth of the Columbia River . . . 1845 and 1846 . . .* (1847), and some other vocabularies cited in the long version. Ultimately, more than fifty dictionaries or vocabularies of Chinook Jargon were published in the Northwest. Thomas, *Chinook,* 3.

33. Hale, *Ethnology and Philology,* 644.

34. Ibid.

35. Chinook Jargon has always been classed as a pidgin and not a creole language—a creole being an artificially created language which then becomes a birth tongue in the second generation. Yet, in Kanaka Village at Fort Vancouver, Hale found that Chinook Jargon was so deeply embedded that it had become creolized. Thus, Hale announced that at the village in 1841 "many young children are growing up to whom this factitious language is really the mother-tongue." Hale, *Ethnology and Philology,* 644. "Chinook Jargon and Native Cultural Persistence in the Grand Ronde Indian Community, 1856–1907" (Ph.D. diss., University of Oregon, 1984) by anthropologist Henry Benjamin Zenk is a compelling study of one other case of the creolization of Chinook Jargon on the

Grand Ronde Indian Reservation of western Oregon in the period between 1856 and 1907.

36. Kanaka Village is treated in Susan Kardas, "'The People Bought This and the Clatsop Became Rich': A View of the Nineteenth-Century Fur Trade Relationships on the Lower Columbia between Chinookan Speakers, Whites, and Kanakas" (Ph.D. diss., Bryn Mawr College, 1971), chs. 4–6, especially ch. 4.

37. Goetzmann, *New Lands*, 295.

38. Horatio Hale, *An International Idiom: A Manual of the Oregon Trade Language or "Chinook Jargon"* (1890).

39. Goetzmann, *New Lands*, 295.

40. Stocking, "Boas."

41. Aside from Boas's own words, quoted below, on his dependence on Chinook Jargon, see the statement by Ronald P. Rohner in Rohner, ed., *The Ethnography of Franz Boas: Letters and Diaries of Franz Boas Written on the Northwest Coast from 1886 to 1931*, trans. Hedy Parker (Chicago: University of Chicago Press, 1969), xxiv.

42. Rohner, ed., *Ethnography*, 19–21, 28.

43. Franz Boas, "Note on the Chinook Jargon," *Language* 9 (1933): 208.

44. Franz Boas, *Chinook Texts* (1894), 5–6. Rohner, ed., *Ethnography*, 120–22.

45. Boas, *Chinook Texts,* 5–6.

46. Thomas Vaughan, ed., *Paul Kane, The Columbia Wanderer, 1846–47* (Portland: Oregon Historical Society, 1971), 25.

47. Maria Tippett, *Emily Carr: A Biography* (New York: Oxford University Press, 1979), 30–32. Emily Carr, *Klee Wyck* (1941; repr. Toronto: Irwin Publishing Co., 1962), 3–11. *Klee Wyck* is Carr's remarkable book of autobiographical sketches.

48. Tippett, *Emily Carr*, 80–81. Carr, *Klee Wyck*, 22–31.

49. Tippett, *Emily Carr*, 157–62.. Paula Blanshard, *The Life of Emily Carr* (Seattle: University of Washington Press, 1987), 187–88, 309n. Carr, *Klee Wyck*, 97–107. On the killing of Kitwancool Jim see Robin Fisher, *Contact*, 208.

50. Theodore Winthrop, *The Canoe and the Saddle* (1863). Timothy Egan, *The Good Rain: Across Time and Terrain in the Pacific Northwest* (New York: Alfred A. Knopf, 1990) uses *The Canoe and the Saddle* as its intellectual point of departure and pays tribute to Winthrop but does not mention Winthrop's attitude to Chinook Jargon.

51. Winthrop, *Canoe*, 6. Anthropologist Henry Benjamin Zenk (see n. 35, above) speaks Chinook Jargon fluently. Having recently heard Dr. Zenk deliver a speech in Chinook Jargon, I am convinced that Theodore Winthrop correctly admired the poetic, euphonious quality of spoken Chinook Jargon. Dr. Zenk delivered his speech at the conference on the Great River of the West: The Columbia River in Pacific Northwest History sponsored by the Center for Columbia River History at Vancouver, Washington, May 1, 1992.

52. Ibid.

53. Franz Boas, "Chinook Songs," *Journal of American Folk-Lore* 1 (1888): 220. Although Boas entitled this article "Chinook Songs" not "Chinook-Jargon Songs," the article was about Chinook-Jargon songs not songs in Chinook proper. Boas followed a practice that was widespread in British Columbia, Washington, and often elsewhere in referring to Chinook Jargon as, simply,

Chinook. In Boas's case as in others the context makes clear whether it is Chinook Jargon or Chinook proper to which reference is made.

54. Boas, "Chinook Songs," 220–21. For the sake of clarity, I have slightly altered the punctuation in the last sentence of the quotation.

55. The songs quoted below are from Boas, "Chinook Songs," 221–24.

56. Ibid., 222.

57. Ibid., 225.

58. Ibid., 224.

7. Lewis and Clark: Meeting the Challenges of the Trail

by Gary E. Moulton

The Lewis and Clark expedition is the most universally known event of American exploration and discovery. Because of this familiarity, there is a tendency to forget the great difficulties faced by the Corps of Discovery. The unparalleled success of the venture and the apparent ease with which it was carried out have caused historians to overlook or underrate the expedition's potential and actual problems. Perhaps these writers are reacting to the exaggeration of fiction and the hyperbole of less serious works. Nevertheless, the physical hardships and dangers of the trail were real. My theme is that the explorers met these physical challenges with determination and with good sense. They were neither foolhardy, nor were they timid. They were deliberate when possible, and quick-witted when necessary; they were as inventive and creative as situations demanded. Ever adaptable to changing conditions, they employed different strategies to meet the varied challenges.

During the nearly two and one-half years that Lewis and Clark and their party were out, they faced numerous challenges. Best known are the dramatic incidents with Indians, especially the facedown with the Teton Sioux and the bloody encounter with Piegan Blackfeet. There were other challenges as well. At times circumstances could tax the morale of the party. The captains' concern about this is reflected in the many references in their diaries to the men's spirit. Also of great concern was the enlisted men's health, especially threatened under their grueling labors.

As critical as these concerns were, however, it was the physical challenge of the trail that influenced so many other aspects of their exploration. As the strain of physical exertion mounted, so did the likelihood of accidents and illness. Exhaustion led to mishaps and mistakes. Burdened by arduous tasks, hampered by inclement weather, and slowed by the hardships of the terrain, the men would begin to feel the press of time. Hurried decisions and rushed judgments under stress could be disastrous. Their cool-headedness in the face of these predicaments accounts for much of the success of the expedition.

Before Meriwether Lewis set out on the expedition, President Jefferson instructed him in the general goals of the undertaking. In some areas he was quite specific, for example, in details about the men's relations with Indians. For the most part, however, his instructions were only general guidelines. Relying on Lewis's judgments, the president gave no recommendations about the daily routine of activities. He trusted Lewis to make the correct decisions in responding to immediate events. The goals of the expedition were Jefferson's, but decisions to accomplish those goals were to be Lewis's.[1]

Jefferson's confidence in Lewis had grown out of a life-long acquaintance. When as a young army officer Lewis had served as the president's private secretary, that confidence increased. Jefferson's choice of Lewis to head the expedition was not one of convenience. It was a deliberate and well-reasoned decision. He knew that Lewis's military experience had prepared him for leading this important assignment, and he trusted him in the work. Lewis, in turn, chose someone of confidence as his co-commander, a companion who could respond to unusual circumstances in a way that would not endanger the party. William Clark's military experiences likewise had prepared him for the rigors of frontier leadership.

The view of Lewis and Clark as cautious and patient leaders has not been universally accepted. Lewis particularly has been portrayed as somewhat rash and impatient. One historian who has examined the reasons for Lewis's suicide has suggested a pattern of rashness throughout the captain's life. Howard Kushner found childhood examples of Lewis's inclinations toward danger and later tendencies to put his life at risk. In explaining this character trait of Lewis's, Kushner used exaggerated terms like "extreme risk-taker," "compulsive pursuit of danger," and "invited rather than avoided danger." Concerning the expedition years, Kushner wrote: "Lewis's actions during his transcontinental explorations demonstrated both his extraordinary courage and his excessive gambling with his life." And he quoted John Bakeless, a Lewis biographer, who stated that "Lewis had most of the narrow escapes."[2]

It is instructive to examine Bakeless's passage.[3] The narrow escape he cites is Lewis's fall down a cliff a few miles out of St. Louis—an incident more readily viewed as an accident than as an example of risk-taking. And is it not the job of explorers to explore? Lewis may have had more narrow escapes, but there is a plausible answer to the occurrences. Lewis was more often on shore, away from the boat party doing naturalist work or reconnaissance duty, while Clark was on board and in relative safety. Lewis's other narrow escapes are also open to more conventional interpretations than willful gambling with his life. He certainly did not seek out a charging buffalo at the Great Falls of the Missouri, nor did he place himself in Pierre Cruzatte's line of fire near the end of the journey. Other members of the party also had their share of misfortune.

One incident that has been viewed as an example of Lewis's rashness calls for some examination. On May 14, 1805, a few days short of the mouth of the Musselshell River, in present Montana, Lewis and Clark were both on shore. Charbonneau temporarily took control of the main pirogue as it moved upriver some distance from shore. Suddenly a squall of wind struck the boat from the side and turned it. Charbonneau, whom Lewis called the "most timid waterman in the world," swung the boat farther around, bringing the wind's full force against the craft's sail, which was jerked from the hands of a boatman. The pirogue tilted on its side and began to fill with water, ready to go under. Cruzatte, an expert boatman on board, proved equal to the situation. Threatening to shoot Charbonneau if he did not reclaim the rudder, he also ordered men to bail water and row toward the shore, where they arrived barely above water.

Lewis, viewing the distressing scene from the shore, shouted orders to Charbonneau but could not be heard. He knew that the endangered boat contained the party's most important articles, including papers, instruments, medicine, and a large share of the Indian trade goods. Realizing the value of the cargo and forgetting himself for the moment, Lewis threw down his gun and prepared to jump into the river and swim the three hundred yards to the boat, when the folly of the idea struck him. All he could do was stand fretfully by. Lewis described his thoughts: "had I undertaken this . . . there was a hundred to one but what I should have paid the forfit of my life for the madness of my project, but this[,] had the perogue been lost, I should have valued but little."

Reason won out over impulse, and rather than rashness, the incident could easily be viewed as restraint on Lewis's part. It is interesting that this sentence has been lightly struck out in the original journal and the confession does not appear in Nicholas Biddle's narrative of the event.[4] Perhaps Lewis felt embarrassed by it later. It is easy to empathize with Lewis; almost anyone would be ready to dash head first into a similar situation without counting the cost. We might be more suspicious of the man's character if such thoughts had not crossed his mind.

Another matter that Kushner mentions is Attorney General Levi Lincoln's concern that Lewis might be too impulsive. Lincoln reviewed Jefferson's instructions to the captain and recommended changes in the wording.[5] His advice was:

From my ideas of Capt. Lewis he will be much more likely, in case of difficulty, to push too far, than to rec[e]de too soon. Would it not be well to change the term, '*certain* destruction' into *probable* destruction & to add—that these dangers are never to be encountered, which vigilance precaution & attention can secure against, at a reasonable expense.

Kushner failed to note, however, that Jefferson, knowing Lewis better than Lincoln, made no change in his instructions, and left matters to Lewis's own discretion. Moreover, at this same time Jefferson was recommending Lewis to his associates as a man of prudence.[6]

Kushner's interpretation of Lewis's character is partly echoed by David Lavender in a recent book on the expedition. Lavender also emphasized Levi Lincoln's assessment of Lewis and repeated it several times as a measure of the captain's character. Like Kushner, Lavender used damning phrases in depicting Lewis's actions, words like "reckless even for him," "impulsive nature," and "always impatient." Lavender seems bent on establishing this opinion of Lewis, even to the point of blaming him for imprudent behavior more rightly connected to Clark.

Lavender described a plan to assist the Mandan Indians in an attack against the Sioux as a strategy "fitted to Lewis's impulsive nature, [although] Clark apparently was its originator." Then within a few paragraphs he has Clark save the day "to keep Lewis's and his grand plan from crumbling."[7]

Lewis may have been impatient but he seems to have realized this trait about himself. While waiting out the melting snows of the Rocky Mountains in May 1806, he chafed at the "icy barrier which separates me from my friends and Country," then chided himself, "patience, patience."[8] Moreover, impatience is not a failing within itself. Lewis was certainly not impatient to the point of putting himself in jeopardy without good cause, and he was also careful about situations in which he placed his men. Lewis and Clark seem conscientiously to have avoided dangerous or deadly circumstances for the party. Nor is there any indication that the captains pushed the soldiers beyond their physical limits. They understood that this was not a wartime military patrol and that it was much more than a regular reconnaissance. In fact, once well on the trail, disciplinary problems disappeared and even soldierly grumbling seems to have ceased. Most common is the remark that the men were "all in good spirits"; the camaraderie of the Corps appears constant and genuine. Compare this to Captain Zebulon Montgomery Pike's characterization of his men as a "Dam'd set of Rascels."[9] It was not simple luck that only one man died (of natural causes) and that a displaced shoulder was the most serious accident to an enlisted man. At the end of the trip Jefferson would observe that Lewis had been as "careful as a father of those committed to his charge."[10]

Lewis and Clark used a number of different strategies as they met the challenges of the trail. Some obstacles called for direct action, others demanded diversion, while still others required complete avoidance. Meeting the three great physical challenges of the trail—the Great Falls of the Missouri, the Bitterroot Mountains, and the Great Falls of the Columbia—called for all of these.

On June 13, 1805, as Lewis walked upstream with an advance party, the men heard a roaring noise and saw clouds of spray that could only come from the Great Falls of the Missouri River.

Hidatsa informants had told them of this place during the previous winter; now they had arrived at the threshold of the Rocky
Mountains. Lewis's elation was great, reflected in his description of the beauty of the "sublime" spectacle, but the presence
of the five cascades and intervening rapids presented a new
problem, for the canoes and supplies must now be portaged
around this barrier. This task would consume an entire month
of precious time and test the endurance and ingenuity of the
Corps as no other episode to this point.

A survey of the area showed that a diversion of about eighteen miles would be necessary to skirt the falls. To transport the
heavy canoes and goods to their upper portage camp beyond
the falls, the captains directed Sergeant Patrick Gass, a carpen-
ter by trade, to construct wagons. Only one cottonwood tree was
found large enough for the twenty-two-inch wheels, so rounded
slabs from its trunk were cut for the purpose. The men im-
provised other carriage parts, such as tongues and axles, from
other nearby cottonwoods and from willows and elders. On one
trip some ingenious fellows even hoisted a sail over the wagon
in order to take advantage of the wind.

The men had to pull heavy loads across ground roughened by
the dried tracks of buffalo and infested with prickly pear cactus,
all of which tormented their thinly moccasined feet. The exertion was so great that at every rest stop they fell down and went
immediately to sleep. Some of the men were exempted from
this labor to hunt for the party's food, but they had to contend
with numerous grizzly bears. Occasional heavy rains drenched
everyone, and large hailstones injured several; rattlesnakes
and mosquitoes were also constant menaces.

Complaining of fatigue, the explorers nevertheless revealed
admirable endurance and patience under such adversity. They
could also display amazing coolness in the face of physical peril.
A torrent of rain and hail on June 29 caught Clark and a small
party near the river. Taking refuge in a ravine, they were
deluged by a wall of water running through the gully and were
nearly swept into the Missouri. Quick action by Clark, who was
waist deep in water himself, saved Sacagawea and her child;
looking back he saw the water rise to a depth of fifteen feet, carrying everything before it, including some of his valuable

equipment. Side-stepping obstacles did not guarantee an easy route, but diversion was the party's only recourse at the Great Falls.

Later that summer, after scaling Lemhi Pass and coming into present Idaho, the explorers were to face the most difficult physical challenge of the entire trip—crossing the rugged Bitterroot Mountains via the Lolo Trail. This challenge called for a carefully calculated strategy, since the most direct route was extremely treacherous, if not impossible. Wisdom called not for direct confrontation; it called for avoidance.

Geographical information obtained from Shoshone Indians about a route to the Columbia River was not encouraging. A reconnaissance by Clark confirmed that the Salmon River, though it did flow toward the Columbia, was unnavigable because of rapids. Moreover, sheer cliffs and precipices on the river made land travel along its banks equally impractical; scarce game and unsuitable timber for canoes were additional deterrents. Evading the direct but dangerous route on the Salmon altogether, the men decided to purchase horses from the Shoshones and cross the mountains at a point farther to the north.

Before the leaders made the final decision, Clark set down on paper the available options. One option involved sending a contingent down the Salmon by canoe, while the main party would travel overland and attempt to stay in touch with the river party. Clark ruled out this plan. He now knew the country well enough to anticipate the problems with such a course. Another consideration reflects the captain's concern about the scarce game in the area. Under this plan the main party would move north along the Bitterroot River toward the Lolo Trail, while a hunting patrol would return to buffalo grounds near the Great Falls to bring back meat via the Sun River. Lewis and Clark had learned of the Sun River route in discussions with the Shoshones, and Lewis would use the trail on his return trip. Clark crossed through this plan, rejecting it, perhaps because of the cost in time and the wide separation of the two parties.

The ultimate choice was actually the first plan Clark had written down. They would cross the mountains on horseback with the help of an Indian guide. Clark's written exercise illustrates a method of decision-making that may have been used throughout the journey, but perhaps more often in thought or in conversation than on paper. The notes also indicate the care with which decisions were made, Clark's soundness of judgment in this choice, and his remarkable understanding of a country he had never seen.

Fortunately, they were able to secure the services of an Indian guide, "Old Toby," who knew of a route over the ranges. Diversion and improvisation at the Missouri's Great Falls was now replaced by avoidance and dependence on Indian assistance in the Bitterroots. The latter part of August and much of September 1805 would be consumed by the overland trek, which would take the party over the rugged Lolo Trail.

The trip over the Bitterroot Mountains via the Lolo Trail was perhaps the severest physical test of the whole expedition. Winter was already beginning in the high country in September, and the party struggled through deepening snow. Lack of game forced the men to kill and eat some of their horses. Pack animals slipped and fell down steep mountainsides. Old Toby misled them at one point, costing precious time. Finally the captains decided to adopt a procedure used previously. Clark would go ahead with a small party to find open country and make contact with friendly Indians. Setting out with six men on September 18, he arrived two days later at Weippe Prairie, an open area in west-central Idaho. Here Clark was the first white man to meet the Nez Perce Indians. The long and difficult trip from mountain pass to meadows dashed all hope of a short portage across the Rocky Mountains and ended dreams of an easy passage to the Orient.

The explorers returned to boat travel after crossing the mountains, now descending the Snake and Columbia rivers. Indians had told the men of falls and rapids on the Columbia, but the explorers could not have anticipated the difficulties to come. In one fifty-five mile stretch, they encountered the most treacherous river conditions of the entire trip. They portaged some of the swirling waters. At other times, eager to reach the Pacific, they plunged directly through the rapids in their ungainly canoes, much to the amazement of Indians who were watching from the shore. Here again they adopted a variety of coping strategies in order to overcome a multiplicity of conditions.

On October 23, 1805, the party entered this spectacular but dangerous stretch of the Columbia. They found a series of three major barriers, created by the stream as it cut through the Cascade Range in its descent to the sea. More than a week of demanding physical effort was required to pass through this part of the river. They made a short, successful portage of their first obstacle, the Celilo, or Great, Falls. Local Indians, on the other hand, maneuvered their own heavily-loaded crafts through the high waters. In addition to battling the river, the men were now set upon by infuriating fleas and irritating body lice.

Immediately below the falls came The Dalles, comprising the short and long narrows of the river. In spite of the "horrid appearance of this agitated gut Swelling, boiling & whorling" as Clark described it, the party was forced to run the narrow passage since no portage was possible. Under the steady hand of Cruzatte the boats and much of the cargo were guided through the straits to the astonishment of onlooking Indians. Non-swimmers walked on shore carrying what they could of valuable supplies. The unperturbed Cruzatte played the fiddle in the evening as the men danced and entertained the locals.

After a few days rest and some drying out of supplies, the party approached the final barrier, the Cascades or Grand Rapids, which they negotiated on November 1–2. Here the river passed through a series of chutes and falls with such velocity that it was again necessary to portage men and equipment. Now somewhat familiar with the routine, the boatmen ran the rapids with little damage to the canoes and without injury to personnel. Lewis and Clark were much relieved at their success and within a few days they could exclaim triumphantly, if prematurely, "Ocian in View! O! the joy."

The challenges faced by Lewis and Clark on their expedition of discovery were probably not new or unique to them. Both had met similar challenges during their military service in the Ohio valley. Leading men on dangerous missions in wilderness settings against potentially hostile Indians was, after all, a task of most young officers of that era. But the transcontinental crossing challenged the captains in ways that earlier experiences could not have totally prepared them for.

The expedition called for difficult decisions under circumstances unmatched on the men's previous assignments and not encountered by their contemporaries. Cut off from the support and reliable advice of seasoned professionals, the captains had to depend on their own good judgment. In this they proved themselves entirely worthy of the president's trust, and they are still to be admired for their resourcefulness and ingenuity. Jefferson could not have wanted better leaders for the young nation's first great venture into western exploration.

Chapter 7 Notes

1. Jefferson's instructions to Lewis, June 20, 1803, in Donald Jackson, ed., *Letters of the Lewis and Clark Expedition with Related Documents, 1783–1854* 2d ed., 2 vols. (Urbana: University of Illinois Press, 1978), 1: 61–66.

2. Howard I. Kushner, "The Suicide of Meriwether Lewis: A Psychoanalytic Inquiry," *William and Mary Quarterly*, ser. 3, 38 (July 1981): 478–79.

3. John Bakeless, *Lewis and Clark: Partners in Discovery* (New York: William Morrow, 1947), 117.

4. Biddle's edition is most readily found in Elliott Coues, ed., *History of the Expedition under the Command of Lewis and Clark* . . . (1893; repr., 3 vols., New York: Dover Publications, 1965). The incident is described in 1: 310–11.

5. Lincoln to Jefferson, April 17, 1803, in Jackson, ed., *Letters of the Lewis and Clark Expedition*, 1: 35.

6. Jefferson to Benjamin Rush, February 28, 1803, in ibid., 1: 18–19.

7. David Lavender, *The Way to the Western Sea: Lewis and Clark Across the Continent* (New York: Harper and Row, 1988), 48, 63, 66, 74, 165, 296. Lavender's most sweeping estimate of Lewis as reckless is found on pp. 383–84.

8. Lewis's entry, May 17, 1806, in Gary E. Moulton, ed., *The Journals of the Lewis and Clark Expedition* 7 vols. to date (Lincoln: University of Nebraska Press, 1983–), 7: 267.

9. Donald Jackson, "How Lost was Zebulon Pike?" *American Heritage* 16 (February 1965): 13.

10. Jefferson's "Memoir of Meriwether Lewis," in Coues, ed., *History of the Expedition under the Command of Lewis and Clark*, 1: xxi.

8. The Men of the Frémont Expedition: Their Backgrounds and Recruitment

by Mary Lee Spence

In the twelve years between 1842 and 1854, John Charles Frémont completed five major expeditions into the West, three of them in the service of the U.S. Corps of Topographical Engineers. During the second, the most famous of all, he traversed that part of the Oregon Trail which is now in southern Idaho. The government had ordered him to connect his survey with those of the Pacific Coast reconnaissances of Commander Charles Wilkes in 1841–42. Consequently, he came to Fort Hall, and, in his progress along the Snake River, described or encamped at such places as American Falls, Shoshone Falls, Kanaka Rapids (his "Fishing Falls"), and Salmon Falls. It was "a melancholy and strange-looking country," he wrote, "one of fracture, violence and fire."[1] Crossing the Snake River at Three Island Ford, near Glenns Ferry, he curved northwest to Fort Boise and out onto the Columbia Plateau.

What of the size and composition of the expedition that crossed Idaho in 1843? Were the men representative of Frémont's other exploring parties? What were their backgrounds and training? How did they view their leader? And what about their commander himself—his education? his training? and his suitability for the tasks at hand?

When the expedition reached Fort Hall, it numbered thirty-nine men, including Frémont, and his black servant, Jacob Dodson, an eighteen-year-old free man. Jacob was also to be a member of the third expedition, which became involved in the conquest of California. A fine horseman, he once rode with Frémont from Los Angeles to Monterey in three days and ten hours, a remarkable ride of some 400 miles, much of it through mountainous country. On his fourth expedition, Frémont took another free black, Jackson Saunders, as his striker, and on the fifth expedition a mulatto, Albert Lea. All three were from the Benton household. Albert would be the Frémonts' servant for a

John Charles Frémont as he looked about 1847. From James Madison Cutts, History of the Conquest of California and New Mexico.

number of years in Bear Valley, California, until 1859, when, after a drastic personality change, he murdered his estranged wife in San Francisco and was hanged.[2]

Arriving with the expedition at Fort Hall, but not as a formal member of it, was Pennsylvanian William Gilpin, newspaper editor and later Colorado's first territorial governor. He wintered in the Willamette Valley and on his return to the United States the next year made reports on the Oregon country which were much sought after. It was not unusual for private persons to travel with the various expeditions, perhaps only a portion of the way as did an "Indian woman of the Snake nation" (and her two children) whose French engagé husband had been shot in the back at Lupton's Fort. At Lupton's Fort, Frémont divided his expedition. The widow accompanied him to the Bear River, while the murderer, Thomas Fallon, later a Bear Flagger and briefly a mayor of San Jose, joined the expedition as a paid *voyageur* and went with the FitzPatrick contingent.[3] The Indian woman seems not to have been a disruption, but private gentlemen travelers could bring danger. As Frémont noted, they were often "not trained to the care and vigilance and self-dependence" which such expeditions required and were "not subject to the orders which enforce attention and exertion."[4]

As was the case with his first expedition, his party consisted principally of Creole and French Canadian *voyageurs* who had become familiar with prairie life in the service of the fur companies in the Indian country, although the trend was beginning toward more American personnel. Five of the men had been with him in the initial expedition to the Wind River Mountains. In general the *voyageurs* received from $.45 to $1.00 per day. Eleven of them were discharged "voluntarily" at Fort Hall on September 20 and paid wages to November 20, which was the time period calculated to permit their return to St. Louis.[5] They were given guns, mounts, and twelve days' provisions to take them into buffalo country. Among those returning were Basil Lajeunesse, a favorite of Frémont's, and his brother François, who had been one of Sir William Drummond Stewart's employees on his journey of 1837. Basil was one of the five who had been on the first expedition, and he would go again on the third only to meet his death at the hands of the Modocs while he and his fellow expeditioners slept at Klamath Lake in 1846.

Two men elected to be discharged in Oregon in order that they might settle there; consequently, after completing his survey of the Oregon Trail and deciding to march in a great arc toward the Southwest, Frémont had but twenty-five or twenty-six men, including a Chinook Indian youth, William Perkins, who was anxious to "see the whites" and make an acquaintance with their institutions. The son of a chief, he knew a few words of English, having lived for some time in the household of H. W. K. Perkins, a missionary at The Dalles. He became very attached to Frémont, but after the party returned to the east, he was sent to Philadelphia to live with a Quaker family, returning the next spring with the third expedition to participate in the conquest of California.[6]

After the second expedition arrived at Sutter's Fort, yet another five were discharged "with their own consent," but not before the pay of two, Oliver Beaulieu and Philibert Courteau, had been docked for stealing sugar from the party's supplies. Frémont would encounter them again in California in 1846 when he bought supplies from Beaulieu and hired Courteau as a cattle guard. Among the five electing to remain in California were Thomas Fallon, who has already been noted, and Samuel Neal, who continued his blacksmith trade with John Sutter. Neal soon claimed a 22,000-acre ranch, Esquon, in Butte County and acquired some local fame for his fine animals.[7]

Apparently deranged by the trials of crossing the Sierra Nevada in mid-winter, *voyageur* Baptiste Deroiser wandered off for many days before returning to Sutter's establishment. Before he completed his fourteen-month circuit of the West, Frémont had a man, Jean Baptiste Tabeau, killed by Indians in the vicinity of present Littlefield, Arizona, on the Virgin River. Another, François Badeau, accidentally shot himself to death; and a third, Alexis Ayot, was crippled for life by a rifle accident in crossing a creek as the expedition neared home.

Listed as a *voyageur* in the financial records for the expedition, Louis Zindel was an immigrant from Germany with nineteen years experience as a commissioned officer of artillery in the Prussian army and skilled in the making of rockets and fireworks. He had charge of the brass twelve-pound howitzer with which the expedition was armed along with carbines, principally Hall's. Frémont had become acquainted with him on the

1839 expedition with Joseph N. Nicollet into the Minnesota country. In the interval, Zindel had opened a grocery store in St. Louis. He did not accompany Frémont on the third expedition, but made tents for it and later moved to Keokuk, Iowa, where he continued in the grocery trade.[8]

Lucien B. Maxwell, who had served the first expedition as a hunter, joined the second at Westport Landing and, for his own personal safety, traveled with it as far as Fort St. Vrain on the South Platte. He was on his way to Taos, and Frémont hoped he would be able to procure there ten or twelve mules, pack them with provisions, and bring them to the mouth of Fountain Creek on the Arkansas River (presently Pueblo, Colorado). Troubles in Taos prevented this, but Christopher Carson joined the group at Pueblo, as did also Charles Town, and Carson was able to obtain the necessary supplies from Bent's Fort some seventy-five miles below. Described by Frémont as a prudent and courageous man, Maxwell was the grandson of trader Pierre Menard of Illinois, was related to the Choteaus, and would marry the heiress of the vast Beaubien-Miranda tract in New Mexico and eventually become its sole owner. He had gone west early to trap and trade and by 1839 was working for Bent, St. Vrain and Company. Just prior to Frémont's first expedition he had resided in an Arapaho village as a trader. Maxwell would also be a member of Frémont's third expedition and play a role in the conquest of California.[9]

Both Charles Town and Kit Carson served as hunters for the expedition. Town, a native Saint Louisan and a friend of the Bents, had been in the West only since 1841.[10] Kit Carson had been Frémont's guide in 1842, a position now being officially filled by Thomas ("Broken Hand") FitzPatrick, who was receiving $3.33 1/3 per day for his services. FitzPatrick had been one of William Henry Ashley's brigade leaders and a partner in the Rocky Mountain Fur Company. During his activities in the fur trade, he had ranged over a vast region of the west, trapping in Oregon, in Blackfoot country, and in the Great Basin. It was while on a trip to the Southwest that he recruited the young Kit Carson for the mountains. When profits from the fur trade began to decline, he went to work as a guide and took the Bidwell-Bartleson emigrant train of 1841 as far as the Bear River in

Idaho and the White-Hastings party to Oregon the following year.[11]

Although listed on the financial vouchers as hunters, Kit Carson and Alexander (sometimes Alexis) Godey, who was picked up near the South Fork of the Platte, were much more than that to Frémont. Indeed, one might say that Carson was pilot and assistant. Born in 1809, he ran off at age sixteen from the saddler to whom he had been apprenticed in Missouri and made his way to Santa Fe with a wagon train. In time Ewing Young employed him as a trapper and he went all the way to California and back in 1829–31. After that he trapped for various outfits or for himself in the Rockies (the 1843 visit to Fort Hall was not his first) until it was no longer possible to make a living at it. Frémont was on a Missouri River steamboat, heading for Kansas Landing to start his first expedition, when he met Carson, who was returning from placing his little Indian daughter with relatives in St. Louis. Recommending himself as a guide, Carson got the job and over the years Frémont developed a real affinity for him.

Younger and less well educated than FitzPatrick, Carson, like many of the *voyageurs*, was at that time unable to sign his name on the pay vouchers, but he could converse in French, Spanish, and several Indian dialects. To Frémont, the older guide was "Mr. FitzPatrick," while the younger man was just plain Carson or, more often, Kit. Harvey Carter speculates that since Fitz-Patrick and one of Frémont's later guides, Joseph R. Walker, had been firmly established in the fur trade, they found it difficult to follow a younger man and that Frémont found it difficult to warm up to them. Whatever the reason, it was the billing Frémont gave Carson in his two official reports, widely published and read, which made the reticent mountain man famous. The fact that Mrs. Frémont and Senator Thomas Hart Benton liked him and paid public tribute to him did not hurt in the creation of the legendary Carson.[12]

As Carson and Maxwell had done, Alexander Godey (1818–89), a Saint Louis Creole, went to the mountains as a youth, trapping for Nathaniel Wyeth and supplying meat to Fort Hall. In the spring of 1836, he and Carson made a hunt on the Humboldt River in the employment of Thomas McKay of the

Hudson's Bay Company. Godey was serving as a hunter at Fort St. Vrain when he and his mule joined Frémont, beginning an association that would be a lengthy one. He would go on the third and fourth expeditions and when the latter was overcome by winter weather in the San Juan Mountains, with ten men dying, Godey was largely responsible for rescuing the survivors who were strung out along the upper Rio Grande. Frémont early recognized his reliability with strong praise: "In courage and professional skill," he wrote, "[Godey] was a formidable rival to Carson and constantly afterwards was among the best and most efficient of the party, and in difficult situations was of incalculable value."[13] Carson and Godey were two of the three that Frémont named many years later who had the mettle to have become marshals under Napoleon, "chosen as he chose men." The third was Richard Owens, expert Ohio gunsmith, who had been with Nathaniel Wyeth in the Oregon country in the mid-thirties, fought hostile Blackfeet and grizzlies alike, stole horses from the Shoshone, and ranged through much of the area between Fort St. Vrain and the Black Hills before he became a member of Frémont's third expedition.[14]

Quite in contrast to such veterans was eighteen-year-old Theodore Talbot, whose role was not designated on the pay vouchers. He came along at the recommendation of the Chief of the Corps of Topographical Engineers and served as a sort of aide to Frémont with a "view to advancement in his profession," presumably the army since he had once attended military school in Kentucky and later made the military a permanent career. The son of a deceased United States senator from Kentucky, Theodore was a Catholic and his social standing was at least upper middle class. He gave evidence of a superior education, being able to quote Horace and Shakespeare and to use phrases in Latin or French.[15]

Then there was Charles Preuss, the topographer and artist for the expedition. He had been born in Germany, studied the science of geodesy, which was just then coming into its own, and begun his professional career as a surveyor for the Prussian government. He emigrated in 1834 and was hired by the U.S. Coast Survey under Ferdinand Hassler, who introduced him to Frémont. This was his second expedition with Frémont and their association was to extend over many years. He was not a happy or well-adjusted man—he hanged himself in 1854—but the extent of his frequent miseries was not revealed until the translation and publication of his western diaries. There he comes across as a dour traveler, unhappy with Frémont, unhappy with hardship and inclement weather. Assuming that his own diaries are in part catharsis, we can place some credence in Frémont's recollections of the man as one who had served him willingly and well, enduring hardships cheerfully and patiently. Occasionally tensions between the two men did surface, as at Fort Vancouver when Frémont offered to accept his resignation. One of the irritants was Frémont's wish to have Preuss make himself "presentable" to the authorities by shaving his beard. "Nothing doing!" Preuss recorded in his diary. "That would be the last straw, to have the disagreeable feeling of a growing beard for two weeks just for the privilege of a few dinner invitations. No! No! I'd rather stay with the Indians in the tent, especially since we have good bread, butter, milk, and potatoes."[16]

Preuss was responsible for the thirteen dramatic lithographs in the first and second expedition reports and he played a major role in drafting the maps that came out of the Frémont surveys and which did so much to change the entire picture of the West. While Frémont was away on his third expedition, Preuss, upon authorization by the Senate, did a map of the Oregon Trail in seven sections so that the wagon traveler could handle one section with ease, even on a windy day. The scale of ten miles to the inch, or approximately 250 miles per sheet, permitted much more detail than that on the 1845 map. Furthermore, printed over the face of the map was the mileage from Westport as well as excerpts from Frémont's reports giving information on game, grass, fuel, and Indians. For example on Section VI, west of Kanaka Rapids, one learned that salmon, fresh and dried, could be obtained from the Indians, and at this location on the Oregon Trail the traveler was about 1,320 miles from Westport Landing.

There were Indians in varying numbers and for varying lengths of periods in all of Frémont's expeditions, primarily serving as guides, hunters, canoeists, and porters. Sometimes it

American Falls. From Frémont's 1845 report.

was not always easy to find a native guide who would venture into strange territory with such a fearsome-looking group as the expeditioners. After leaving Klamath Lake in December 1843, Frémont encountered great difficulty in obtaining guides, and, once persuaded, they sometimes deserted. Of two Washoes who had been enticed, an amused Frémont noted: "Our guides wore out their moccasions; and putting one of them on a horse, we enjoyed the unusual sight of an Indian who could not ride. He could not even guide the animal, and appeared to have no knowledge of horses."[17]

Coming home from California with him the next Spring were two Tularé Indian *vaqueros* who subsequently went with him on both the third and fourth expeditions.[18] In addition, on the third he had the services of nine Delaware hunters, two of whom were chiefs—Swanuck and Sagundai. One of the nine, Crane, was killed by Modocs at Klamath Lake and the others joined the California Battalion.[19]

Sagundai negotiated the contract by which ten Delaware hunters were to go on the fifth expedition—receiving two dollars per day and furnishing their own animals. Frémont was to provide the ammunition and saddles. Actually as many as twelve Delawares and four Wyandotts seemed to have served, some only briefly, but always they constituted one-half the per-

Thousand Springs, near Hagerman, Idaho. Labeled "outlet of sub-terranean river" in Frémont's 1845 report.

sonnel of the reconnaissance force. Carvalho records that he never saw "a more noble set of Indians," that most were six feet tall, and that most spoke English and all understood it. Although they maintained a separate camp and were under the command of their own captain, they seemed to have been very much integrated into the work of the expedition. Frémont sent eight of them back from California by sea, but one died before reaching St. Louis.[20]

In terms of personnel, the second expedition was fairly representative of the two other government surveys which Frémont led. The first, with its limited objective of the South Pass, had been smaller; the third, with approximately sixty-two men when he entered California, was much larger and less dominated by the creoles. Persons with Hispanic names were beginning to replace French Canadians as laborers. Recruiting for the first and second expeditions seems to have been informal, perhaps through contacts with fur companies or even *voyageur* friendships. When Frémont recruited for his third expedition, he gave notice through the papers that those who wished to accompany him could meet him at the Planters Warehouse, one of the largest in Saint Louis, where he would explain the objects, duties, and pay of the expedition. He was swamped with applicants (there were forty-two for the position of artist alone) and had to hold the meeting in the open. Theodore Talbot described the situation:

I walked round to the place of meeting about this time with Mr. Bent to see what was going on. The whole street and open space was crowded. We could only trace the Captain's motions by the denser nucleus which moved hither and thither. They broke the fences down and the Captain finally used a wagon as his rostrum but it was impossible for him to make himself heard. Each one being unwilling to allow his neighbor the advantage of having a word with or even being seen by Frémont.[21]

Talbot feared that some who would render little service had been signed on because of the influence of their friends. And indeed, the expedition was not too far out before ten to fourteen men turned back, perhaps dissatisfied with the strict discipline.

The fourth and fifth expeditions, financed by private means, were constituted somewhat differently. Three businessmen, who hoped to see railroad tracks stretch westward from St. Louis to the Pacific, underwrote some of the costs; Frémont and his father-in-law, Thomas Hart Benton, may have also put in money.[22] Frémont asked veterans of previous expeditions to join him, and sixteen or almost one-half of the total force that entered the San Juan Mountains had been with him earlier. Some were undoubtedly paid; others seem to have hoped, a hope perhaps encouraged by Frémont, that Congress would appropriate money after the survey was completed in order to compensate retroactively.[23]

Among the veterans who stepped forward was the ex-commander of Sutter's Fort, Edward Kern of Philadelphia, who had served as Frémont's artist and topographer on the third expedition. Kern also volunteered the services of two of his brothers, Richard, himself an artist, and Benjamin, a trained physician. Both Edward and Richard had studied and taught at Franklin Institute and were well grounded in science as well as drawing, excellent training for the precise recording expected of an artist-explorer in the West. Ben was a graduate of Pennsylvania Medical College and went as the expedition's doctor and naturalist. All three brothers were members of the Philadelphia Academy of Natural Sciences and no doubt expected to send to eastern colleagues a wealth of information about new flora, fauna, and fossils. All three were curious-minded and enterprising; perhaps they would settle in California or return with newly honed skills. To a friend, Richard Kern cavalierly explained the trip across the continent as "an opportunity to improve myself [in] landscape painting."[24]

Other veterans coming forward were Godey; Preuss; Henry King, from the gentry of Georgetown; Charles Taplin of St. Louis, who had obtained a regular commission in the army after serving on both the second and third expeditions; and Raphael Proue, a *voyageur* who would be making his fourth trip with Frémont. New recruits included botanist Frederick Creutzfeldt, probably a friend of Preuss; Micajah McGehee, a young graduate of Transylvania University and the son of a Mississippi judge and planter; Julius E. Ducatel, the son of the state geologist of Maryland; and Captain Andrew Cathcart, who was searching for game and excitement. Cathcart was the descendant of a wealthy Ayrshire family and had served in the 10th and 11th Hussars before leaving the British army in 1846.[25]

These few examples should be sufficient to indicate that the fourth expedition was composed largely of gentlemen and artisans rather than of artisans, trappers, and *voyageurs*, as had been true of the three previous expeditions. Many were independent spirits; some were paying their own way, perhaps even supplying their own equipment. They did not take orders easily and they resented the fact that on the trail they were sometimes expected to do the work of muleteers.[26] Furthermore, quite a few were greenhorns, and some were very young and inexperienced in the survival techniques of the West.[27]

As for the fourth, funding for the fifth expedition was private. Financial vouchers for this expedition are not extant either, but there is evidence that all the men were promised compensation, and perhaps Frémont's authority was greater.[28] It was a small expedition—only twenty-one men (including Frémont) and fifty-four shod animals—when it left Bent's Fort. Frémont was acting as his own guide, but had with him a photographer-artist, Solomon Nunes Carvalho, and three engineers, including F. W. Egloffstein, a Prussian baron, who later became a member of the surveys of E. G. Beckwith and Joseph C. Ives.[29] The size was reduced even farther when for health reasons Carvalho and Egloffstein withdrew at Parowan.

What about the education and training of the leader of these five expeditions? Frémont, a South Carolinian, had a good grounding in classics and mathematics and a B.A. degree from the College of Charleston, which had been bestowed seven years after the institution had dismissed him for "incorrigible negligence." He had taught mathematics to midshipmen on board the USS *Natchez*, worked as surveyor along the route of the projected Charleston, Louisville, and Cincinnati Railroad, and had been the assistant of Captain William G. Williams of the U.S. Corps of Topographical Engineers in the survey of the Cherokee Indians' lands in Georgia, Tennessee, and North Carolina. Frémont remembered the latter as a strenuous survey of forest and mountain country, made hurriedly in midwinter, but here he found the path he was destined to walk. In December 1837, he applied for a commission in the U.S. Corps of Topographical Engineers; a few months later, Captain Williams was instructed to come to Washington as soon as the survey was completed and to bring the applicant with him. South Carolinian Joel R. Poinsett, now Secretary of War, requested that the twenty-five-year-old Frémont be assigned as a civilian assistant to the distinguished French scientist Joseph Nicolas Nicollet, who was about to embark upon an examination of the northern territory lying between the Mississippi and Missouri rivers. The survey into the Minnesota country would require two expeditions, and it was while he was away on the first that Frémont's commission as a lieutenant in the Topographical Corps was approved.

The Corps of Topographical Engineers, as a separate unit with its own chief, but under the Secretary of War, was officially created in 1838, and only seventy-two officers would serve between that date and its official ending in 1863. Of these seventy-two, all but eight had been graduated from the Military Academy at West Point, which at the time had a heavy emphasis on engineering, with liberal arts playing little part in the course of study.[30] Frémont was one of the non-West Pointers, and later he and his close associates became convinced that he had encountered prejudices and paid a heavy penalty for not having entered the army through the gates of the academy. On the other hand, his army critics were equally convinced that his rapid advancement was due to his political connections. One prospective voter, taking note of Frémont's bid for the presidency in 1856, no doubt reflected the views of many Americans when he wrote, "I should not be ill-pleased to learn, that he has made himself what he is, unaided by a college of any sort."[31]

The two-year expedition with Nicollet and the subsequent labors on the report and map of that survey "proved to be Frémont's Yale and his Harvard," as William Goetzmann has noted.[32] Under the French scientist, Frémont learned sophisticated methods of geodetic surveying, including using the barometer to measure altitude, a considerable amount of geology, how to manage an expedition, and care in taking observations. No doubt his mentor encouraged him to read the works of world-renowned geographer Alexander von Humboldt, and his knowledge of plants must have been enriched through contact with Charles Geyer, the botanist for Nicollet's 1838 foray and later for Frémont's Des Moines River survey.

Nicollet was pleased with his pupil and wrote to Poinsett that he had "justified on all points the high hopes you had of him." He went on to add:

In all the courses of our campaign, it is not only in science that I have tried to develop the ideas of Mr. Frémont, but also [I have tried to present to him] the large views of politics, commerce, farming, and so on which the regions we have explored may offer in the future to the government and people of the United States. At the least opportunity, I made him a part of my long studies and the results of my experience.[33]

With respect to the "large view of politics," this aspect of Frémont's education received strong reinforcement from western expansionists, especially Senator Thomas Hart Benton, who became his father-in-law in 1841.

We know the instruments Frémont took with him on the second expedition; we also know that he carried a daguerreotype camera, but the device was so new and unperfected that he was unable to use it successfully. We are unable to name the books he actually carried; he certainly had astronomical tables, probably some botanical reference materials, and one or more books on mineralogy. He makes no mention of the reports of other explorers or travelers; possibly he had with him the accounts and maps of John Kirk Townsend (1839) and Samuel Parker (1838) of their travels across the Rocky Mountains and into Oregon or even the Nicholas Biddle narrative of the Lewis and Clark expedition. He and Preuss collected plants, rocks, minerals, and fossils. These would not be analyzed and catalogued in the field, but would be later by trained and increasingly specialized scientists in the East—part of the nineteenth-century liaison, though somewhat furtive, between the federal government and science.

Out of Frémont's background came a solid body of formal knowledge, critical in helping to make him a perceptive observer. On the Columbia Plateau he saw that some of the sedimentary rocks had been metamorphosed by contact with the lavas and that zeolites had formed in the gas cavities of the lava. He noted that the Oregon Territory was geologically different from the rest of the country, partly because of the lava flows and partly because of the Columbia River. Upon seeing submerged trees at one place in the Columbia he immediately recognized that their drowning was the result not of rising waters, but of complicated land-sliding, and upon examination he was able to find the actual shear surfaces on which the slides had occurred. He was the first to describe and explain so succinctly the great climatic differences between the east and west sides of the Cascade Mountains, but probably his greatest scientific contribution, besides his and Preuss's maps, was the conceptualization and naming of the Great Basin as a geological and geographical entity. Because he explored the area's perimeters, he knew that no rivers ran from it to the sea, although large streams flowed in; his perceptive analysis of this phenomenon was the first recognition of the great power of evaporation in the region. His comparison of the Great Basin with the interior of Asia was an apt one.

Frémont brought to exploration not only formal knowledge, field experience, and keen perception, but also enthusiasm, imagination, and an ability to capture the grandeur and charm of the natural environment and to involve his readers vicariously in the exciting adventures of the expedition. Written jointly with his wife, his reports were not only for his superiors but for the American people, and they hit their mark. "I have never been so delighted with any Book in my life," exclaimed one excited enthusiast. Some thought he ranked with Daniel Defoe and that his second expedition was more important than Lewis and Clark's in its "breadth and variety" of discoveries, although at least one reader detected a preoccupation with image, a "passion for seeming," on the part of the hero.[34] Made a public idol by his reports, Frémont in the years to come would feel obliged to live up to that image, leading him to make some questionable, even foolish decisions.

Frémont's later career brought endless criticisms, but what about the explorer, the Frémont of the 1840s? What kind of a leader was he? How did he view his men and vice versa? If we ignore the jealousy, politics, and struggle for authority that came out of the war in California, there were virtually no complaints by his own men until 1848, save Preuss's to his private diary. However, until his nomination for the presidency in 1856, he is known largely through his own writings and those of his wife and father-in-law. It is rather extraordinary that five expeditions, involving at least 175 men, left so few letters and journals by the participants. None at all relating to the first three were published during his lifetime. Two men noted that he prohibited the keeping of journals, which was in contrast to the government-sponsored Lewis and Clark expedition wherein sergeants were ordered and the enlisted men urged to keep journals. Of course, the personnel of the first three Frémont expeditions was of a kind not likely to write. The fourth was composed of a larger number of educated men and their trials so horrendous, with ten men dead and charges of cannibalism, that public criticism was perhaps inevitable, especially with Richard Kern openly fanning the flames.[35] Like the Kerns, Captain Cathcart withdrew from the expedition but seems not to have been as bitter as they were, and later presented Frémont with a handsome steel-mounted sword.

In conclusion, what can be said about the men of Frémont's five expeditions? First, many had no formal education, but a practical acquaintance with life. Frémont recognized that the *voyageurs* and his various trapper-guides—Thomas FitzPatrick, Kit Carson, Joseph R. Walker—were masters of an environment that the government was trying to penetrate and understand. He learned from them and he appreciated their knowledge of the country that he had been sent to map. The West was a vast region, yet quite a number of "his" men already knew each other, with Carson often the connecting link: Carson and Maxwell, Carson and FitzPatrick, Carson and Godey, Carson and Owens, Carson and Walker. Furthermore, many of the men who went with him went not once, but twice, and sometimes three and even four times as in the case of Raphael Proue. Frémont was a man to stir deep loyalties. He held military rank for the three government expeditions, but all the men were civilians and worked together as a tightly knit group, almost by an unwritten code. The fourth was more heterogeneous in nature and, after Frémont went for relief in the San Juans, it splintered into groups. The reports do not indicate disciplinary problems; no doubt the presence of such respected mountain men as Carson, FitzPatrick and Godey would have had a calming effect on the rowdy. Uncomplaining himself, Frémont in public had nothing but praise for his men, and only with the failure of the fourth, in private letters to his wife (which were published immediately in the *National Intelligencer*), did he question the courage of his men and lash out at his guide, Old Bill Williams, and the faithful Proue, who laid down in the trail and froze to death.[36] Long after the expeditions were concluded, Carson related: "The hardships through which we passed I find it impossible to describe, and the credit which he deserves I am incapable to do him justice in writing."[37]

Chapter 8 Notes

1. Much of the information for this chapter comes from the correspondence, reports of expeditions, memoirs, and financial vouchers of John C. Frémont as printed in *The Expeditions of John C. Frémont*, edited by Donald Jackson and Mary Lee Spence (Urbana: University of Illinois Press, 1970–84). Volume 1 of the work is cited as Jackson and Spence, volume 2 as Spence and Jackson, and volume 3 as Spence. The initials JCF and JBF are used for John C. and Jessie Benton Frémont. This particular citation is from JCF's 1843–44 Report in Jackson and Spence, 528.

2. On Dodson's later service as a messenger in the Senate, see Washington *Daily National Intelligencer*, March 30, 1849; for the controversy concerning Lea's sentence, see San Francisco *Alta California*, Feb. 26–28, March 1–3, 1861, which includes an article by JBF.

3. JCF's 1843–44 report in Jackson and Spence, 453; Theodore Talbot, *The Journals of Theodore Talbot, 1843 and 1849–52, with the Frémont Expedition of 1843 and with the First Military Company in Oregon Territory, 1849–52*, ed. by Charles H. Carey (Portland: Metropolitan Press, 1931), 24, 28.

4. 1843–44 report in Jackson and Spence, 431. This is an oblique reference to a gentleman, Frederick Dwight, who traveled with the expedition for about three months. In 1845, when he was forming his third party, Frémont wrote Archibald Campbell that he was restricted "solely to the engagement of hired men" save for the procurement of interpreters in the more remote regions (Jackson and Spence, 424). Perhaps this order took care of the problem of "gentlemen" travelers.

5. Frémont wrote: "The early approach of winter, and the difficulty of supporting a large party, determined me to send back a number of the men who had become satisfied that they were not fitted for the laborious service and frequent privations to which they were necessarily exposed, and which there was reason to believe would become more severe in the further extension of the voyage" (1843–44 report in Jackson and Spence, 519). Basil Lajeunesse returned for family reasons.

6. JCF's 1843–44 report and Caspar Wistar to T. Hartley Crawford, May 5, 1845, in Jackson and Spence, 576–77, 417–18.

7. Hubert H. Bancroft, *Register of Pioneer Inhabitants of California, 1541–1848* (repr. Los Angeles: Dawson Bookshop, 1964); 1843–44 report in Jackson and Spence, 656–57. Sutter speaks of adopting a tin currency impressed with a stamp made by Neal, which he used in trade with the Indians (Erwin G. Gudde, *Sutter's Own Story* [New York: G. P. Putnam's Sons, 1936], 56).

8. JCF's memoirs in Jackson and Spence, 50; Zindel family member to Frances Stadler, Missouri Historical Society.

9. Maxwell's early years in the West are shrouded in mystery. Reports that he worked for the American Fur Company or that he kept a store in Hardscrabble are erroneous, according to Harvey L. Carter, "Lucien Maxwell," in LeRoy R. Hafen, ed., *The Mountain Men and the Fur Trade of the Far West*, 10 vols. (Glendale, Calif.: Arthur H. Clark Company, 1965–72), 6: 299. The date of Maxwell's marriage is sometimes given as May 27, 1842, sometimes as June 3, 1844. The most recent biography of the famous New Mexico rancher is Lawrence R. Murphy, *Lucien Bonaparte Maxwell, Napoleon of the Southwest* (Norman: University of Oklahoma Press, 1983); for services with Frémont, see JCF's reports in Jackson and Spence, 144–45, 198, 428, 430–31, 436, 445–46, and JCF's memoirs in Spence and Jackson, 20, 34–35, 120.

10. Town was killed by Apaches and Utes in Manco de Burro Pass, east of Raton, in 1848, and Maxwell was wounded. For a sketch of Town, see Janet Lecompte, "Charles Town," in *The Mountain Men and the Fur Trade*, ed. by LeRoy R. Hafen, 1: 391–97.

11. LeRoy R. Hafen and W. J. Ghent, *Broken Hand: The Life Story of Thomas FitzPatrick, Chief of the Mountain Men* (Glendale, Calif.: Arthur H. Clark Company, 1954).

12. For a recent biography of Carson, see Thelma S. Guild and Harvey L. Carter, *Kit Carson, A Pattern for Heroes* (Lincoln: University of Nebraska Press, 1984). The process by which Carson's reputation was built is traced in Harvey L. Carter, *'Dear Old Kit': The Historical Christopher Carson with a New Edition of the Carson Memoirs* (Norman: University of Oklahoma Press, 1968), 3–46. Carter indicates Carson may have been placing his daughter with his sister; Frémont indicates a Catholic convent school (John Charles Frémont, *Memoirs of My Life* [Chicago: Belford, Clarke, 1887], 74).

13. JCF's 1843–44 report in Jackson and Spence, 452. Harvey L. Carter has brought scattered biographical details about Godey together in a little article entitled, "The Divergent Paths of Frémont's 'Three Marshalls,'" *New Mexico Historical Review*. JBF to JCF, Jan. 22, 1889 (Southwest Museum), gives details about Godey's death and his surviving fifth wife, a twenty-one-year-old Mexican woman.

14. Frémont, *Memoirs*, 427.

15. A brief biographical sketch of Talbot is contained in *Soldier in the West: Letters of Theodore Talbot During His Services in California, Mexico, and Oregon, 1845–53*, edited by Robert V. Hine and Savoie Lottinville (Norman: University of Oklahoma Press, 1972); Charles H. Carey has edited *The Journals of Theodore Talbot, 1843 and 1849–52, with the Frémont Expedition of 1843 and with the First Military Company in Oregon Territory, 1849–52* (Portland: Metropolitan Press, 1931).

16. Charles Preuss, *Exploring with Frémont*, translated and edited by Erwin G. and Elisabeth K. Gudde (Norman: University of Oklahoma Press, 1958), 97–98. The introduction to the diaries contains a biographical sketch of Preuss.

17. JCF's 1843–44 report in Jackson and Spence, 616.

18. Ibid., 671. A third *vaquero* deserted near the San Joaquin River (ibid.), 657, 660. The names of the two Indian boys who went east were Juan and Gregorio. For their presence on the third and fourth expeditions, see JCF's memoirs in Spence and Jackson, 5, and JCF's notes on the 1848–49 expedition in Spence, 52. A third Indian on the fourth expedition was Manuel, a Christian Indian of the Cosumne tribe in the Valley of the San Joaquin. He seems to have come East with JCF in 1847 and was known to JBF (JCF to JBF, Jan. 27, Feb. 17, 1849, in Spence, 82).

When JCF went for supplies for his starving party in the San Juans, he encountered, on the fifth day out, a Utah who guided him to the Red River settlements in the neighborhood of present Questa, New Mexico (JCF to JBF, Jan. 27–Feb. 17, 1849, in Spence, 79).

Preuss notes that Carson purchased a twelve- or fourteen-year-old Paiute for $40 at Utah Lake when he was returning with Frémont's second expedition. "He is to eat only raw meat, to get courage, says Kit, and in a few years he hopes to have trained him, with the Lord's help, so that he will at least be capable of stealing horses" (Preuss, 134). At the end of the third expedition, Thomas Breckenridge brought east a fourteen-year-old Indian boy who had been given to him by his mother (Thomas E. Breckenridge, MS and typescript, Western Historical Manuscripts Collection, University of Missouri).

19. JCF's memoirs in Spence and Jackson, 112. In a certificate dated March 21, 1857, JCF lists eight Delawares who were with him. The ninth, a small boy, acted as a page or equerry and is not listed. Moreover, JCF notes that when his exploring party converted to a military character, the Delawares were offered an additional two dollars per day and as veterans would be entitled to land warrants (Memorial of the Delaware Indians, 58th Cong., 1st sess., Senate Doc. 16, pp. 159–60 [Serial 4563]).

20. JCF's agreement with the Delaware hunters, in Spence, 382–83. Sagundai did not go on the fifth, but one veteran of the third did so.

The roster of the Indian personnel is compiled from Carvalho and from the unpublished diary of James F. Milligan, who withdrew from the fifth expedition at Bent's new fort. Carvalho never mentions the Wynadotts and gives the Delaware count as ten (Carvalho in Spence, 385, 392 456). Brigham Young's *Journal History*, Feb. 20, 1854, records the arrival of twelve Delaware hunters in Parowan, making no mention of Wyandotts. For a report of the arrival of the Delawares in St. Louis at the end of the fifth expedition and interviews with them, see *Missouri Republican*, June 6, 1854, and *Daily Missouri Democrat*, June 7, 1854.

21. Talbot to Mary, June 4, 1845, printed in Spence and Jackson, 9. On the number of artist applicants, see Robert V. Hine, *Edward Kern and American Expansion* (New Haven, Conn.: Yale University Press, 1962), 6.

22. Robert Campbell seems to have advanced him $5,000 (Thomas H. Benton to James Buchanan, Aug. 20, 1848, printed in Spence, xxii); Thornton Grimsley, a saddler, and Oliver D. Filley, a Dutch oven manufacturer, provided saddles, packs, and camp equipment (Charles W. Upham, *Life, Explorations and Public Services of John Charles Frémont* [Boston: Ticknor and Fields, 1856], 273). After the disaster in the mountains, Edward Kern reckoned that Frémont's own loss (from whatever sources) must have been between $8,000 and $10,000 (Edward Kern to Mary Kern Wolfe, Feb. 10, 1849, Henry E. Huntington Library).

23. Thomas E. Breckenridge, Reminiscences, ms. and typescript, Western Historical Manuscripts Collection, University of Missouri.

24. Quoted by David J. Weber, *Richard H. Kern: Expeditionary Artist in the Far Southwest, 1848–1853* (Albuquerque: University of New Mexico Press,

1985), 26. Weber points out that Dick Kern "seems to have possessed some of the Romantic restlessness that characterizes many men of his generation" (ibid). Biographical details on Benjamin Kern may be found in Weber and in Hine's *Edward Kern*.

25. For brief biographical information on the thirty-three men who made up the fourth expedition, see Spence, 52–58.

26. Sometime after mid-February 1849, Edward Kern wrote to his sister Mary that JCF had broken faith with them (Henry E. Huntington Library).

27. William Brandon's *The Men and the Mountain* (New York: William Morrow & Co., 1955) is a gripping account of the fourth expedition's battle with the winter and the mountains.

28. A final payment to Egloffstein was for $100 (JCF to George Engelmann, Aug. 20, 1854, in Spence, 493–94). Carvalho, who left the only account of the expedition, writes that JCF paid for his board in Parowan and supplied him with the means to reach home (Spence, 464). The Delawares later alleged that JCF had not met all his financial obligations to them.

29. For biographical information on Carvalho, see Joan Sturhahn, *Carvalho: Portrait of a Forgotten American* (Merrick, N.Y.: Richwood Publishing Co., 1976); on Egloffstein, see Robert Taft, *Artists and Illustrators of the Old West, 1850–1900* (New York: Charles Scribner's Sons, 1953). A second engineer was Oliver Fuller of St. Louis who died on the expedition. The third engineer, Max Strobel, had just withdrawn from the northern railroad survey headed by Isaac I. Stevens, having been employed to aid the artist John M. Stanley (Spence, 404).

30. William H. Goetzmann, *Army Exploration in the American West, 1803–1863* (New Haven, Conn.: Yale University Press, 1959), 12–14.

31. George W. Bradburn to George W. Wright, April 26, 1856 (George W. Wright Papers in the possession of M. A. Goodspeed, Chevy Chase, Md.).

32. Goetzmann, *Army*, 70.

33. Edmund C. Bray and Martha C. Bray, translators and eds., *Joseph N. Nicollet on the Plains and Prairies* (St. Paul, Minn.: Minnesota Historical Society, 1976), 230–31.

34. George P. Hammond, ed., *The Larkin Papers* (Berkeley: University of California Press, 1951–64), 5: 291; JBF to JCF, June 16, 1846, in Spence and Jackson, 150; *United States Magazine and Democratic Review*, 17 (July 1845): 77; Ralph Waldo Emerson, *Journals and Miscellaneous Notebooks*, edited by William H. Gilman et al. (Cambridge, Mass.: Harvard University Press, 1960–62), 9: 431.

35. Richard Kern censured JCF in the Quincy, Illinois, *Whig*, May 22, 1849, and Edward Kern wrote family members that JCF "loves to be told of his greatness" and was prone to believe "the reports of the meanest in the camp." He added that Frémont would have had them continue on to California with him, "for he did not wish a man of his with any influence to remain here. The greatest dread he has at present is that a true and correct account of the proceedings *above* [in the San Juan Mountains] and *here* [Taos] may be made public." (E. M. Kern to Mary Kern Wolfe, mid-Feb. or March 1849, Henry E. Huntington Library).

36. Privately, he intimated to John Torrey, the botanist, that Creutzfeldt had failed to label some plants and permitted others to get wet repeatedly, and to George Engelmann, a scientist in St. Louis, he expressed disappointment in Egloffstein who "has many good qualities but is not a good topographer for such service as we are engaged in" (Spence, 571, 494).

37. Carter, *'Dear Old Kit,'* 121.

9. Isaac I. Stevens and the Expeditionary Artists of the Northern West

by David Nicandri

Few men have cut as wide a swath through the early history of Washington as did its first territorial governor, Isaac I. Stevens. More has been written about Stevens than all other territorial governors combined. Indeed, if ever a regional example were needed to make the argument that the past has pointed relevance to contemporary concerns, the Stevens Indian treaties recommend themselves. Although the governor is best known for his Indian policies, lately greater attention has been brought to the governor's career as an explorer.

Stevens's work as leader of the northern-most Pacific railroad survey in 1853, under whose auspices he first came west, was very much wrapped up with the treaty-making for which he is justly known. Running topographic lines in 1853, the governor laid the foundation for his treaty tour, the bulk of which occurred in 1855. When that later expedition came to pass, the governor's mind never strayed far from his dreams of a railroad that would catapult Washington Territory, and no doubt himself, into national prominence.

Whatever else might be said about Stevens, he had a sense of history. This comes through in his lengthy and detailed narratives and also in his penchant for having artist-illustrators assigned to his various expeditions. In an age before sophisticated photography, only the illustrator's pen, ink, and wash (later transformed into duotoned lithographs) could provide visual information about exotic new lands or history in the making.

The best known of the artists associated with the several expeditions led or instigated by Stevens was John Mix Stanley. Born in upstate New York, Stanley followed in the footsteps of the far better-known George Catlin. Both helped popularize the notion of the Vanishing American by preparing and exhibiting their collections of Indian portraiture, imagery thought to be all the more valuable because of the presumed inevitable extinction of the native peoples.

133

Stevens hired Stanley as artist for the governor's railroad survey party that left St. Paul in the spring of 1853. Part of Stanley's appeal, aside from his considerable artistic talent, was the fact that he was one of the few members of the Stevens party to have previously been in the Northwest. In 1847 he crossed the path of yet another famous Indian artist, Paul Kane. Indeed, Stanley just barely missed the fate of the Whitmans, and later served as the substitute father for those famed orphans, the Sager children (who had been at the mission at the time of the Cayuse attack), when the refugees floated down the Columbia under the protection of Peter Skene Ogden.

Of all the railroad survey parties commissioned for the "Grand Reconnaissance" (as William Goetzmann phrased it) of the western interior, none had their exploits more lavishly illustrated than the Stevens team. Stanley's views of the romantic West—the pristine wilderness, exotic trading posts, the native encampments—were, at one level of analysis, snapshots of history illustrating the trail from Minnesota to Puget Sound.

Stevens's eighty-six-man contingent left St. Paul in late May of 1853. On July tenth, in present-day east-central North Dakota, the expedition reached buffalo country—and in a grand

Buffalo in east-central North Dakota by John Mix Stanley. From the Pacific Railroad Reports, Vol. 12, Book 1. Courtesy Washington State Historical Society, Tacoma.

manner. Accompanying one of Stanley's most famous sketches, a lithograph of buffalo, Stevens wrote in awestruck tones: "I had heard of the myriads of these animals inhabiting these plains, but I could not realize the truth of these accounts till to-day, when they surpassed anything I could have imagined...." After brief encounters with the Red River hunters, an amalgamated population of Chippewa, Sioux, and Euro-Americans— and the Assiniboines (depicted in a scene by Stanley that illustrates the ritual distribution of presents)—the Stevens party reached the American Fur Company's Fort Union, at the confluence of the Yellowstone and Missouri rivers. This fort was a significant milestone because it allowed the party to refresh itself, but it also represented the gateway to the territory of the vaunted Blackfeet, whose legendary temperament posed a serious threat to Stevens's dream of a railroad.

Three hundred seventy-five miles and several weeks later, the Stevens party arrived at the last outpost before the Rocky Mountains, Fort Benton, home to a dozen American Fur Company men who traded with the Blackfeet. After using this fort as a base camp for numerous explorations of the northern passes, Stevens crossed the divide and for the first time set foot in the then enlarged Washington Territory. At the crest itself Stevens halted the party for a short ceremony, which one writer colorfully related: "To all interested cottontails and larger game within earshot, Stevens issued a proclamation announcing the existence of Washington Territory and creating its civil government, which was himself."

The principal objective in the intermontane Bitterroot Valley was Fort Owen, formerly St. Mary's Village of the Jesuits. Here Stevens was resupplied by elements of the expedition's western division, which had started from Fort Vancouver under the overall command of captain, later general, George B. McClellan.

Descending the west side of the Bitterroot chain, Stevens came upon the Jesuit mission just east of Lake Coeur d'Alene. Today we know it as Cataldo Mission. It is the oldest piece of formal architecture extant in the state of Idaho and was designed and built in 1848 by Father Ravalli. It was in this vicinity that Stevens had hoped to encounter McClellan himself, but

Cataldo Mission. From the Pacific Railroad Reports, *Vol. 12, Book 1. Courtesy Washington State Historical Society, Tacoma.*

that was not to occur until the governor arrived in the Colville district near Tshimikain Mission northwest of Spokane.

Pushing ahead, Stevens, Stanley, and others reached Fort Walla Walla, a Hudson's Bay Company post, on November first. From there, keeping an eye toward the navigability of the Columbia, Stevens pressed on ahead of the overland party by quickly descending the river in a canoe, reaching Fort Vancouver on November fifteenth, effectively the end of the exploratory trail.

Lately, a new, what might almost be termed revisionist, artistic interpretation has emerged regarding the lithographs from the Stevens report. A phrase that has developed some currency among those trying to recast western art history runs to this effect: it is not so much what's *western* in western art that makes it important, rather, it is what this body of work says about American art history that gives it value. Now even this view, recently held as radical because it minimized the conventional role of western art as document, has itself been transcended by the intellectual vistas opened up by Barbara Stafford's *Voyage into Substance: Art, Science, Nature and the Illustrated Travel Account*, published in 1984.

Stafford argues that illustrations of new and sometimes exotic topographic features encountered by European explorers during their voyages in the eighteenth and nineteenth centuries, though on the surface unassuming, were in fact a more rigorous mode of aesthetic expression than the more rhetorical landscape paintings produced in studios before or since. Fitted under Stafford's rubric, the views of the northern West contained in Stevens's report can be unfolded to reveal a third level of significance: not merely the documentation of particular sites at a point in time, not just representations of an artistic mode, but additionally, indications of the deepest currents of scientific interest and natural philosophy.

Lithic phenomena had the most appeal in the aesthetic of scientific exploration. Basaltic outcroppings attracted unusual interest because of the scientific controversy surrounding their origins. Volcanism was laden with philosophical implications because it called into question the immutability of divine creation and the putative lastingness of metamorphosis. Both the isolated mountain and mountain chains evidenced the energy that allowed inanimate matter to shape itself.

On the other hand, it is the very absence of edifice that gives the plain its visual interest. The plains were disadvantaged geologically compared to a mountain's observable potential since

Kettle Falls. From the Pacific Railroad Reports, *Vol. 12, Book 1. Courtesy Washington State Historical Society, Tacoma.*

the layers of earth did not reveal themselves. The power of the plain lay not in the spectacle of elevation, but in its ability to hold things, like buffalo or people like Stevens and his scientist cohorts—men stunned by the immensity of it all.

Another good example of the dynamism of nature and its corresponding aesthetic is the cataract, important because it shows water's ability to sculpt the earth. The sketch of Kettle Falls may be the most scientifically informed of any in the Stevens report, combining as it does the density of rock, the erosive power of water, and a primal man.

The pictorial interest in forests lay in their vegetative energy —a vitalist chord that harmonized well with Enlightenment theories of a living universe. Here matter is clearly alive. Indeed, the texture and organic intensity of the forest scene depicting a meeting between Stevens and the Nez Perces overpowers the human element.

There remains one last category of Stevens's artistic "patronage" to consider—the ethnographic realm. As mentioned earlier, before setting out on the railroad survey to Washington Territory from St. Paul in the spring of 1853, Stevens had already separated the expedition into his, the eastern, and a western division. George McClellan commanded the western division and had two major responsibilities. He was to personally lead an exploration of possible railroad routes through the Cascades, and a smaller detachment of McClellan's led by Lt. Rufus Saxton was to resupply the Stevens party with food and pack animals in the Bitterroot Valley.

In Saxton's command was an otherwise obscure German immigrant infantryman, Private Gustav Sohon, who, it was discovered, had significant artistic talents. Stevens, who already had with him Stanley, saw in Sohon the source of additional topographic views for his railroad report, and assigned Sohon to a detachment that stayed in the interior during the winter of 1853–54. Eventually a dozen landscape scenes of the inland Northwest prepared by Sohon were included in Stevens's monumental final report on explorations. In some respects Sohon's drawings surpass the work of Stanley, the expedition's official artist.

Stevens intended to give an account of his treaty operations

Nez Perces. From the Pacific Railroad Reports, *Vol. 12, Book 1. Courtesy Washington State Historical Society, Tacoma.*

much like his encyclopedic railroad survey. Knowing that dramatic illustrations would greatly enhance the value of a treaty-tour narrative, and now familiar with Sohon's "great taste as an artist," the governor secured Sohon's services from the army. Sohon joined the Stevens treaty party when it headed toward eastern Washington in the late spring of 1855, the governor having already completed his tour of Puget Sound. Stevens never lived long enough to complete his treaty account, but Sohon's remarkable drawings have been preserved by the Washington State Historical Society.

The view of the Nez Perce arriving on the Walla Walla council grounds was the first event to be depicted by Sohon. Their grand entry put the Stevens party in awe of them, which was precisely the effect intended. On the day after his arrival, Stevens and his co-commissioner representing Oregon, Joel Palmer, banqueted the Nez Perces under an arbor built specifically for that purpose. The numerous, militarily powerful, and long-friendly Nez Perces held the balance of power at Walla Walla, and Stevens went out of his way to ingratiate himself to them. Sohon's sketch of a formal council session at Walla Walla shows the American commissioners and their retinue facing outward toward the Indians seated in semi-circular rows. Contrary to the victimologists who have seen the Indians as the pitiful pawns of Isaac Stevens's dominating personality, the Indians at Walla Walla were not totally powerless. Because of the recalcitrance of native leaders like Peo Peo Mox Mox, the treaty commission was forced into what for them was a major concession—the creation of a third reservation on the plateau for the Cayuse, Walla Walla, and Umatilla Indians.

The most tragic figure arising out of the Walla Walla Council was Kamiakin. The irony in Kamiakin being looked to by Stevens as a head chief is that within the Yakima tribe he was considered somewhat of an upstart because his father was a Palouse. During the council Kamiakin stated that he had influence over only Yakima and Palouse, but the treaty he signed contains a long list of mid-Columbia tribes that not only were absent, but had gone without notice of the proceedings. The severe consequences of Stevens's fictive Yakima Confederacy became apparent with the outbreak of war within a year.

After a tumultuous few weeks in Walla Walla, Stevens headed for his next council at Hell Gate near Missoula, at a site known to the Indians of the Bitterroot Valley even into the twentieth century as the place "where the trees have no lower limbs." Here the governor resorted to outright subterfuge to gain a treaty with the Flathead and Pend D'Oreille Indians. The source of Stevens's duplicity lay in his anxiety to meet the powerful Blackfoot and related bands to the east.

Among these were the Blood Indians, shown arriving at the

Walla Walla Council of May 1855, Governor Stevens with Indians. Courtesy Washington State Historical Society, Tacoma.

Blackfoot Council held at the mouth of the Judith River in central Montana, brandishing a flag given them by the governor at the time of his railroad expedition. Historically resistant to white passage through their country, the Blackfeet, Stevens thought, held the key to a pacified northern west—one factor in the general practicability of his railroad route and political dreams. Stevens had fretted for two years over what he perceived to be the pivotal Blackfoot Council, but it took only two days in October to conclude what the Blackfeet henceforth referred to as Lame Bull's treaty, after the principal chief of the

Sohon's drawing of Blackfeet Indians. Courtesy Washington State Historical Society, Tacoma.

Old Koutaine, Blackfoot chief, sketched by Sohon. Courtesy Washington State Historical Society, Tacoma.

Piegan band. Stevens had a placid meeting with the Blackfeet because this treaty did not involve the cession of land or reservations.

Soon after this triumph, Stevens's entire treaty system collapsed when word reached him that the so-called Yakima War had erupted. Rejecting advice that he return to Puget Sound via the Missouri River, New Orleans, and the Isthmus, Stevens confronted the situation head on. He chose an unconventional early winter crossing of the Bitterroot Mountains, as opposed to his expected return along the Clark Fork route, to achieve the element of surprise.

Storming into the Spokane River Valley, Stevens convened the last of his eastern Washington councils. The Spokane Council of December 1855 was significant because true dialogue between Stevens and an Indian leader, Spokan Garry, occurred there. Garry, having been educated in Canada by the Hudson's Bay Company, could speak English fluently. Thus, Stevens heard native views unmediated by trade jargon or faulty translation. Stevens, content simply to keep the Spokan and neighboring peoples neutral in the Yakima War, withstood Garry's verbal barrage. Ultimately the governor was given a protective escort through the war zone to the relative safety of The Dalles by a Nez Perce guard.

As with the topographic art from the railroad survey, the imagery prepared by Sohon has a value that transcends its original intended use as illustrative material for a written narrative. Sohon's Indian portraiture has a scientific quotient too, in this case furtherance of the nascent discipline of ethnology. Sohon in effect carried the Bodmerian tradition westward by preparing drawings rich in anthropological detail and related clothing, ornament, hairdress, and ceremonial paraphernalia.

Perhaps Sohon is most like Bodmer in that his drawings depict the Northwest chiefs as individuals, avoiding the opposite stereotypes so common in the nineteenth century of the skulking and noble savages. Sohon's portraits are typified by a few crisp lines and shadings that cumulatively render the image with a life-like, three dimensional quality. From the perspective of social science, Sohon's drawings are a model of ethnographic depiction. His documentary technique—providing variations on names and keys to their pronunciations, color codes for garments, and tribal affiliations, plus dating his sketches—all presaged later anthropological conventions. Each portrait is like an archaeological specimen, carefully unearthed and logged in.

By far the least well-known artist associated with the Stevens expeditions, if he is known at all, is Lieutenant Johnson K. Duncan, who served as an aide to McClellan in the western division of the railroad survey. McClellan's route eastward took him across the difficult southern flank of the Cascades. Once east of the mountains the party turned north, reached Fort Okanogan, and then headed east again linking up with Stevens near Colville. A graduate of West Point and veteran of the late Seminole conflict in Florida, Duncan is credited with the design of the Washington territorial seal and later served in the Confederate army. His art work, which to my knowledge has never been exhibited or published, is in the National Anthropological Archives of the Smithsonian.

Duncan's art can be differentiated from that of Stanley and Sohon in several ways. Duncan was the only one to attempt depicting native material culture. More substantively, Duncan prepared sketches of native women, such as Tee-ra, a Spokane girl, and Sa-mil-a-ka-mie, both of whom were sketched near Fort Okanogan. Marie and Marion were half-bloods whom Duncan encountered near Fort Colville. Indeed Duncan even drew a sketch of a young girl, Nelly, the granddaughter of the prominent Yakima Chief Ow-hi. This tendency stands in stark contrast to the male/chieftainly bias of Sohon.

Stevens never thought the Puget Sound and Lower Columbia Indians were important enough to have an artist depict them, as he would with the tribes on the Columbia Plateau via Sohon's artistry. Thus it is only in Duncan's depiction of Sni-nu-wit and Ya-ka-tow-itz that we are provided a brief glimpse of Chinook Indians, probably encountered in the vicinity of Fort Vancouver. Duncan also made a sketch of Joe, a cross between the Nisqually people of Puget Sound and the Yakima, an intimation of family relationships that would take on some importance to the Americans in the winter of 1855 when the Yakima War spread across the mountains to Puget Sound.

In one more departure from Sohon, Duncan's depiction of the great Yakima chief Ow-hi seems completely infused with the psychology of inter-racial tension that was reaching yet another crescendo when McClellan and his men trooped across the Columbia Plain in the summer of 1853. I draw this conclusion by comparing Duncan's drawing of Ow-hi to the one prepared by Sohon of the same man at the time of the Walla Walla Council nearly two years later. This is made even clearer with Duncan's sketch of Qual-chan, Ow-hi's son, both of whom met a sad fate at the hands of the sadistic George Wright in the concluding phase of the Spokane War of 1858.

Tee-ra. National Anthropological Archives, Smithsonian Institution, Washington, D.C.

Nelly, granddaughter of Ow-hi. National Anthropological Archives, Smithsonian Institution, Washington, D.C.

Chinook Indians. National Anthropological Archives, Smithsonian Institution, Washington, D.C.

Ow-hi. National Anthropological Archives, Smithsonian Institution, Washington, D.C.

Ow-hi. Courtesy Washington State Historical Society, Tacoma.

Qual-chan, son of Ow-hi. National Anthropological Archives, Smithsonian Institution, Washington, D.C.

Today, in both the popular and academic press, Isaac Stevens receives bad reviews. Certainly I have not intended to offer a historiographical brief on behalf of his personality or policies. Nevertheless, posterity, especially historians having an interest in the early art of the West, owe much to this man. Given the fact that the Lewis and Clark expedition, unlike its contemporaneous counterparts in maritime exploration, did not systematically produce drawings of the landscapes encountered in the trek across the continent, we owe the first substantive views of the northwestern frontier to the man who followed in their footsteps fifty years later. With the possible exception of Paul Kane, no more significant body of imagery was produced in the greater Northwest before the era of sophisticated photography than that which flows from the direct or adjunct influences of Isaac Stevens.

10. Anthropological Exploration in the Great Northwest, 1778–1889 and After

by Douglas Cole

Anthropological description and study of the Great Northwest began with initial coastal exploration by Spanish, Russian, and British expeditions, notably those of Malaspina, Lisiansky, and Cook. Although hundreds of ships came to the coast bringing fur traders, few left with anything scientifically valuable except as incidental notes in their logs. With these earliest explorations, the most striking pattern of the entire period was already set—governmental sponsorship of scientific, including anthropological, investigations. Science was, of course, subsidiary to national economic and diplomatic strategies, and only in exploration sponsored by governments did it find any real place. Government vessels stayed longer in a single harbor and, as in the case of Cook and Malaspina, they carried explicit instructions to learn as much as they could about the aboriginal peoples. Naval officers, even crews, were interested in such things to a degree not usually found among the profit-motivated traders.

The same generalization can be made about land-based exploration and trade. The continental traders tended to write more than their maritime counterparts, but the major ethnological contribution came from the government-sponsored expedition of Meriwether Lewis and William Clark. "Guided by Jefferson's precise instructions and their own curiosity, expedition ethnographers amassed a virtual library of information about the Indians. Journal entries, vocabularies, drawings, maps, artifacts, population estimates—all hold priceless knowledge about Indian ways from the great river to the western sea." Again, they established a baseline, capturing "an essential part of American life on the edge of profound change."[1]

The results of these early expeditions were descriptive of manners, morals, and material culture, providing detailed accounts of subsistence, dress, and territorial and political

149

organization, and were extremely valuable in these matters. The expeditions, however, give little information on social organization or religion. George Gibbs's later comment about coastal literature applies to the whole region: "Of the externals of savage life on the Oregon coast, there are many graphic and full accounts," he wrote in the 1850s, "but an insight into their minds is not so easy to reach...."[2]

After Lewis and Clark, one has to wait almost forty years for another significant anthropological exploration and it came, not surprisingly, in the form of a major governmental expedition—the Wilkes or United States Exploring Expedition. The Wilkes expedition is notable for the appearance, for the first time in the Northwest, of a person specifically named as ethnologist (actually "philologist"), a young Harvard graduate, Horatio Hale, who accompanied the expedition on its voyage through the South Pacific, to the Oregon Territory, and to the tip of South America.

Hale is significant in a number of ways. He is the first "professional," and his concerns, as reflecting his time, were philological. Most important, he became in a very significant way, the father—perhaps more accurately the grandfather—of Northwest anthropology, the lineal ancestor of Franz Boas and through Boas, of Lowie, Teit, and others who later made important contributions to the anthropological investigations of the region.

Born in New Hampshire in 1817, Hale was admitted to Harvard at age sixteen, receiving his appointment to the Wilkes Expedition, for reasons not quite clear now, on the day of his 1837 graduation. After a long tour of the South Pacific, the expedition arrived on the Oregon Territory coast in 1841, and Hale spent three months in travels and researches there, dependent largely upon missionaries, including Marcus Whitman, and Hudson's Bay Company traders. Upon his return to the United States, he published his results. *Ethnography and Philology* suffered from many defects.[3] "I was then," he wrote in his later years, "a young man of twenty-four, fresh from College, and ethnological science was far behind the present stage."[4] The vocabularies were thin, too often received from non-native speakers, but the most glaring impression which a reader today receives is of the enormous ethnocentricity of his views and of the harshness of his judgments of Indian character. The Oregon Indians, he wrote, were "among the ugliest of their race," "of moderate intelligence, coarse and dirty in their habits, indolent, deceitful, and passionate"—indeed, "grossly libidinous."[5] He came later to see the error of his views, regretting "that I rated the character of those Indians too low."[6]

Ethnography and Philology, despite its defects, was an immense addition to knowledge of the region's peoples and offered a basic framework of ethnic distribution. His Pacific islands and Australian work largely synthesized information already known, but in the Northwest,

Hale obtained the first information of any kind on many of the numerous Indian languages there, and on the basis of these materials he published the first linguistic classification of the Indian groups of this large and important area. The linguistic map of native North America, which had previously had a large blank in the West, was now substantially filled in.[7]

At the same time that Hale was in Oregon, I. G. Voznesenskii was in Russian America collecting material (largely artifacts and drawings) for the Imperial Academy of Sciences Museum. His ethnological collections were perhaps the largest of any single Northwest collection at the time and the sponsorship, as much museum as governmental, was a harbinger of future patterns.[8]

After the Wilkes expedition with its full-time professional, we are dependent for almost the same length of time (that is, for another forty years) on yet another kind of anthropologist, the earnest dilettante, self-taught but often with a great deal of sophistication. Yet even these characters—George Gibbs, W. H. Dall, the brothers Krause, James G. Swan, A. P. Niblack, and Myron Eells—were usually dependent upon government patronage. The circumstances of each was different.

Favored with political connections to New York Whigs, George Gibbs found a variety of patronage appointments, often involving Indian treaty commissions, after moving west in 1850.[9] Living in the West inspired him to collect native vocabularies and to enter into correspondence with Henry

Schoolcraft. Appointed geologist and ethnologist with the Pacific Railway Survey directed by Isaac Stevens, he prepared a thirty-four-page report on the Indians of Washington Territory that was concerned mostly with population estimates and with recommendations for government policy, especially toward the eastern Washington Indians as yet little affected by settlement. West of the Cascades, he condemned the inattention given to natives, but noted that "but a few years will elapse before a universal escheat will preclude the necessity of any purchase."[10] After moving East in 1861, he made a connection with the Smithsonian where he furthered study of Native American languages by translating Father Pandosey's Yakima grammar and various vocabularies collected by himself and by others, and, most notably, carefully expanding his work on the natives of western Washington.

Gibbs's "Tribes of Western Washington and Northwestern Oregon," published posthumously as part of the first volume of the government's *Contributions to North American Ethnology* carried Major John Wesley Powell's appreciation of its "thorough and conscientious work."[11] The study, some eighty-four pages, plus vocabularies, is a solid, descriptive ethnology of distribution, population, customs, and society. The tone of depopulation and decay among coastal Indians remained, and the characterization, as "nations whose life is almost altogether sensual," follows Hale (to whom Gibbs was not actually greatly indebted).[12]

Gibbs's "Tribes" was preceded in the same volume by W. H. Dall's "Tribes of the Extreme Northwest," an expansion of Dall's earlier *Alaska and Its Resources*.[13] Dall's knowledge of Alaskan natives came largely from his experience as director of the scientific corps of the Western Union Telegraph Expedition, part of that company's attempt to link North America and Europe by telegraph over the Bering Strait. Even though it was privately sponsored, Dall's scientific work was afforded every cooperation by government agencies, including the Smithsonian. "Tribes of the Extreme Northwest" is actually several papers on the distribution and classification of ethnic stocks, on archaeology of the Aleutians, on the origin of the Eskimo, and with vocabulary lists. Dall, like Gibbs and others of the late nineteenth century, was primarily concerned with labels and territory, although the pioneer archaeology, with its careful attention to stratification, is, for its time, almost unsurpassed.

Dall's research was, despite his Smithsonian connections, a corporate venture. The Tlingit expedition of Aurel and Arthur Krause was also non-governmental, sponsored as it was by the Bremen Geographical Society and wealthy merchants of that Hanseatic city. The Krauses, natural scientists from Berlin, stopped in Washington to consult Dall and others at the Smithsonian and then, after a summer on the Chukchi Peninsula, spent the winter of 1881–82 in Alaska's Tlingit country. Although primarily naturalists, the monument of their expedition is Aurel Krause's 1885 *Die Tlinkit-Indianer*.[14] Krause's report, which "has not been superseded by any modern ethnography,"[15] became the first monographic treatment of a single stock within the area. It is exemplary in its breadth. Krause paid the usual attention to material culture and devoted a chapter to language, but gave extraordinary attention to ceremony, religion, and mythology. Much of this was the result of the presence at Haines of Sarah Dickinson, the mission-educated native wife of the Northwest Trading Company agent. Even more unusual is the chapter devoted to "missions and effort at civilization."

James G. Swan was a Bostonian who left his wife and family to pursue a pioneer career in Washington Territory. Born in Massachusetts in 1818, Swan left a business and a family to sail in 1850 to the golden land of California. A few years later he turned up in Willapa Bay, where he helped Governor Stevens negotiate with Indian bands at Chehalis, a position he converted into a secretaryship to Stevens in Washington, D.C. Moving back to the West in 1858, he settled in Port Townsend, taught Indian school for awhile in Neah Bay, by which time he had made a connection with Joseph Henry at the Smithsonian, who moved him into scientific activity by playing upon his vanity. For someone piecing together a hand-to-mouth living as journalist, ticket agent, notary, probate judge, and occasional counselor in admiralty law—"performing odd jobs of simple literacy in a society where simple literacy was in demand"[16]— becoming a correspondent to the Smithsonian gave Swan a measure of flattering prestige. In 1875 Henry and Assistant

Secretary Spencer Baird found an opportunity to give Swan a major assignment to collect native materials for the great Philadelphia Centennial Exposition. Although Swan also published small studies of the Makah and Haida, his major work was in ethnological collecting, and he sent east an enormous quantity of coastal material that makes up the core of the Smithsonian's Northwest Coast collections.

A. P. Niblack was a young Annapolis graduate seconded to the Smithsonian's National Museum for a time and then allowed, while serving the summers of 1885 through 1887 in northern waters for the U.S. Coast and Geodetic Survey, to compile a remarkable descriptive ethnology of the observable culture of the natives.[17] The ensign's work drew upon Dall and the early publications of Franz Boas and George Dawson, but he was influenced in his general organization and material culture emphasis by Otis T. Mason of the U.S. National Museum. Theoretically, Niblack attempted to link part of his work with Mason, but also with British social evolutionists James G. Frazer, John Lubbock, and Herbert Spencer. He owed a personal indebtedness to Swan, which he generously returned. Characteristic of Niblack was his concern with material culture, a product of his familiarity with Swan's National Museum collections. He emphasized the observable culture, and he acknowledged that he contributed little on philology or mythology, subjects which needed to be covered systematically and in the winter months.

Niblack, Swan, and Gibbs all worked under government sponsorship. Myron Eells did not. A Presbyterian missionary to the Puget Sound Salish, about whom he wrote a series of articles in the 1880s and 1890s, Eells stands as a major exception to government-sponsored science in this period. While many missionaries wrote about their charges and a number compiled vocabularies, even dictionaries and sometimes grammars, none from this generation (and only Father A. G. Morice in the next) left behind anthropological work of the caliber provided by Rev. Eells.

Eells was a prolific writer, publishing dozens of articles in his lifetime, but his large work, "The Indians of Puget Sound," remained unpublished until 1985.[18] A good observer (though hardly immune from bias), he was also a generally sympathetic one. Like most amateurs of his generation, his contribution lies in describing external culture, and yet he is best at "reporting the rapid and thorough cultural changes going on under his eyes."[19]

The Pacific Railroad and Forty-Ninth Parallel surveys were the only American government surveys that more than touched on the Northwest proper. While Clarence King, J. W. Powell, George M. Wheeler, and Ferdinand V. Hayden were doing their monumental surveys to the south—and in the process turning some geological surveyors into anthropologists (Powell himself, W. H. Holmes, and W J McGee)—the Geological Survey of Canada was working its own way west. Incorporation of the Northwest Territories into the Dominion in 1869 and the adherence of British Columbia as a province in 1871 necessitated its own expansion north and west.

In 1875 George M. Dawson, a diminutive young Montreal geologist trained in London, arrived in the Pacific province for the first of a number of field seasons. Although his preoccupation was necessarily geology and mining, Dawson, like Powell, spent time and energy as an anthropological researcher, publishing important studies of the Haida, Kwakiutl, Interior Salish, and Yukon Indians, and a set of comparative vocabularies compiled with the assistance of retired Hudson's Bay physician W. F. Tolmie.[20]

While Dawson was working on the northern side of the international boundary, Albert S. Gatschet, quite a different kind of scientist and the first full-time professional anthropologist since Hale, was working among the Klamath in Oregon. Born in Switzerland and educated at Bern and Berlin in classical philology, Gatschet began work on the Oregon group in 1877, the first year of his employment by J. W. Powell's Rocky Mountain Survey. He transferred from the Survey to Powell's new Bureau of Ethnology at its founding in 1879 and worked as a philologist with the Bureau until his death. Powell's needs—his desire for a full classification of Indian languages north of Mexico—determined that Gatschet's services for the Bureau would be scattered across the continent. He was responsible for southeastern languages, but was also sent by Powell to the Apaches, the Comanches, the Cree, the Modoc, and the Shoshone, then reassigned to a phonetic comparison of the forty-odd Algonquin dialects. His landmark, *The Klamath Tribe and Language of Oregon*, published only in 1890 but based on more than a decade of episodic field research and careful office analysis, was his only major published work. It was a significant milestone: the first tribal monograph for the region south of Alaska, the first full linguistic study, and the first significant published collection of mythological texts recorded in the native language (with interlineal translations). Franz Boas, another European-trained scientist, described Gatschet's Klamath study as "by far the best grammar of an American language in existence." Gatschet was, Boas said, "by far the most eminent American philologist, away ahead of us all. If he had done nothing else but that he would have justified his work."[21]

Gatschet's *The Klamath Tribe* was ready for publication just as Idaho and other northwestern territories were receiving statehood. It might have served as the end point of this paper were it not for Gatschet's close associate, Boas himself. Twenty years younger, Boas was German born and educated. His initial work was among the Baffin Island Eskimo, but, attracted to the problems of American Indian anthropology by the presence of a group of visiting Bella Coolas in Berlin in 1885, he undertook in the following year, at his own initiative and expense, a field trip to their native British Columbia. His resulting report attracted the attention of that grandfather of Northwest anthropology, Horatio Hale, living in Ontario and active again in anthropological circles, a leading figure in Canadian anthropology.

At the British Association for the Advancement of Science's (BAAS) 1884 Montreal meetings, Hale and Dawson had helped to establish a committee to investigate the Dominion's Northwest tribes, seen to be in danger of rapid disintegration with the impending completion of the Canadian Pacific Railway. The committee, though under the formal chairmanship of Oxford's E. B. Tylor, was run largely by Hale. It accomplished little until Hale, frustrated by his age from distant fieldwork, approached Boas for the task, asking for an account of the linguistic stocks, full descriptions, and an ethnographic map.[22]

Beginning, then, in 1887 and extending over the next ten years, Boas made five trips to British Columbia under the committee's auspices. Sponsored by the BAAS, the society's contribution was matched each year by the Canadian government. In 1889, while teaching at Clark University, Boas deputized his first doctoral student, A. F. Chamberlain, to do work among the Kootenay.

Boas, who soon made himself the leading scholar of the Northwest, did not restrict himself to British Columbia. Securing support from Powell's Bureau of Ethnology, he worked among Oregon Indians at the Siletz and Grande Ronde reservations, among the Salish of Puget Sound, and especially among the Clatsop and Kathlamat Chinook, aided there by the remarkable Charlie Cultee.

In his work for the BAAS, Boas was required to secure "a general synopsis of the ethnology of the whole of British Columbia, according to linguistic stocks."[23] Boas, who wanted more independence and more focus on his own interests on the central and north coast, fought the restrictions imposed by Hale, who insisted on a general survey before monographic treatment of single groups. Boas would later come round to the usefulness of the approach. The work was fragmentary, but "the opportunity which I have had to become acquainted with so many different tribes was very welcome."[24]

Hale, as Jacob Gruber pointed out, remained tied to his own experience with the Wilkes Expedition of fifty years before. He had given a comprehensive outline of Oregon linguistics, and he now wanted Boas to repeat that treatment, including a British Columbia ethnographic map comparable to his Oregon one. Hale, as Gruber sympathetically concluded, "involved himself vicariously in Boas' work" and "saw the activities of the younger man as an extension of his own work which had begun, but was never finished, a half-century earlier." Boas was his successor, and he conducted the relationship as "master to student, almost of father to son."[25]

The brief irritation between the two, it must be noted, was over research strategy, not over anthropological ideas. Hale's views had been formed in the days of P. E. Duponceau, Albert Gallatin, and John Pickering, in the pre-evolutionary period of American anthropology. He was skeptical of racial categories and his own hierarchy of peoples was based upon linguistic, not evolutionary, principles. Although his ideas were somewhat rigid and occasionally eccentric, they did not clash with Boas's.

Boas's work for the BAAS and the Canadian government continued until 1897 when, in the final year of the North-Western Tribes committee, his work overlapped with the first season of the Jesup North Pacific Expedition sent out by New York's American Museum of Natural History where Boas was now a curator. For Boas, the Jesup Expedition was a continuation of the systematic work of the BAAS committee, though that committee's annual resources of $1,000 was small in comparison to the ample pocketbook of millionaire Morris K. Jesup and the organization, experience, and personnel of the American Museum. Now with an institutional base at the New York museum and at Columbia University, Boas was able to accomplish many of his ambitions. He did more than any other single anthropologist in filling the remaining gaps in Northwest Coast ethnology. The Jesup Expedition researched the Interior Salish, Haida, Bella Coola, Chilkotan, and Kwakiutl of British Columbia, the Quinault and Quileute of Washington State, and the Tlingit of Alaska.[26]

At least as important, Boas launched the "Vanishing Tribes of North America" project. Most Northwest anthropological work, including Boas's own, had until now been done among the coastal Indians. By the turn of the century, they were far better known in almost every way than interior Indians. Boas's "Vanishing Indians" changed much of that by sending out young anthropologists, mostly trained by himself at Columbia University, into the western field. Roland Dixon, A. E. Kroeber, Livingston Farrand, Clark Wissler, H. H. St. Clair, Pliny Goddard, and Edward Sapir, among others, were dispatched between 1899 and 1906 to study tribes which Boas thought were in danger of imminent destruction. "If we do not collect this material," wrote Boas, "our failure to do so will be held up to our generation as a constant reproach."[27] Using such an appeal, he secured appropriations from Jesup and other benefactors and eventually from general museum funds. Some of the work was necessarily superficial, but among Northwest tribes visited were the Shoshone and Bannock by Kroeber; the Alsea, Siletz, Klickitat, Yakima, Quinault, Quileute, Nez Percé, Umatilla, and

Cayuse by Farrand; the Shoshone, Coos, and Tikelma by St. Clair and Dixon; and Sapir did work on Upper Columbia groups. In addition, Boas used the project to secure additional material from resident George Hunt among the Kwakiutl and Nootka, from James Teit among the Interior Salish on both sides of the border, and from Henry Tate among the Tsimshian.

Boas's dispatched crew were a new generation of professionals, trained in linguistics and ethnology in the seminars of Columbia and the study collection of the American Museum. "The time is past," Boas emphasized in 1901, "when anthropological work may be intrusted to good advantage to a man whose scientific judgment and knowledge in other branches of science can stand in place of a good training in anthropology. We shall never get beyond the standpoint of amateurs as long as we adhere to this antiquated method."[28]

After Boas's 1905 resignation from the museum, Clark Wissler, his student and successor, carried on the work, though with different emphasis. Wissler sent Robert Lowie to the Lemhi Reserve in Idaho to begin his important work among the Shoshone and sponsored the Nez Percé work, initiated by the Peabody Museum at Harvard, of Herbert Joseph Spinden. Wissler's own interests centered on the Blackfeet, and most of the American Museum's work in the next decades concentrated on tribes east of the continental divide, notably research on the Blackfeet and Gros Ventre by Kroeber, Wissler, and Lowie, on the Assiniboine and Plains Cree by Lowie, and on the Sarcee by Pliny Goddard.

Though Boas's museum resignation lost him that important source of research funding, he retained his base at Columbia University and continued his connection with the Smithsonian's Bureau of American Ethnology. This allowed him to support western research by his students and others, including Leo J. Frachtenberg (Coos and Umpqua), Herman Haeberlin (Puget Sound), Gladys Reichert (Coeur d'Alene), Leslie Spier (Klamath), Melville Jacobs (Northern Sahaptin), Erna Gunther (Puget Sound), Archie Phinny (Nez Percé), Helen Codere (Kwakiutl), Viola Garfield (Tsimshian), Marian W. Smith (Puyallup and Nisqually), and Frederica de Laguna (Tlingit, Eyak, Chugash). Almost all of this group of Boas students has now passed on, though, at least in de Laguna's case, the dedication to anthropological research continues. Indeed, Dr. de Laguna has recently revised our knowledge of the Tlingit by editing the massive manuscripts of George Thornton Emmons for a monograph begun in 1888 but never fully completed. Emmons, the son of a Wilkes expedition naval officer, served himself with that service on the Alaska coast. Best known previously as an artifact collector for museums, Emmons, through de Laguna's retrieval, now ranks as an important ethnologist as well.[29]

Beyond the detail of individual names and publications is the overwhelming importance of governmental sponsorship throughout most of the nineteenth century. Without the Wilkes Expedition, the Smithsonian Institution, and the Bureau of American Ethnology, little work would have been accomplished in exploring the anthropology of the Northwest. Similarly, without the Geological Survey of Canada and the Canadian government's matching grant to the BAAS, our knowledge of the natives of British Columbia would have been greatly impoverished. Only later, after about 1895 or so, does the modern museum and, with it private philanthropy, have a significant effect. The West is enormously indebted in this latter regard to the American Museum and its benefactors, notably Jesup, the Huntingtons, and Henry Villard. The nineteenth century, however, was primarily the age of government ethnology, followed by a period of museum explorations, succeeded only later by university work.

Nineteenth-century anthropology put a premium on philology and, to a lesser but still significant extent, upon mythology. Almost all the contributors to Northwest anthropology mentioned here collected vocabularies, and the primary concern of some of the major figures, notably Hale, Gibbs, Gatschet, and (with qualification) Boas and his students, was upon language. This linguistic concern came partly from the European inheritance, from the impressive successes of Indo-Germanic linguistics in showing affinities and tracing origins and connections in the years after Jacob Grimm's *Deutsche Grammatik* of 1819. By that time there was already an American school of philology, represented preeminently by Gallatin, and the two merged in the study of American Indian languages. Henry Rowe Schoolcraft saw language as the most promising instrument to solve the puzzles of the origins and history of American aborigines. "I consider language to be the most important monument of the American Indian," wrote Gatschet in his Klamath monograph. "Archaeology and ethnography are more apt to acquaint us with *facts* concerning the aborigines, but language, when properly investigated, gives us the *ideas* that were moving the Indian's mind, not only recently but long before the historic period."[30] Hale considered that "the mental facilities of a people are reflected in their speech."[31] To Boas, linguistic research enabled a reconstruction of the history of the culture of a people and of its admixtures and migrations.

At the same time, philology was a natural entry point to ethnology and ethnological classification, a way to bring a framework, no matter how elementary, to an uncharted territory. Hale's map, which filled in the blank left in Gallatin's 1836 classic "Map of the Indian Tribes of North America," was the first, followed by the refinements of Gibbs, Dall, Boas, Niblack, and Dawson. The end of our centenary period almost coincides with the publication of J. W. Powell's great 1891 classification of American Indian languages north of Mexico and its accompanying map. By then, linguistic classification, save some dialectic shadings, was virtually complete. The next generation, largely Boas-trained linguists, would work on intensive study rather than territorial boundaries, though classification, in terms of affinities, would continue among both "lumpers and splitters."

The concern for mythology among Gatschet and Boas, and later with Hale, also had its roots in European scholars' concerns with Indo-Germanic folklore. Here, too, was a tool through which one could trace historical affinities and contacts and, as with language, find a key to the study of Indian psychology. Mythology, wrote Boas, was "of great importance, as it reveals customs which easily escape notice" and was the best means of tracing the history of tribes by revealing traces of the past when each group possessed its own independent culture.[32] The collecting of mythological texts and contributions to the *Journal of American Folk-Lore* became almost obligatory to Boas's students.

Alongside this concern with philology and folklore was an interest in Indian material culture. Few of these people, Boas possibly excepted, was greatly exercised to produce systematic study of Indian basketry, weapons, or clothing, but virtually all (Hale seems the exception) collected artifacts or specimens for museums, collections which provided the basis for such studies. Swan, Gibbs, Dawson, Niblack, Eells, and Boas (and all his students) were collectors who captured the material heritage of the Indians for their own and for the future use of anthropological scholars.

This leads to another theme. By the 1870s all features of western American anthropological study were motivated, and increasingly so, by the urgency of salvage, by the realization that time was essential. Civilization was everywhere pushing the primitive to the wall, destroying his material culture, leaving the language and legends forgotten, even destroying the stock itself. The BAAS committee had been formed with this now-or-never idea, and Boas was always compelled by the urgency of the task. The work, he wrote, "if not undertaken now, will never be done, because the languages, customs, and types of Indians will disappear with the present generation."[33] They had not disappeared by 1899 and in many respects they still have not. But this urgency to salvage what was still to be saved was the imperative that led governments, capitalist philanthropy, and later university researchers into the field.

The mission was only partly successful. Some coastal groups, the Chinook and Kalapuya, for example, were so shattered or decimated that little was recordable even in Gibbs's day (though Boas later and Verne Ray even later secured a great deal) and reconstructions are greatly dependent upon early exploration and fur-trade descriptions. Interior Indians were affected by intensive contact only later, but the opportunity provided by the interval was not often enough used. Practically nothing, for example, was known of the Shoshone when Lowie arrived in 1906, and those on the Lemhi reservation had already been confined there for thirty years and were about to be moved to the more remote Fort Belknap.

Finally, I wish to note the continuity of personality. Students, we all know, are not made in their mentor's image, but Hale did lead to Boas, who led to his own students, people such as Kroeber, Lowie, Wissler, Sapir, de Laguna, Jacobs, Spier, Garfield, and Reichert. They, in their turn, supervised and influenced students—anthropologists like Cora Du Bois, Catherine McClellan, Julian Stewart, Demitri Shenkin, and Samuel Barrett. Important work stands outside this genealogy, and I do not wish to overemphasize the Hale-Boas legacy. Both men had their limits and placed constraints on others' work, but the continuity is there between the first and second centuries of anthropological exploration of the Northwest.

Chapter 10 Notes

1. James P. Ronda, *Lewis and Clark among the Indians* (Lincoln: University of Nebraska Press, 1984), 254. The vocabularies, unfortunately, have now disappeared.

2. Gibbs, "Tribes of Western Washington and Northeastern Oregon," *Contributions to North American Ethnology* 1 (1877): 236.

3. *United States Exploring Expedition, during the Years 1838–1842, under the Command of Charles Wilkes, U.S.N.*, 6 (Philadelphia, 1846).

4. Hale to Boas, 1 March 1888, Boas Papers, American Philosophical Society.

5. "Ethnography and Philology," 198, vol. 6, of the *United States Exploring Expedition During the Years 1838, 1839, 1840, 1841, 1842* (Philadelphia: Lea and Blanchard, 1846).

6. Hale to Boas, 1 March 1888, Boas Papers.

7. Adrienne L. Kaeppler, "Anthropology and the U.S. Exploring Expedition," in Herman J. Viola and Carolyn Margolis, eds., *Magnificent Voyages: The U.S. Exploring Expedition, 1838–1842* (Washington: Smithsonian Institution Press, 1985), 147.

8. See E. E. Blomkvist, "A Russian Scientific Expedition to California and Alaska, 1839–1849," translated by Basil Dmytryshyn and E. A. P. Crownhart-Vaughan, *Oregon Historical Quarterly* 73 (June 1972): 100–70.

9. See Stephen Dow Beckham, "George Gibbs, 1815–1873: Historian and Ethnologist," Ph.D., UCLA, 1969.

10. Gibbs, "Report of Mr. George Gibbs to Captain McClelland on the Indian Tribes of the Territory of Washington," *Reports of Explorations and Surveys . . . in 1853–4*, House Exec. Doc. 91, 22d Sess., 33d Cong. (Washington, D.C.: 1854; repr., Fairfield: Ye Galleon Press, 1967), 28.

11. Department of the Interior, *U.S. Geographic and Geological Survey of the Rocky Mountain Region* (Washington, D.C.: GPO, 1877), viii.

12. Ibid., 163.

13. (Boston: Lee and Shepard, 1870).

14. Aurel Krause, *Die Tlingit—Indiana* (Jena: Hermann Constenoble, 1885). See also Aurel and Arthur Krause, *Zur Tschuktschen-Halbinsel und zu den Tlinkit-Indianern, 1881/82: Reisetagebücher und Briefe von Aurel und Arthur Krause*, edited by Ella Krause (Berlin: Dietrich Reimer Verlag, 1984).

15. Erna Gunther, "Preface" to Aurel Krause, *The Tlingit Indians: Results of a Trip to the Northwest Coast of America and the Bering Straits*, translated by Erna Gunther (1885; repr. Seattle: University of Washington Press, 1956), iii.

16. Norman H. Clark, "Introduction" to Swan, *Northwest Coast* (Seattle: University of Washington Press, 1957), xx.

17. Albert P. Niblack, "The Coast Indians of Southern Alaska and Northern British Columbia," *Report of the United States National Museum* (1888), 227–386.

18. George Pierre Castile, ed., *The Indians of Puget Sound: The Notebooks of Myron Eells* (Seattle: University of Washington Press, 1985).

19. William W. Elmendorf, "Myron Eells as Ethnographer: An Appraisal," in ibid., 454.

20. See Douglas Cole and Bradley Lockner, eds., *The Journals of George M. Dawson: British Columbia, 1875–1878* (Vancouver: University of British Columbia Press, 1989), 18–22.

21. Papers of the 1903 Investigation of the Bureau of American Ethnology, Boas Papers, quoted in Curtis M. Hinsley, "The Development of a Profession: Anthropology in Washington, D.C., 1846–1903," Ph.D. diss., University of Wisconsin, 1976, 240.

22. Hale to Boas, 30 January 1887, Boas Papers.

23. Hale to Boas, 21 May 1888, Boas Papers.

24. Boas to parents, 15 January 1891, Boas Papers.

25. Gruber, "Horatio Hale and the Development of American Anthropology," *Proceedings of the American Philosophical Society* 3 (1967): 26, 29.

26. See Aldona Jonaitis, *From the Land of the Totem Poles: The Northwest Coast Indian Art Collection of the American Museum of Natural History* (Seattle: University of Washington Press, 1988).

27. Boas to Archer M. Huntington, 18 May 1904, American Museum of Natural History.

28. Boas to Zelia Nuttall, 20 November 1901, American Museum of Natural History.

29. George Thornton Emmons, *The Tlingit Indians*, edited with additions by Frederica de Laguna and a biography of Jean Low (Seattle: University of Washington Press; New York: American Museum of Natural History, 1991).

30. *Klamath Indians*, vii.

31. Hale, *The Iroquis Book of Rites* (1883; repr. Toronto: University of Toronto Press, 1963), 99.

32. Clark lecture, 1888, 5, Boas Papers.

33. Boas to Morris Jesup, 1 December 1899, American Museum of Natural History.

11. A Taxonomy for Discovery

by Martin Ridge

Almost everyone knows a good deal about discovery and exploration in America. If you were asked to name a significant explorer or discoverer, most would say Christopher Columbus, or, if you are a Scandinavian, Leif Ericson. For most people, there is no distinction between explorers and discoverers, and the words are used almost interchangeably.

But there is a difference. Discovery is finding out about something that we did not know existed either through searching, or studying, or just plain good luck. But discovery is a tricky term. Columbus may have discovered America for the people in Europe but certainly not for the American Indians who were already there. Therefore, discovery must be seen in two contexts: the intellectual context of the world of the discoverer and the context of the discovered, which may be entirely different. Discovery also means publicizing what is found and being given credit for calling it to the attention of people who also knew nothing about it. That is why Leif Ericson's reputation suffers. He may have stumbled on or even stepped foot on the North America landmass before Columbus, but he never publicized that fact. Unlike discovery, which can be haphazard, exploration is systematic. An explorer tries to find out more about something or someplace that his intellectual world already knows exists.

Regardless of definitions, we tend to lump explorers and discoverers together. They intrigue us. We want to know what they did, what made them tick, and how they fit in together in time, in importance, and in the history of human development. When we teach children, we portray discoverers differently—they are heroes. Whatever their personal shortcomings, they are singled out in our history classes to teach us the ingredients of greatness. To go where no one had ever gone before, whether in thought or action, meant taking great risks and confronting

165

prejudice and ignorance, as well as physical and often life-threatening danger. Take the case of Columbus. Although it seems almost patently obvious today, the idea of sailing west to reach the East defied common-sense logic in the fifteenth century. If Columbus did not have to convince educated men and women that the world was round, he certainly worked hard at convincing his rough-and-ready sailors that what he had in mind was possible. Samuel Eliot Morison makes much of the fact that he kept a double set of ship's log books—one so he knew where he was and another so he could deceive his crew if they wanted to know where they were. Ironically, the bogus ship's log books, says Admiral Morison, proved more accurate than the real ones; Columbus actually deceived himself. Columbus may not have been the best navigator in Western Europe, but he was a genuine discoverer because he not only challenged simple-minded, popular conventions with determination and courage but also faced actual danger by sailing his fleet of tiny ships across the Atlantic Ocean and finding continents unknown in his intellectual context. If Columbus is a good example of a discoverer, I think we can agree that discoverers are courageous, whether they cross oceans of water or oceans of prejudice and ignorance to accomplish their goals.

The real questions about both explorers and discoverers is why they do what they do, and whether there is any pattern or tradition into which each can be fitted. These two ideas are in one sense inseparable. Even explorers and discovers are not unique unto themselves. They constitute parts of different and sometimes overlapping and possibly even conflicting traditions. Unless we recognize such traditions, the history of discovery and exploration can turn into a jumble of eccentric and unique and perhaps interesting events that makes little overall sense to someone interested in the history of human development. Even chronological divisions are not always helpful because the epoch of one society may mean little to another. We ask ourselves what difference does this discovery make and what does it mean? Each individual's activities, whether discoverer or explorer, regardless of accomplishment or daring, may be fascinating in itself, but in the end it may seem disappointingly narrow. We need to organize human activity—to impose order on the past—before we can make sense of it. Historians need to know how discoveries fit together before they can fully appreciate them. The process of integrating discoveries is an intellectual enterprise.

Therefore, let me suggest a very direct and obvious set of examples that may give exploration and discovery in America a somewhat new twist that I hope will also explain my title, "A Taxonomy for Discovery."

Discoverers and explorers are in a sense followers of ideas that can most often be associated with a distinct time and place in history or with a particular man. Here are four ways, in terms of traditions and the men they represent, to organize the history of exploration and discovery. Although they certainly do not embrace all varieties of discovery and exploration, they are handy ways to begin thinking about the subject. First are the sons of the European age of enterprise and commerce; second, the sons of the Apostle Saint Paul; third, the sons of Carl Linne, often called Carolus Linnaeus, the great Swedish botanist; and fourth, the sons of the Baron Alexander von Humboldt—the historian William Goetzmann called them the children of von Humboldt—who is sometimes called the father of modern geography and earth science. The later two traditions are obviously sub-categories of what is often called the scientific revolution.

Of the four, perhaps the most well known are the sons of the European age of commerce and enterprise. These were men *essentially* driven by the desire for economic gain and profit, both for themselves and for their countries. The first generation of this group looked for new trade routes from Europe to what they called the Indies, and they discovered continents, ransacked native kingdoms in Africa, South and Central America, and India, enslaved non-white women and men, and attempted to establish European empires wherever they encountered peoples with lesser technical knowledge or governmental skills. They were men of intense personal ambition, questing not only for great wealth and power but also for fame, if not immortality. Their life stories are fabulous, and often tragic.

Two excellent examples of this kind of man are Christopher Columbus and Robert Cavalier, better known as Sieur de La-Salle. The story of Columbus is now legend. He sought financial backing for a voyage to the Indies and was in the end supported by Queen Isabella of Spain, although he would have been willing to sail for the king of Portugal or perhaps any other monarch who would have put up the money. Columbus struck a shrewd bargain with Ferdinand and Isabella of Spain. He, indeed, wanted to find a sea route to the Spice Islands, but he also insisted that if he succeeded in reaching the Indies he be made ruler over those territories, that he secure a large percentage of all the wealth Spain would gain from the lands discovered by his voyages, and that he be granted the hereditary title of Admiral of the Ocean Seas.

Alas, his bargain was not honored. He went to his grave a well-to-do but not a rich man. He was a keenly disappointed man because the king of Spain proved far from willing to surrender so large a share of the New World's plunder to his servant. Columbus's disagreement with the king can be traced in legal documents—mostly depositions—where the facts and issues are all explained. After reading them it would not be unfair to conclude that Columbus was so single-minded that he saw in America only a source of wealth and potential power, both of which he thought he was entitled to by contract, and both of which he wanted to convey to his children.

Columbus served the king of Spain; Robert Cavalier, Sieur de LaSalle, the king of France. He is not as well known as Columbus, but he is equally interesting and illustrative of men driven by an insatiable personal ambition to found and control an empire. LaSalle was the first white man to travel the length of the Mississippi from where it joins the Ohio River to its mouth. He was a remarkable explorer who could as easily find his way through the uncharted wilderness of the American heartland as he could along the winding streets and alleys of Paris. Like Columbus he sought wealth—for him it was through control of the fur trade with the Indians and French domination of the Mississippi Valley—and like Columbus he was to suffer acute disappointment. He led an expedition to found a city at the mouth of the Mississippi River but missed the estuary and landed instead near Matagorda Bay in east Texas. Always a cold and strong-willed man, LaSalle never held the trust and loyalty of his men. He was always plagued by desertions, mutinies, and treacherous colleagues. In the end, he was murdered by some of his own men who feared he had misled them by luring them into the trackless grasslands of the Gulf plains.

Just as Columbus was reviled by rivals and betrayed by his king, during his lifetime LaSalle was also harassed. He was always in debt to partners who wanted immediate dividends for their investment. La Salle died deeply in debt to French investors, saved from obscurity by his personal courage and the determination that gave France a claim to the middle of the continent, and also because his biographer was Francis Parkman, one of the nation's leading romantic narrative historians of the nineteenth century.

Columbus and LaSalle epitomize the discoverers and explorers of the European age of enterprise and commerce that began in the fifteenth century and continued for almost four hundred years. Wealth, power, glory, and empire were the watchwords of these men, and their names are emblazoned on pages of our traditional history books—from Magellan, the first man to circumnavigate the globe, to John Cabot, the first man to sail to America under a charter from an English king, from the *conquistadores* Cortez and Pizarro, who suppressed the Aztec and the Inca, to Francisco Coronado, the so-called Knight of the Pueblos and the Plains, who struck northward from Mexico in search of the fabled seven cities of gold and eventually wandered lost in the Kansas prairie only to find nothing but impoverished Indians. These men sailed and searched for economic gain and exploitable resources. The list of their names can be carried forward to include Daniel Boone, who explored Kentucky; Zebulon Pike, who searched the upper Mississippi River; Stephen Long, who believed the Great Plains were an American Desert; Lewis and Clark, who pioneered a route to Oregon; and a host of others. Unfortunately, their followers sometimes brought with them dreaded diseases that wiped out native populations.

In saying that these men often sought glory, wealth, or power and served national interest, I do not wish to belittle them or demean their achievements. They were often empire builders. In the process of seeking wealth and extending the power of their employers or nation-states, they actually provided chance and change for less-advantaged individuals who would otherwise have known little opportunity for both economic success and political power.

There were also cultural by-products of their endeavors. Perhaps the examples that most readily come to mind are the wonderful and beautiful maps that were prepared by cartographers who read the reports of the explorers and studied their crude charts. Today copies of these maps are immensely popular—every interior decorator has a bundle—and the originals are in the great libraries of the world. A fine example is Mercator's view of the world.

There is some irony in the fact that part of the justification for establishing the European-centered empires in America rested in the Christian tradition. The lands of non-Christian rulers were considered fair game for conquest. In the wake, if not in the immediate company of the first explorers, came the second kind of discoverer, the sons of the Apostle Paul—the Christian missionaries. All too often one forgets that the kings of Europe took quite seriously their role as defenders and propagators of

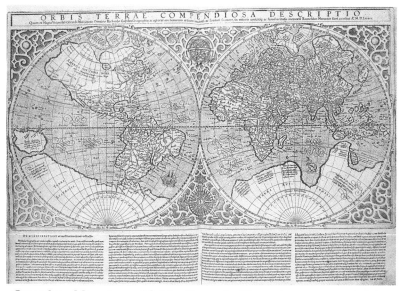

Gerardus Mercatore, "Orbis Terrae," Atlas sive cosmographicae meditationes de fabrica mundi and fabricati figura *(Duisburgi, 1595).* Courtesy the Henry E. Huntington Library and Art Gallery.

the faith. This was especially true in Spain, but the French also turned much of their empire in America over to various religious orders to explore and control because the native population was depicted as heathen, economically underdeveloped, and culturally backward. To the sons of Saint Paul fell the task of not only shattering Indian idols and icons, but also of finding new people to Christianize and to introduce to the European way of life and the white man's goods.

French missionaries acted with a good deal more independence than those of Spain. French Canadian Jesuits kept meticulous if sometimes fanciful accounts of their experiences and tell of daring and dangerous expeditions deep into the heart of the American West by various priests and lay brothers—such as Marquette—who first explored the Great Lakes, the Ohio River, and the lower Mississippi River Valley. Some French priests suffered torture and death at the hands of Indians who found Christianity distasteful or who thought the missionaries were the friends of their enemies, but this did little to deter other missionaries who sought out new tribes to convert.

It is true that the Jesuit priests ousted the Sulpician fathers from New France because they may have been as interested in economic gain through the fur trade as in saving souls, but there can be no denying that their dearly bought knowledge of the wilderness and its riverways and portages gave the French an initial lead in the struggle for control of the North American continent. The Jesuits were the frontline shock troops not only of French Catholicism but also of empire because they exercised a powerful influence over the Indian population and could recruit it in times of war with the Protestant English or against hostile Indian peoples. The vestiges of the French missionary activity are found throughout areas where the first French empire spread. Moreover, the missionaries had a lasting impact among Canadian Indians who assimilated French Catholicism. The French missionaries were true explorers seeking new lands and new people, and they often went virtually alone into the wilderness.

The Spanish sons of St. Paul were as venturous as their French counterparts, and they certainly confronted equal hardships and often suffered martyrdom in America. Like the

French, the Spanish missionaries, also, came from rival religious orders. But regardless of religious order—whether Jesuit or Franciscan—they were, even more than the French priests, the shock troops of Christianity and empire. The kings of Spain considered themselves, especially after driving the Moors from Europe, as primary propagators of Roman Catholicism. There is no doubt of their sincere desire to see Catholicism spread throughout America. Priests accompanied virtually all Spanish exploring expeditions. Moreover, the Spanish developed the mission system, which was part of a method for controlling and expanding their frontier borderlands by pacifying the Indians. On the borderlands of North America, for example, Spanish missionaries operated out of a chain of tiny religious compounds; like a string of beads they extended from northern Florida westward to the Pacific Ocean and from Mexico City northward to San Francisco Bay. The names of Spanish missionaries—such as Serra and Kino, especially, plus a host of others—are virtually household words in California, while the names of the Spanish missions that dotted early maps of the American South and West now as often identify well-established towns and cities as long-gone but once-thriving communities. This is true not only in the United States but also in Central and South America. It would have been true for Oregon and Washington had not the English thwarted the Spanish advance at Nootka Sound.

The Spanish missionaries were more tightly controlled than those of France and seldom acted independently of military authorities. They could not, as could the French Jesuits, vanish into the dense woodlands to seek out and establish contact with unspoiled Indian tribes in quest of converts. Father Junipero Serra, for example, traveled north into California in the company of the experienced Spanish soldier/frontiersman Don Gaspar de Portola. Very often the padres, however, whether Franciscans or Jesuits, although they accompanied military exploring expeditions, did break away and act on their own to establish posts to work with the Indians. They preferred to explore new areas away from civilian or military communities because they wanted to find uncontaminated Indians and keep them from corrupt secular influences. The Spanish missionaries in North America seem to have had a strong Jansenist streak, that is, they were puritanical in habit and had grave doubts about the basic goodness of man. For them the way to make Christians of Indians meant to give them a new way of life that would be compatible with their new faith. It would be based on an ideal Christian existence, a life dedicated entirely to maintaining the church and its rigorous religious practices. This is what the mission was intended to do. But geography, technology, and culture thwarted the hopes of the Spanish missionaries. They often met Indians who lived marginally because the land was poor, and they lacked the tools and skills to develop it. It took great labor to attempt in a generation to refashion the lives of these poor souls and often, even with coercion, little was accomplished. They also encountered tribes that had learned to ride horses and were fierce nomadic fighters. They were unyielding in the face of Christianity, and efforts by priests to penetrate their lands frequently resulted in a slow, tortured death. Moreover, the Spanish dealt with Indians as different as the settled Creek of the East, the Comanche and Apache of the high plains, the Navaho of the desert Southwest, and the California tribes of the Pacific seaboard.

The Spanish missionaries, like their French counterparts, are often accused of seeking economic gain and exploiting and oppressing the Indian. The subject is one on which experts disagree, not so much over the evidence but how to interpret it. By today's standard the degree of man's inhumanity to man in the past is deplorable; in the context of that time there may be reasons to dissent from such a view.

The Spanish missionaries more than any other explorer group tried to change the Indian both materially and spiritually. The French did not attempt anything so daring and with good reason. They not only encountered fierce tribes but also lacked the physical power to dominate them. They were, therefore, more likely to try to accommodate Christianity to Indian customs. Thus, the French missionaries were far less destructive of the Indian way of life so long as the Indians accepted the outward symbols of Catholicism. Ironically, they dealt with peoples they could best attract with material goods. They could not compel the concentration of population as could the Spanish.

Instead the French mastered the languages and the customs of the Indians they met. They wrote detailed accounts of Indian practices and behavior, and these proved valuable then and are of immense value today. The French missionaries were in a way pioneer ethnographers. Their knowledge of Indian ways, their willingness to accommodate to their environment, and the fact that they were not settlers who took land allowed them to explore vast areas of the interior of the continent.

English and American missionaries of a later period should never be viewed as discoverers. They were explorers in the narrow dictionary sense but were in no way comparable to the French or Spanish. From the outset the English and American missionaries were identified with eventual white settlement, from New England's preachers to Marcus Whitman in the Northwest. The English and American sons of Saint Paul sought to save souls and also to exercise social control over what were seen from almost the outset as a hostile, morally corrupt, and potentially dependent peoples. Their goal was the integration of the Indian into the general population by remaking the Indian into a white man, but one with fewer vices. The English and American missionaries had many virtues but they were not explorers.

The sons of Linnaeus claim no one nationality. They were men who came from Europe or were reared in America and whose area of discovery was not in land but in nature. They were rarely interested in the course of empire, or in personal profit, or in men's souls. Linnaeus deserves the title of father for these naturalist explorers not because he was a first but because he proposed a useful method of classification of plants and animals—a taxonomy. He first enumerated the principle for defining genera and species, and he adhered to a uniform use of the binomial system of naming plants and animals (and I might add rocks). For example, to identify tea, we would say *Camellia*, its genus, and *sininsis*, its species. It is possible to have many species within one genus. This eliminated confusion and made classification simpler. Linnaeus lived from 1707 to 1778 and during his lifetime was widely acclaimed throughout Western Europe and America for his achievements as a taxonomist. The fact that his system was crude and misleading in its simplicity should not be held against him. What should be noted is that he worked when men began increasingly to look at America not only as a place to save souls or seek economic opportunity but also as a continent with seemingly endless varieties of entirely new life forms. His work more than anyone else's encouraged the search for new life forms.

Plants were sent from America to gardens and to botanists all over the world, and perhaps the greatest organized transfer of life forms from one continent to another continent was underway. Now, the way was open for a new kind of explorer—someone who made discoveries in nature, identified unique plant life, established gardens to study it, and communicated with other amateurs and professionals throughout the world about American flora and fauna. I cannot overestimate the excitement of this new era of exploration and discovery. Strong national feelings sometimes became involved. For example, the French naturalist, the Comte de Buffon, although a farsighted scientist, speculated that animal and plant life in America was an inferior form. Everything in the New World was smaller, less vital, weaker, and less developed. Thomas Jefferson responded to Buffon by compiling data to refute this canard, and he won the argument. The story is told that Benjamin Franklin at a dinner party in France asked all Americans present to stand along with his French host to prove that native-born Americans towered over their European friends. American life forms were different; they were not just at an earlier stage of evolution. Armchair explorers speculated about the meaning of plant and animal life that existed in America and tried to identify and classify it. In fact, the years after Linnaeus could well be described as the years when science was simply discovery and taxonomy.

In discussing the naturalists who explored America, the list is so long and impressive it is difficult to single out a few from among the scores of men who collected, described, and catalogued everything from azaleas to woodpeckers. I cannot even mention American paleontologists who debated the nature and origin of prehistoric life in North America or the many kinds of classifiers of American life forms. For purposes of discussion let me turn to botanists and zoologists. Among those who deserve special mention is John Bartram, a Pennsylvania Quaker who established the first botanical garden in America. Virtually every European with a scientific interest in America corresponded with him or visited with him and his equally dedicated son, William. They were part of that charmed Philadelphia intellectual circle that included Benjamin Franklin; Alexander Wilson, America's leading ornithologist; and Dr. Benjamin Rush.

The Far West also attracted distinguished naturalist explorers. Take, for example, Thomas Nuttall, a young Yorkshireman who came to America, found employment at Bartram's garden and was fascinated when he saw the specimens collected by Lewis and Clark on their journey to Oregon that were displayed in Charles Wilson Peale's museum in Philadelphia. Nuttall later set out for the villages of Mandan Indians on the upper Missouri River. He was so dedicated a collector of plant life that he was once found by an Indian 100 miles from the Mandan post, almost at death's door, wandering in search of specimens. The zeal of these naturalist explorers knew no limits. Throughout the late eighteenth and nineteenth century they scoured the continent in search of flora and fauna that had not been classified or made available for study. Nuttall and the Bartrams, good sons of Linnaeus, are part of a tradition of inquiry that is still active as naturalists search the ocean depths and isolated locations for previously unidentified life forms.

These early naturalists had an unusual problem. They could transport plant and animal specimens, but when they came to write about what they knew and saw, words were inadequate. The wonders of American flora and fauna beggered description. The answer was to draw pictures from life. Some of the most remarkable studies of plants, animals, and birds resulted from this effort. My personal favorite among the artists who drew animals and plants from life is Mark Catesby, who came to America, worked in Virginia, Georgia, and the Carolinas, and produced astonishingly attractive pictures. John Bartram helped get Catesby's studies published in London. Catesby was a fine artist and a gracious writer. Catesby's frog—the Leopard Frog—taken from volume 2 of *The Natural History of Carolina, Florida, and the Bahama Islands*, was published in London between 1731 and 1743. American frogs captivated Europeans. A

Mark Catesby, "Frog" in The Natural History of Carolina, Florida and the Bahama Islands. . . . *(2 Vols. London, 1731–43). Courtesy the Henry E. Huntington Library and Art Gallery.*

young Swedish naturalist, Peter Kalm, observed shortly after his arrival in America—and it was September—"For besides this all the trees are yet green, and ground is still as much covered with flowers, as in our summer. Thousands of frogs croaked all night long in the marshes and brooks." Catesby's published pictures are not as large as those in John James Audubon's elephant folios, but they are equally attractive and neoromantic. And if I pass over Audubon too quickly it is because he is so well known. He, too, belongs to the draw-from-life school. I should add that most of these men shot and mounted their specimens before they drew them. Contemporary lovers of wild life should think twice about admiring Audubon.

It would be a gross error to think that all of the drawing-from-life artists belonged to the early period in American history or that they all lived in the East. The trans-Mississippi West attracted artists who were for years overlooked and are now finally recognized for their true worth. Let me mention only a few because they represent a shift in focus. Alfred Jacob Miller, Karl Bodmer, and George Catlin were as interested in native people and landscape as Catesby and Audubon were in plants and animals. Miller was among the best trained American artists, having been educated at the Ecole des Beaux Arts in Paris. While visiting in New Orleans his life took a dramatic turn when he joined the western expedition of Captain William Drummond Stewart, a Scottish nobleman who became his patron. He produced not only outstanding sketches but also remarkable portraits. Karl Bodmer, a Swiss artist of distinction, went west with his patron, Prince Maximilian of Wied. He, like Miller, was a highly trained artist, gifted as both portraitist and landscape artist. He returned to Europe after his stay in the West, where he was there associated with the Barbizon School of painters in France. They painted the quiet landscape of the French countryside rather than the robust American landscape. Both Bodmer and Miller were deeply touched by the Romantic era in which they lived.

I take up George Catlin last, although he was born and worked earlier, because he is very special. A lawyer and self-taught portraitist, Catlin's life changed when he saw a delegation of Indians in Philadelphia. He wrote of their "silent and stoic dignity" and saw them as "lords of the forest." He determined to preserve the history and culture of these people through illustration. Today, no one would deny his success, but when he produced his work many people doubted the truthfulness of his art. As an artist, despite his romanticism, Catlin is a pioneer American ethnographer. He developed an almost abstract-like style that allowed him to work with great speed and yet capture the essence of a person or scene. It is difficult to deny that a romantic view of nature touched Catlin, but his depiction also captured the paradox of the benign and the cruel, the nomadic and the sedentary, the strong and the vulnerable.

Catlin, Bodmer, and Miller, each in his own way, saw the Indian as part of America's natural setting, although each would insist no doubt that the Indian was indeed a human being and not merely part of the native fauna. Yet in drawing Indians they were presenting them as part of the American record. They are more the sons of Linnaeus than of any aesthetic goddess. They were essentially taxonomists, part of the exploration that led to identifying and classifying an important part of the New World. They were like many early historians of the West who saw the Indian as part of the environment—worthy of study before it was swept away by a modernizing tide.

The last group of explorers and discoverers are the sons of Baron Alexander von Humboldt, who was something of a universal man—statesman, traveler, and naturalist—and the father of modern geography. His primary interest was more in earth science than in life science. For example, he helped delineate the isothermal lines for maps to show temperatures throughout the earth, and he also used diagrams and maps as a means to demonstrate the connections and interrelationships among all things in nature. Above all, these relationships were grounded not in impressions but in mathematical forms. If Linnaeus sought to classify plants and animals, von Humboldt wanted correct measurements of the earth's surface. Questions about the proper location of rivers and their sources intrigued him, and he shared a wide interest with many educated men who felt that knowledge of the physical world was inadequate.

His followers among explorers and discoverers may well have been men of strong ambition and ego, but scientific knowledge as well as the quest for great personal wealth and national power remained their goal. That they would seek self-aggrandizement through their contribution to knowledge is doubtless true. This led to generations of meticulous surveys of the continent, some of which are still continuing, as the land is measured and the landscape is charted. Von Humboldt's followers differed from earlier explorers who often did not know what lay before them. The later explorers were educated civil engineers and geologists, preparing maps for future railroads, defining boundaries, investigating parts of the so-called Great American Desert like the Staked Plains of eastern New Mexico that had not been thoroughly mapped, and seeking accurate information about the land itself.

Much of this great work was done under the auspices of the government of the United States. Congress authorized the United States Army Topographical Corps to survey all feasible routes for a transcontinental railroad. There were expeditions led by Captain, later Civil War General, George B. McClellan across the Northwest and Lieutenant A. W. Whipple along the Mexican border. Captain John Gunnison started what might be seen as a representative party because it included a physician, a

Alexander Von Humboldt, "Chimborazo" in Vues des Cordillèras et Monuments des Peuples Indigènes de l'Amerique *(Paris, 1810). Courtesy the Henry E. Huntington Library and Art Gallery.*

trained geologist, a botanist, and a trained artist. In the days before photography, artists were an essential component of most
parties, and the reports of these expeditions, when published,
were not only valuable scientific treatises but remarkable
works of art. There was a tragic side to this expedition. Before it
ended, Gunnison, his topographer/artist Kern, and his botanist
Creuzefeldt, were slain by Indians. Even in the nineteenth century, exploration had its perils.

Exploring expeditions were also led by well-educated geologists and elementary environmentalists of both courage and
genius as well as by military officers. The government established the United States Geological Survey, and it rivaled the
army's Topographical Corps. Two of its best-known directors
were John Wesley Powell, who explored the Colorado River,
and Clarence King, who examined a vast swath of land from the
Sierra to the Rockies along the 40th meridian. It is only fair to
say that the scientific work in the West produced sharp competition in the scholarly and governmental communities. Government agencies vied with one another for contracts to explore
the West. It may be startling to realize that the government was
spending a larger share of its national revenue in the nineteenth century on studying the West than it was on space exploration in 1978. Geologists, topographers, paleontologists, engineers, soldiers, and artists were all involved. Little wonder
that the mapping of America—and it lasted for more than half a
century—was as vital an age as that of the voyages of Columbus.

A substantial part of this era of measurement and description,
as I have noted, touched directly the lives of American artists. I
do not wish to leave the impression that American artists had
previously ignored their national landscape. In fact, quite the
contrary. The Hudson River School of American artists concentrated on presenting first the eastern mountains and later other
grand scenes in a strongly romantic fashion. They tried to
depict an American landscape in terms equal to the grandeur
presented by European landscape artists.

Von Humboldt did, however, have a profound impact on
these artists, especially one of the very best of them—Frederick
Edwin Church of Hartford, Connecticut. Von Humboldt pleaded
for painters who would capture in aesthetic form what the

geographers and surveyors were seeing. He wanted, for example, the brilliance of the South America he had visited and written about presented to a new audience in aesthetic form. Church read von Humboldt, went to the Andes Mountains, and painted his version of one of von Humboldt's sketches. The results are worth seeing, and they show the difference between the physical scientist as artist and the artist as interpreter of the physical world. They indicate Church's power as an artist but even more the American fascination with transferring the magnitude of statistical measurement into an aesthetic comparable to that of Europe.

I have now set out for you four possible ways of looking at and thinking about the discovery and exploration by Euro-Americans: they are the advocates of profit, enterprise, and empire; the proponents of the evangelical spirit; the classifiers of human organisms; and the measurers of the physical world. In examining these four approaches and providing a few examples, I hope some evocative questions have been raised.

Discovery and exploration are not dead subjects. We live in a time of great exploration and discovery. As we examine our past and our present and think of how and why men and women dare to go in thought and action where no one has ever been, how they confront public prejudice and ignorance, how these acts are expressed in art and literature, and how our lives and

Frederick Edwin Church, "Chimborazo" from the Virginia Steele Scott Collection. Courtesy the Henry E. Huntington Library and Art Gallery.

values are affected by their efforts, we should have multiple frameworks of understanding. As men and women look deeper into the oceans, into the heavens, into the nature of life, and into themselves, is it fair to ask why? And if the past can serve as a guide, we can say that wealth, fame, moral values, science, national self-interest, curiosity, and aesthetic expression have been overriding motivations. Will they continue to be? Yes.

No act in history, regardless of daring and greatness, stands alone; it is part of a past. When Enrico Ferme, the Italian physicist, first split the atom in a manner that made the atomic bomb possible and opened the atomic age, a secret message was sent from his University of Chicago laboratory to Washington, D.C., with the announcement. But despite its secret nature, it was not in code; it was in plain English. With a profound sense of the history and tradition of discovery, the author of the message wrote: "The Italian navigator has discovered the New World."

Part II

Exploration History in Print and in the Field

12. Exploration History: A Publisher's Overview

by Patricia Knapp

If you were to take a poll among the staff members at the University of Nebraska Press asking whose name comes to mind when they think of exploration history, you might get a couple of votes for James Ronda or William Goetzmann or Bernard DeVoto, but the majority would go without hesitation to two major figures in exploration history—Meriwether Lewis and William Clark. The staff has been thinking about, planning around, praising, and cursing these two men for over eleven years now and will continue to do so for probably eleven more. Think of it—they have already outlasted one director, one production manager, two acquisitions editors, two sales managers, and an entire warehouse crew, and the press has only made it half way through their journals.

I want to present an overview of one publisher's experience with publishing one piece of exploration history—or Nebraska's history of publishing Volume One of the journals, the *Atlas of the Lewis & Clark Expedition.*

Nebraska's involvement with the journals began in June 1977 when David Gilbert, director of the press at the time, read a review essay by Ernst Stadler in *Papers on Language and Literature.* In his essay, entitled "Let Him Keep Also a Diary," Stadler said: "It took America a century to have one of its treasures, the original journals of Lewis and Clark, published. Since the publication of Thwaites's edition, a plethora of written material about Lewis and Clark has become available, but readers and scholars still have to rely on that 1904–1905 edition. We are still waiting, 170 years after the writing, for a fresh and complete edition of the journals of Lewis and Clark." That is precisely the sort of comment that good editors look for and act upon, and Gilbert is a good editor, so he and Steve Cox, Nebraska's editor-in-chief at the time, decided to determine just how much scholarly interest there was in a new edition of the journals.

187

The first person they contacted was Donald Jackson, who replied to Cox's query by referring him to an article in the *Bulletin of the Missouri Historical Society*. The article was a transcription of a speech Jackson had made to the Society in 1967, a speech which he called pointedly enough, "Some Advice for the Next Editor of Lewis and Clark." Jackson had closed with this statement: "When we have found a man who is willing to undertake all these diverse tasks, and have found a university or a society or a foundation which is willing to support him as he does his work, and when finally we have a publisher who goes eagerly into the process of publishing the result while realizing that multi-volume editions seldom pay for themselves—then we should be on our way toward having what the world has needed for 150 years, a complete and modern edition of the journals of Meriwether Lewis and William Clark."

Jackson said to Cox, "I came out strongly for a new edition [ten years ago].... It was my thought at the time that I might undertake it, but Frémont got in the way and then [Washington]." Even though he had not been able to get around to the task himself, Jackson still firmly believed there was a need for a new edition.

Jackson was exactly right about the three prerequisites to a new edition of the journals: a scholar, an institution, and a press. As it happened, however, he articulated them in reverse order. With equally strong encouragement from other scholars, like Ray Wood and John Logan Allen, the University of Nebraska Press made the first move by deciding to "go eagerly into the process of publishing the result." It was the press that sought an institution willing to support a scholar during the long editing process, with the matter of finding a scholar reserved until last.

In August 1977, Jackson came to Lincoln to discuss the project at length with the press editorial staff. During the course of this series of discussions, another entity at the University of Nebraska became involved. The Center for Great Plains Studies had been established the year before by a group of professors interested in developing an interdisciplinary framework unique to our region. They envisioned the Center as a catalyst for the intellectual exploration of all aspects of the Plains environment:

the land, the wildlife, the peoples, and the cultures. Put those words together just right—exploration-plains-land-wildlife-peoples-cultures—and you can see why the scholars searching for a project to give their Center an identity felt a new edition of Lewis and Clark should come from Lincoln. The acting director of the Center, Paul Olson, and the Center's board of directors happily accepted responsibility for overseeing development of the project.

Don Jackson had just retired and did not feel that he was in a position to undertake editing the journals himself, but he did agree to serve as a consultant for the project and immediately began to lay some essential groundwork. The first step was to identify all of the institutions holding materials relevant to a new edition and the second was to determine what level of cooperation they were willing to extend to the project. Jackson also wrote the first draft of the successful grant application to the National Endowment for the Humanities for support of the research aspect of the project.

Now that there was a publisher committed to publishing the results, and an institution willing to support a scholar while the editing was completed, it was at last time to find a scholar willing to devote what would essentially be an academic lifetime to editing Lewis and Clark. Gary Moulton was hired as editor of the new edition in July 1979, two years and one month after Gilbert first read Stadler's essay. Tom Dunlay was hired as assistant editor soon after, and the two men, along with a number of associates and consultants, immediately began work on the first volume of the new edition, the *Atlas of the Lewis & Clark Expedition.*

The decision to begin the new edition of the journals with the *Atlas* was unanimous. Everyone involved in the project agreed that Thwaites's atlas was the part of his edition most in need of revision. Thwaites had published fifty-three maps, but he made no concerted effort either to annotate or to evaluate those maps. The editorial apparatus he offered was cursory at best, and at worst wrong. He misidentified a number of the maps and omitted or overlooked others. In addition, more Lewis and Clark maps had been discovered or identified since Thwaites had gone to press in 1905. All in all, there were fifty-two "new" maps waiting to be published, forty-two of them for the first time.

There was a second unanimous sentiment: everyone agreed from the beginning that they wanted the finest facsimile-size reproductions that care and attention could produce. They wanted the reader to be able to envision each and every contour of the land just as Clark had mapped it, and to be able to enjoy each and every handwritten caption, like the one Bartlett pointed out on map fifty-eight: "6 men killed a brown bear which was near catching several of them."

To get that kind of quality a printer must shoot production negatives directly from the original documents. Reproducing only reproductions will yield nothing better than secondhand quality; therefore, a critical component of the success of this project would be printer access to the original maps.

The time frame was extremely important at this point. By the spring of 1982 we had two deadlines in our sights, and we knew that meeting the first would determine whether or not we could meet the second. The first deadline involved the Joslyn Art Museum, which held thirty-four of the original documents we wanted in the *Atlas*. The museum agreed to let the maps out of their custody if they were returned by August tenth, the date the maps were scheduled to go on display (the documents were to remain on display through the end of the year). The second deadline arose because we wanted *very much* to have something to show for all of our talk about the journals in time for the annual meeting of the Lewis & Clark Foundation in April 1983. Our printer advised us that if we wanted books for the foundation meeting, then we had to have all the materials in his hands by November 1, 1982. This meant we had to get to those Joslyn maps before they went on display or we could not get the material to the printer in time for spring books. Well, we made the first deadline, but we could not make the second.

The press, it should be remembered, is a department within a publicly funded institution, or in essence a state agency. That meant we were required by law to solicit at least three bids on each of our printing jobs. To actually obtain the bids the press would send a requisition to the university's central purchasing office detailing all specifications for the job and request that the purchasing department solicit bids from specific printers. Purchasing would then shuffle some paper, advertise the job locally, and send the specifications to the out-of-state vendors we had suggested, wait at least thirty days, shuffle some more paper, and then eventually notify us of who had won the bid. We could not officially authorize any work on the project until that little dance was done.

We could not send the requisition to purchasing until we had prepared the composition specifications, and we could not prepare specifications until we had the manuscript in hand. The manuscript was scheduled to arrive during the last week of April 1982. If we were going to do all of the design work necessary to prepare composition specifications, go through the bidding process, have the maps photographed by the printer, and have them returned to the Joslyn before August tenth, then we would have to be prepared.

And we were. To be honest, we knew who the printer *had* to be at least a year before the manuscript arrived. Recall that Don Jackson began laying the groundwork some five years earlier, and Steve Cox had been building on that foundation ever since. For example, we knew from the beginning that the Library of Congress had two maps we needed, and we discovered very early that they would not allow a printer to remove those maps from their custody. They would provide photographs of the originals. The same was true with the National Archives and the four maps we needed from them. Finally there was the Missouri Historical Society with five originals; they would send photographs also.

On the other hand, there was the Library of the Boston Athenaeum, which agreed to ship the one original they had to our printer, subject to our obtaining adequate insurance. Joslyn, as I mentioned earlier, had agreed to lend us their thirty-four originals provided they were back for display by August tenth. Last, there was the Coe Collection at the Beinecke Rare Book Library at Yale University. The administration there said, "This project is so important that we'll let you take the eighty-one maps that you want out of our collection on one condition: they will go to Meriden Gravure in Meriden, Connecticut. Meriden is the only printer in the whole entire world to whom we will relinquish control of our documents." Eighty-one of an anticipated 128 maps gave Yale voting control of the stock in this project, and that is how we knew what the outcome of the bidding process had to be.

The manuscript arrived right on schedule, passing from Steve Cox's hands into the hands of our production department on April 24, 1983. Specifications were prepared, a requisition naming three carefully chosen printers went to purchasing (we felt certain that no local companies would bid on this one), and on July fourteenth purchasing notified us that Meriden had in fact won the bid. The maps from the Joslyn had already been shipped by air freight, heavily insured, to Meriden. Our production manager said good-bye to purchasing, dialed Meriden, and the staff there immediately began shooting. They were finished with the Joslyn maps on August 4, returning them in plenty of time for the display. The first deadline had been met.

Later in August, George Miles, the curator of the Western Americana collection at the Beinecke, began to hand-carry the maps from his collection over to Meriden in thirds. That way if disaster struck away from home, they would still have two-thirds of their collection intact. Disaster did not strike, and everything went smoothly. Meriden completed their work on the Yale maps by the end of October, and a single map from the Boston Athenaeum posed no problem.

However, there was still the matter of those three institutions which insisted on providing reproductions rather than the originals. John Peckham, president of Meriden, had provided detailed written instructions in May on preparation of the continuous tone negatives and prints essential to achieve the quality we wanted. Steve Cox had been in contact with individuals at each of the three institutions since the late 1970s, talking with them at length to clarify not only production standards but editorial standards as well. In other words, "Here's the quality we need, and here's why we need it."

The requisition for the maps from the Library of Congress was sent to our purchasing office on June 28, and the requisition for the National Archives maps on June 30. We ordered the maps from the Missouri Historical Society on August 2. There followed a long period of letters, phone messages, and memos.

Each and every one of the reproductions had to be returned for reshooting because not one of the institutions used the techniques or the materials that we had requested. In at least one instance, the reproduction had be to returned twice. The upshot was that the last reproduction was not sent to Meriden until January 24, 1983, seven months after it was ordered. Needless to say, the November 1 deadline had been missed and the Lewis and Clark meeting happened without the *Atlas*.

The first batch of finished books arrived on June 29, 1983. Each one of the atlases weighs 8.5 pounds, fairly begging for comparison with an overdue baby, and I understand it was difficult to tell who was acting more like the expectant father— Gilbert or Cox. But at long last the *Atlas of the Lewis & Clark Expedition* was a reality. Only eight more volumes to go!

I would like to note one thing for future researchers. I think it would be interesting to know just how much money the insurance companies realized as we shipped the original Lewis and Clark maps around the country. It would be no small amount of change, I am sure.

13. Keeping It in Perspective: Getting Exploration History into State and Local Journals

by William L. Lang

As explorers probe the less known or the truly unknown, they travel through profoundly unfamiliar worlds. Their explorations are never born without lineages. They are the offspring of earlier ventures, and exploration is never conducted in an intellectual vacuum. Explorers venture out with their heads filled with assumptions, expectations, and all that comprises their cultural milieu, from the climate of opinion to the status of scientific knowledge, so the study of exploration is, as William Goetzmann has recently called it, also an investigation of an "intellectual landscape."

That phrase includes two critical points of reference in exploration history—ideas and the age they dominate, and territory and the space it fills or time and space, the two essential components of perspective. Goetzmann's phrase is also a good place to begin talking about publishing exploration history in local journals and delineating why perspective, with all its meanings, is such a key ingredient.

Let's begin with landscape. During the first decades of this century, when *Oregon Historical Quarterly, Washington Historical Quarterly,* or *Contributions to the Montana Historical Society* published Northwest exploration history, usually from diaries, journals, and letters, their readers could still look out on a land that had been lightly disturbed. Dams had not changed the look of the Columbia River and interstate highways had not flattened mountains, spanned canyons, or straightened curves on the landscape, taking us away from historical travel routes. Before those "improvements" to the landscape, geographical references meant more. We could still watch salmon leap and Indian fishermen net them on the Columbia; outside Helena, Montana, we still had three switchbacked mountain roads to carry us over the Continental Divide.

194

With these changes in mind, authors writing exploration history should take care to describe the landscape. Beyond orientation, these descriptions give readers some sense of the difficulties explorers faced and some means to measure their achievements. More than that, accurate portrayals of geography convey a sense of immediacy that melds the truth of our everyday observations of the landscape with the actions of explorers a century or more earlier.

John Logan Allen's brilliant essay on Lewis and Clark's critical decision at the Marias is a good example of an article that succeeds in giving readers geographical perspective.[1] After outlining the captains' sense of geography, including the historical basis for their preconceptions and misconceptions, Allen carefully gives the lay of the land at the junction of the Marias and Missouri rivers. His description of the surrounding mountain ranges, the shape of the riverbanks, and the look of the land substantially enhanced his interpretation of the captains' achievement. The perspective he provides in carefully drawn geographical descriptions underscores the importance of the event, which is one of the most dramatic sequences in the expedition's history.

Today's highway runs near the junction of the Marias and Missouri, but you cannot see the confluence from the road and few people bother to hike to the location. It is just out there somewhere on the land. As with road signs that direct motorists' attention to some general landscape with a legend, such as: "Indians and U.S. Cavalry clashed *near* here on...," nonspecific or minimal geographical descriptions leave readers to create an imaginary landscape or superimpose a celluloid image of Indian-white warfare on the farmer's field in front of their windshield. The perspective is lost and the point the author is trying to make is also often diminished or lost.

Nothing graphically enhances perspective in exploration history better than cartography. Although authors writing exploration history work directly with maps and know their importance, they often forget to link their text to maps. They forget what an enormous gap there is between the reader's understanding of geographic relationships and the reality of the nineteenth- or eighteenth-century West. Following the peregrinations of one of the fur trappers, for example, can be next to impossible *without* a modern topographical map in hand. Thinking in cartographic terms and describing events and sequences with map graphics in mind can keep readers in step with Jim Bridger or Osborne Russell as they charted the Rockies.

In period maps—one of our basic sources—there is another dimension of historical perspective that needs mention in this discussion. As the magnificent atlas volume of the new edition of the *Journals of the Lewis & Clark Expedition* demonstrates, maps are documents that orient us in time as well as space. How much did the explorers know? How much did they see? And how accurately did they see it? These questions and their answers are part of broader inquiries about how we know the details of exploration history.

The principal sources of exploration history—journals, diaries, fragments of autobiographies—offer another kind of perspective. Short of dropping into an abyss of antiquarian detail, authors should include the provenance for exploration history documents. It is hard to think of a better proof of the importance of provenance than Donald Jackson's editing of the *Letters of the Lewis and Clark Expedition,* but in journal literature Ray Wood and Gary Moulton's article on the Maximilian maps comes to mind as an excellent example of this same concern for documents.[2]

The story of Maximilian's maps and their derivation from William Clark's maps of the Missouri and Yellowstone rivers is fascinating documentary history, but in the authors' hands it becomes an expanded history of *our* understanding of this portion of the Lewis and Clark Expedition. Wood and Moulton also keep readers in touch with modern place names and locations. This article is specifically about a group of documents, but the authors' careful delineation of the relationships between our knowledge of exploration, the sources of that knowledge, and what it can tell us about the nature of exploration point up how important these relationships are in understanding the total context of exploration history.

Part of that total context is the intellectual part of Goetzmann's intellectual landscape. As Thomas Kuhn and Daniel

Boorstin have brilliantly reminded us, the discoveries that have been made over the centuries were made within a circumscribed world of understanding. The expectations of Humboldt, Darwin, or Meriwether Lewis were nurtured, and the surprise of discovery was at least as much in looking and finding something beyond their circle of ideas as the content of the discovery itself.

In exploration history the connections in ideas are often reflected in the connections between people. Context is served when authors include the "begats" of those connections in their descriptions and explanations of exploration history because this colors in the full portrait of exploration and draws the lines that connect discovery in the Northwest with people and ideas quite remote from the region. It underscores the truth that the history of exploration and discovery is *never* just local or even regional history. Readers of state and local journals need to know that.

A good example of an article that traces out those connections in exploration history is Jim Ronda's description and interpretation of the beginnings of the Astorian enterprise.[3] By tracing the intellectual and economic links between key personalities in the development of the great Astorian gamble, Ronda parts the veil for readers and lets them look in on the development of an idea that resulted in exploration, settlement, and international political conflicts. As isolated as Astoria might seem to today's tourists—and surely as it must have seemed to its inhabitants in 1813—its history is directly connected to the world. Without that perspective of time—the incubation and development of an idea—the accomplishment of enterprise in an unknown and remote place loses its impact. Ronda's attention to perspective enhanced that slice of exploration history.

In our desire to get the most accurate and detailed articles on exploration history in our state and local journals, if we pay a bit of extra attention to keeping perspective—time, ideas, spaces, personalities, and the land—our readers will learn more and we will better serve the muse.

Chapter 13 Notes

1. John Logan Allen, "Lewis and Clark on the Upper Missouri: Decision at the Marias," *Montana, the Magazine of Western History* 21 (Summer 1971).

2. W. Raymond Wood and Gary E. Moulton, "Prince Maximilian and New Maps of the Missouri and Yellowstone Rivers by William Clark," *Western Historical Quarterly* 12 (October 1981): 372–86.

3. James P. Ronda, "Astoria and the Birth of Empire," *Montana, the Magazine of Western History* 36 (Summer 1986): 22–35.

14. On the Trail of Lewis and Clark Today

by Robert Carriker

In January 1985 the National Endowment for the Humanities included on its roster of forthcoming Summer Seminars for School Teachers a month-long course entitled, "The Search for Knowledge in Nineteenth-Century America: Elliott Coues's *History of the Expedition Under the Command of Lewis and Clark.*" As the director of that seminar I received many letters of inquiry. One especially memorable response came from a teacher in western Massachusetts who challenged me to believe that he was blood relative not only of Meriwether Lewis and William Clark but Sacajawea as well, and, further, that he owned twin buffaloes whose names memorialized you-know-who.

Assuredly, the clever teacher who created such a novel, attention-getting device overstated his credentials. Perhaps it was instinct, perhaps it was experience, but in either case it did not take this teacher very long to conclude that inasmuch as there were only fifteen seats in the seminar, something beyond the ordinary letter of application would be required. Indeed, 228 persons ultimately applied for the seminar. The large number of applications, I believe, had less to do with the academic reputation of the director, or even with the fact that the National Endowment for the Humanities would subsidize each participant, than it did with the popularity of the subject matter. There simply were large numbers of teachers from every state in the union who had a great interest in, but very little real knowledge of, the Lewis and Clark Expedition. American history textbooks normally limit their coverage of Lewis and Clark to one paragraph or less, yet the interest of teachers would have had them fill several volumes.

Since that first seminar in 1985 it has been my pleasure to direct two additional NEH Summer Seminars on the Lewis and Clark Expedition. In 1987, and again in 1991, groups of fifteen professional educators traveled to the Gonzaga University

199

campus in Spokane, Washington, seeking the opportunity to study the lives and legacies of "The Captains" by using a common text in an academic environment.

The NEH Summer Seminars for School Teachers (SSST) originated in 1983 as a response to the growing national concern about the academic energy of America's front line of teachers. Impressed with the results of the Summer Seminars for College Teachers (SSCT) program that had begun a decade earlier, William Bennett, the chairman of the NEH, ordered his staff to create a program that would at once reward the best elementary and secondary teachers in the nation, encourage others to imitate their excellence, and, in a direct way, intellectually recharge the batteries of school personnel. The result was the SSST program.

Fifteen seminars were offered in 1983 for 226 teachers. The immediate and positive response encouraged the NEH to boost the number of seminars to fifty or more beginning the next year. As a result, at the conclusion of its tenth year of operation in 1992, more than 7,600 American teachers had participated in 511 seminars. Selection is competitive, and successful applicants each receive a stipend ranging from $2,450 to $3,200 depending on the length of the four-, five-, or six-week seminars. In short, the SSST program recruits the best teachers in America and entices them back to a college campus for study with like-minded individuals and a university professor in a field of common interest in the humanities. The SSST has been called the most successful program for teachers ever devised by a bureaucratic agency—a left-handed, but well-intentioned compliment.

As early as the 1960s the United States Department of Education began to sponsor Summer Institutes for elementary and secondary teachers, and the NEH does so now, too. Summer Seminars, however, are unlike other programs in at least one very important way. SSST programs stress the pure joy of learning. No college credit is given; the incentive is merely to profit from an intense, systematic, and thorough study of one or more important texts in the humanities. The text may be *The Canterbury Tales, Beowulf,* or works by John Locke, James Fenimore Cooper, or Thoreau. There are no limits except that each seminal work selected as the core reading for the seminar must be thought provoking. Within the scope of each seminar there is time for reading, writing, and formal and informal discussion, but, unlike Summer Institutes, there is no allotment of time for curricula planning or other pedagogical concerns. Summer Institutes affect the institution; Summer Seminars influence the seminarian. Because of this distinction, teachers of all disciplines, not merely those whose teaching assignments fall within the content limits of the subject matter, are eligible and welcome to the SSST program. Thus, when I offered an SSST centering on Elliott Coues's *History of the Expedition Under the Command of Lewis and Clark*, participants included persons from the disciplines of American and European history, English literature and grammar, trades and industry, biology, chemistry, psychology, art, and religion.

In the three summers the Lewis and Clark SSST has been offered at Gonzaga University, it has become the most oversubscribed seminar in the program. More than 1,100 teachers have inquired about the subject matter of the seminar, of whom 579 subsequently applied, a return rate of fifty percent, whereas the overall figure for the entire program is less than fifteen percent. Why is the subject matter of this seminar so compelling to teachers? The answer, I think, lies in a statement once made by the late Donald Jackson, editor and author of three important works on Lewis and Clark. Every generation, Jackson decided, discovers Lewis and Clark for itself, and each generation thinks it is the first to do so. Certainly that is true of the current generation that will live to see the bicentennial celebration of the Corps of Northwest Discovery in the year 2005.

The study of western exploration history in general, and the Lewis and Clark Expedition in particular, is alive and well as both a vicarious adventure and a scholarly pursuit. The Lewis and Clark Trail Heritage Foundation, an organization of so-called "buffs" interested in the exploits of the Corps of Northwest Discovery, now has some 1,500 members, more than belong to the Western History Association. Expertly guided tour groups take to the trail in increasing numbers every summer, some sponsored by university alumni groups, and others organized by individual professors. The Smithsonian Institution offered Lewis and Clark oriented horseback trips into the mountains of Idaho several times in recent years, but eventually their commercial enterprise yielded to the luxury accommodations of the cruise ships. Sven-Olof Lindblad's Special Expeditions of New York City and two Portland-based outfitters now annually book some 4,000 passengers on six-day Columbia and Snake river cruises entitled, "In the Wake of Lewis and Clark." Individual travelers are also exploring the captains' route in increasing numbers, casually visiting some of the eighty nationally registered historical sites associated with the expedition. Many travelers are assisted by two helpful guide books, Dayton Duncan's *Out West* (1987) and Gerald Olmsted's *Fielding's Lewis & Clark Trail* (1986). Another book, David Lavender's recent best-seller, *The Way to the Western Sea: Lewis and Clark Across the Continent* (1988), is so energetically written it allows armchair adventurers to feel the uneven, dusty trail beneath their feet and the sting of salty ocean spray in their faces without ever leaving home! The choices are many.

Meanwhile, on the academic side, new volumes probing various aspects of the Lewis and Clark Expedition, some quirky and entertaining, others insightful and thoughtful, continue to be written and read. Two examples will suffice. James Ronda's literate and perceptive volume *Lewis and Clark Among the Indians* has not only changed forever the way Lewis and Clark's expedition will be perceived in classrooms across the country, it has sold nearly 15,000 copies since its publication in 1984. Secondly, it is significant that all seven of the text volumes prepared thus far by Gary Moulton in his new edition of *The Journals of the Lewis & Clark Expedition* (1983–) have sold out and been reprinted at least once, even though the University of Nebraska Press has increased the press run from 1,500 copies for the early volumes to 2,500 copies. Clearly, Lewis and Clark is an "in" subject, a "hot ticket," and elementary and secondary teachers, with their enthusiasm for academic settings, are part of the phenomena.

The NEH SSST on Lewis and Clark lasts for four weeks, and in that time the participants complete three assignments. First of all, everyone reads all 1,364 pages of Elliott Coues's *History of the Expedition Under the Command of Lewis and Clark.* This narrative of the Lewis and Clark expedition was prepared by Nicholas Biddle and Paul Allen and first published in 1814. In 1893 Coues edited the Biddle/Allen volumes, more than doubling the size of the narrative in the process. Coues's edition serves the seminar as the common text from which discussion arises. In that capacity, it is at once a very wise choice for a seminar, and a very poor choice. The dominant feature of Coues's edition is that he has extensive footnotes in the areas of botany, zoology, ethnology, geology, and linguistics, precisely the areas in which Lewis and Clark wrote so voluminously in their journals. On the other hand, in many instances his footnotes are a fount of misinformation. But even that limiting factor has value for a seminar. Participants learn early on that Coues's volumes are not a substitute for the "real thing," the original journals of Lewis and Clark, and so no discussion of an event is considered complete until both editions of the original journals, those by Ruben Gold Thwaites (1904) and Gary Moulton, are researched. In addition, many of the topics brought up for discussion can be referred to the hundreds of authoritative books and articles authored about the expedition over the past fifty years in the fields of natural history, cartography, and cultural relationships. The goal of the seminar is not merely to retrace the trail through Coues's eyes, but also to open to participants new ways to evaluate the accomplishments of the most enlightened explorers to thus far penetrate the farthest northwest quadrant of the trans-Mississippi West.

A second requirement of the seminar is that every participant must annotate one or more maps dealing with the route of the expedition. Some choose a modern-day highway map on which to follow the progress of the Corps of Discovery. Another option is to laminate a copy of William Clark's 1810 "Map of Lewis and Clark" (one comes with each set of the Coues volumes), and then make their own adjustments on Clark's imaginary geography, a vision of the West that remained standard on American maps for thirty years after its drafting. A third possibility is to annotate a unique, poster-sized map of the Columbia River as it was at the time of Lewis and Clark. This is a special map that was prepared for the seminar by a Gonzaga graduate who is now a cartographer with the Central Intelligence Agency.

Finally, there is the requirement most eagerly looked forward to, and later best remembered by all participants, the field trip on the Lolo Trail. After two and one-half weeks of book work in the classroom, the seminar eagerly takes to the trail. Because of its importance to the expedition and its remoteness to the average traveler (and the exotic sound of its name!), SSST seminars go to the Lolo Trail in the Bitterroot Mountains of Idaho. Participants spend their first night in Missoula, Montana, and the following morning drive over the Lolo Pass on U.S. Highway 12. At the Powell Ranger Station the paved roadway is left behind and the vans head straight up Parachute Hill, a seemingly perpendicular incline, on Forest Service roads. When the crest is reached it is possible to follow the ancient Nez Perce pathway commonly called the Lolo Trail for ninety-nine miles. Because at least half of the participants in any given seminar turn out to be novice hikers and/or virgin campers, it is prudent to transport everyone in two fifteen-passenger vans. Moreover, as a federally supported program the field exercise should not be of such a nature as to limit access by handicapped persons.

In the course of a journey along rain-rutted and rock-pitted Forest Service Road 500, the Lolo Motorway constructed a half-century earlier by the Works Progress Administration, it is possible to visit thirteen certified Lewis and Clark sites. Several of the sites are only a few yards from the roadway, but the majority require a hike varying in distance from several hundred yards to several miles. Everyone is invited to experience at least one hike in the ruts of a trail blazed by the Nez Perce and followed by Lewis and Clark, and, in three days in the mountains, I estimate that those who take full advantage of the opportunities accomplish about twenty-five miles of walking in moderate to rugged terrain. The two most popular hikes involve a climb to the summit of Spirit Revival Ridge, for a wondrous view of distant prairies, and a stroll through the bear grass between the Smoking Place and the Sinque Hole.

During the course of three trips to the Lolo Trail, the seminar has had its share of awkward occasions, both on the road and in the office of rental car companies. Not surprisingly, the company from which the vans were rented the first year would not agree to cooperate the second year, and the same disapproval took place the third year from the second company, so ultimately Gonzaga University motor pool vans, unreliable as they can be, were pressed into service in 1991. In fairness to the rental agencies it should be noted that Forest Service Road 500 can exhaust even the best-maintained vehicles.

Sharp rocks shredded a tire on one van, and the elevation of the road, reaching 7,000 feet at one point, strained the capacity of another vehicle's radiator. In 1985 the weather was hot and exceedingly dry, with the result that powdery dust overwhelmed the engine filter on a van and choked the carburetor to the point where it simply "died." Mercifully, the demise of the van occurred on U.S. Highway 12, shortly after coming down from the mountains. In 1987 neither heat nor dust posed a problem, but snow and ice did. On July 18, in mid-afternoon, the seminar was vexed by a freak blizzard that covered the ground with hail, coated windshields with ice, and sent everyone scurrying for cover. Reluctantly, the seminar had to abandon the high ground—Lewis and Clark called such a maneuver a "retrograde march"—lest first-time campers perish from the cold. Through the intercession of our guide and companion, Duane Annis of the Clearwater National Forest, we took refuge in some firefighter cabins located on the banks of the Lochsa River. In the morning the vans once again ascended the road to the top of the mountain, and we resumed our journey.

During each one of the three field trips one or more persons—all of them men—managed to get lost. Teachers seem to revert to student-type conduct when they join a seminar of their peers, and in each group there were two types of high-risk hikers: those who wanted to march on ahead of everyone else, oblivious of the fact that they did not know where they were going, and those who hung to the rear, ostensibly to snap one of those once-in-a-lifetime photos without interference by the group as a whole. One group of five teachers once took a shortcut that turned out to be a five hour "lost-cut."

Elementary and secondary teachers in American schools are bullish on Lewis and Clark and have been for some time. The present NEH-sponsored seminar and a similarly structured course offered by Carlos Schwantes and Steve Brunsfeld at the University of Idaho, are, in fact, third generation offspring of courses developed by other professors. Professor John Caylor of Boise State University offered a Lewis and Clark course for his students in the 1970s for several years prior to his death. Professors Steven Ambrose of the University of New Orleans (with a special interest in the Lolo Trail), Stephen Dow Beckham of Lewis and Clark College in Portland (with a special interest in the Columbia River), and Harry Fritz of the University of Montana (with a special interest in the Missouri River Wild and Scenic Waterway) followed his lead. Professor Schwantes and I, in turn, have followed their trail.

The response with which students and teachers have accepted the current Lewis and Clark courses at Gonzaga University and the University of Idaho is, I think, clear evidence of both the enduring quality of the subject matter and the unflagging interest in it by educators. And the future looks good as we begin the countdown for the bicentennial of the Corps of Northwest Discovery. If scholars continue to produce invigorating inquiries into the exploration of the American West and Lewis and Clark, then the programs at Gonzaga University and the University of Idaho will continue to find creative ways to bring those ideas to the attention of the elementary and secondary teachers, and ultimately the students, of this nation.

Suggestions for Further Reading

"The Adventures of Alexander Ross in the Snake Country," *Idaho Yesterdays* 14 (Spring 1970): 8–15.

Allen, John Logan. *Passage through the Garden: Lewis and Clark and the Image of the American Northwest.* Urbana: University of Illinois Press, 1975.

Anderson, Bern. *Surveyor of the Sea: The Life and Voyages of Captain George Vancouver.* Seattle: University of Washington Press, 1960.

Andreyev, A. I. *Russian Discoveries in the Pacific and in North America in the Eighteenth and Nineteenth Centuries,* Carl Ginsberg, trans. Ann Arbor: J. W. Edwards, 1952.

[Appleman, Roy E.] *Lewis and Clark: Historic Places Associated with their Transcontinental Exploration (1804–06).* Washington, D.C.: Department of the Interior, 1975.

Bakeless, John. *Lewis and Clark: Partners in Discovery.* New York: William Morrow, 1947.

Barkan, Frances B., ed. *The Wilkes Expedition: Puget Sound and the Oregon Country.* Olympia: Washington State Capital Museum, 1987.

Bartlett, Richard A. *Great Surveys of the American West.* Norman: University of Oklahoma Press, 1962.

Beaglehole, J. C. *The Life of Captain James Cook.* Stanford: Stanford University Press, 1974.

——, ed. *The Journals of Captain James Cook on his Voyages of Discovery,* 5 vols. in 4. Cambridge: Published for the Hakluyt Society at the University Press, 1955–74.

Beals, Herbert K., ed. and trans. *For Honor and Country: The Diary of Bruno de Hezeta.* Portland: The Press of the Oregon Historical Society, 1985.

——, ed. and trans. *Juan Perez on the Northwest Coast: Six Documents of His Expedition in 1774.* Portland: Oregon Historical Society Press, 1989.

Boorstin, Daniel J. *The Discoverers.* New York: Random House, 1983.

Broughton, William Robert. *A Voyage of Discovery to the North Pacific Ocean.* New York: De Capo Press, 1967, repr. of 1804 ed.

Caruthers, J. Wade. "The Sea-Bourne Frontier on the Northwest Coast, 1778–1850," *Journal of the West* 10 (April 1971): 211–52.

Chittenden, Hiram Martin. *The American Fur Trade of the Far West,* 2 vols. Lincoln: University of Nebraska Press, 1986, repr. of 1935 ed.

Chuinard, Eldon G. *Only One Man Died: Medical Aspects of the Lewis and Clark Expedition.* Glendale: Arthur H. Clark Co., 1979.

207

Clark, Malcolm, Jr. *Eden Seekers: The Settlement of Oregon, 1818–1862.* Boston: Houghton Mifflin, 1981.

Clark, Charles G. *The Men of the Lewis and Clark Expedition.* Glendale: Arthur H. Clark Co., 1970.

Cline, Gloria Griffen. *Peter Skene Ogden and the Hudson's Bay Company.* Norman: University of Oklahoma Press, 1974.

Cole, Douglas. *Captured Heritage: The Scramble for Northwest Coast Artifacts.* Seattle: University of Washington Press, 1985.

Cole, Jean Murray. *Exile in the Wilderness: The Biography of Chief Factor Archibald McDonald, 1790–1853.* Seattle: University of Washington Press, 1979.

Conner, Daniel, and Lorraine Miller. *Master Mariner: Capt. James Cook and the Peoples of the Pacific.* Seattle: University of Washington Press, 1978.

Cook, Warren. *Flood Tide of Empire: Spain and the Pacific Northwest, 1543–1819.* New Haven: Yale University Press, 1973.

Coues, Elliott, ed. *New Light on the Early History of the Greater Northwest: The Manuscript Journals of Alexander Henry and David Thompson, 1799–1814,* 3 vols. New York: F. P. Harper, 1897.

Criswell, Elijah Harry. *Lewis and Clark: Linguistic Pioneers.* Columbia: University of Missouri Press, 1940.

Cutright, P. R. *Lewis and Clark, Pioneering Naturalists.* Urbana: University of Illinois Press, 1969.

———. *A History of the Lewis and Clark Journals.* Norman: University of Oklahoma Press, 1976.

Cutter, Donald C. *Malaspina and Galiano: Spanish Voyages to the Northwest Coast, 1791 and 1792.* Seattle: University of Washington Press, 1991.

Davies, K. G., ed. *Peter Skene Ogden's Snake Country Journal, 1826–27.* London: Hudson's Bay Record Society, 1961.

Dawson, Jan C. "Sacajawea: Pilot or Pioneer Mother," *Pacific Northwest Quarterly* 83 (January 1992): 22–28.

DeSmet, P. J. *Letters and Sketches with a Narrative of a Year's Residence Among the Indian Tribes of the Rocky Mountains.* 1843, repr. in Reuben Gold Thwaites, ed., *Early Western Travels,* vol. 27. Cleveland: A. H. Clark Co., 1906.

———. *Oregon Missions and Travels over the Rocky Mountains in 1845–46.* Fairfield: Ye Galleon Press, 1978, repr. of 1847 ed.

DeVoto, Bernard, *The Course of Empire.* Boston: Houghton Mifflin, 1952.

———, ed. *The Journals of Lewis and Clark.* Boston: Houghton Mifflin, 1953.

Dicken, Samuel N., and Emily F. Dicken. *The Making of Oregon: A Study in Historical Geography*. Portland: Oregon Historical Society, 1979.

Dillon, Richard. *Meriwether Lewis: A Biography*. New York: Coward-McCann, 1965.

Dixon, Captain George. *A Voyage Round the World*. London: Geo. Goulding, 1789.

Douglas, David. *Journal Kept by David Douglas During His Travels in North America, 1823–27....* London: W. Wesley, 1914.

Elliott, T. C., ed. "David Thompson's Journeys in Idaho," *Washington Historical Quarterly* 11 (April and July, 1920): 97–103, 163–73.

Engstrand, Iris H. W. *Spanish Scientists in the New World: The Eighteenth-Century Expeditions*. Seattle: University of Washington Press, 1981.

Exploration of the Northwest Coast. 19th Cong., 1st sess. H. Report 35. Washington, D.C. 1826.

Fisher, Raymond H. *Bering's Voyages: Whither and Why*. Seattle: University of Washington Press, 1977.

——. *The Russian Fur Trade, 1550–1700*. Berkeley: University of California Press, 1943.

Fisher, Robin. *Vancouver's Voyage: Charting the Northwest Coast*. Seattle: University of Washington Press, 1992.

——, and Hugh Johnson, eds. *Captain James Cook and His Times*. Seattle: University of Washington Press, 1979.

——, and J. M. Bumsted. *An Account of a Voyage to the Northwest Coast of America in 1785 & 1786 by Alexander Walker*. Seattle: University of Washington Press, 1982.

Franchère, Gabriel. *Narrative of a Voyage to the Northwest Coast of America in the Years 1811, 1812, 1813, and 1814 or the First American Settlement on the Pacific*, trans. and ed. by J. V. Huntington. 1854, repr. in Reuben Gold Thwaites, ed., *Early Western Travels*, vol. 6. Cleveland: A. H. Clark Co., 1904.

Galbraith, John S. *The Hudson's Bay Company as an Imperial Factor, 1821–1869*. Berkeley: University of California Press, 1957.

Gates, Charles M., ed. *Five Fur Traders of the Northwest; Being the Narrative of Peter Pond and the Diaries of John Macdonnell, Archibald N. McLeod, Hugh Faries, and Thomas Connor*. Minneapolis: Published for the Minnesota Historical Society by the University of Minnesota Press, 1933.

Gibson, James R. *Imperial Russia in Frontier America: The Changing Geography of Supply of Russian America, 1784–1867*. New York: Oxford University Press, 1976.

———. *Otter Skins, Boston Ships, and China Goods: The Maritime Fur Trade of the Northwest Coast, 1785–1841*. Seattle: University of Washington Press, 1992.

Glover, Richard, ed. *David Thompson's Narrative, 1784–1812*. Toronto: The Chaplain Society, 1962.

Goetzmann, William H. *New Lands, New Men: America and the Second Great Age of Discovery*. New York: Viking, 1986.

———. *Army Exploration in the American West, 1803–1863*. New Haven: Yale University Press, 1959.

———. *Exploration and Empire: The Explorer and Scientist in the Winning of the American West*. New York: Knopf, 1966.

Gough, Barry M. *Distant Dominion: Britain and the Northwest Coast of North America*. Vancouver: University of British Columbia Press, 1980.

———. "James Cook and the Origins of the Maritime Fur Trade," *American Neptune* (July 1978).

———. *The Northwest Coast: British Navigation, Trade, and Discoveries to 1812*. Vancouver: University of British Columbia Press, 1992.

———. "The Northwest Company's 'Adventure to China,'" *Oregon Historical Quarterly* 76 (December 1975): 309–31.

Griffin, Walter R. "George W. Goethals, Explorer of the Pacific Northwest, 1882–84," *Pacific Northwest Quarterly* 62 (October 1971): 129–41.

Gunther, Erna. *Indian Life on the Northwest Coast of North America as seen by the Early Explorers and Fur Traders During the Last Decades of the Eighteenth Century*. Chicago: University of Chicago Press, 1972.

Hafen, LeRoy R., ed. *The Mountain Men and the Fur Trade of the Far West; Biographical Sketches . . .* , 10 vols. Glendale: A. H. Clark Co., 1965–72.

Haines, Francis D., Jr. "Francois Payette, Master of Fort Boise," *Pacific Northwest Quarterly* 47 (April 1956): 57–61.

———. "The Relations of the Hudson's Bay Company with the American Fur Trader in the Pacific Northwest," *Pacific Northwest Quarterly* 40 (October 1949): 273–94.

Harmon, Daniel Williams. *A Journal of Voyages and Travels in the Interiors of North America*. Toronto: AMS Press, 1904.

Hawke, David F. *Those Tremendous Mountains: The Story of the Lewis and Clark Expedition*. New York: Norton, 1980.

Hayden, Willard C. "The Hayden Survey," *Idaho Yesterdays* 16 (Spring 1972): 20–25.

Hayes, Edmund, ed. *Log of the Union: John Boit's Remarkable Voyage to the Northwest Coast and Around the World, 1794–1796*. Portland: Oregon Historical Society, 1981.

Henry, John Frazier. *Early Maritime Artists of the Pacific Northwest Coast, 1741–1841*. Seattle: University of Washington Press, 1984.

Hopwood, Victor G., ed. *David Thompson: Travels in Western North America, 1784–1812*. Toronto: Macmillan of Canada, 1971.

Hough, Richard. *The Last Voyage of Captain James Cook*. New York: William Morrow, 1979.

Howay, Frederic W. *Voyages of the "Columbia" to the Northwest Coast, 1787–1790 & 1790–1793*. Portland: Oregon Historical Society Press, 1990.

Hussey, John A. *The History of Fort Vancouver and its Physical Structures*. Tacoma: Washington State Historical Society, 1957.

Irving, Washington. *The Adventures of Captain Bonneville, U.S.A., in the Rocky Mountains and the Far West*, Edgeley W. Todd, ed. Norman: University of Oklahoma Press, 1986, repr. of 1837 ed.

Jackson, Donald. *Among the Sleeping Giants: Occasional Pieces on Lewis and Clark*. Urbana: University of Illinois Press, 1987.

——, and Mary Lee Spence, eds. *The Expeditions of John Charles Frémont*, 3 vols. and map portfolio. Urbana: University of Illinois Press, 1970–84.

——, ed. *The Journals of Captain Nathaniel J. Wyeth's Expeditions to the Oregon Country, 1831–1836*. Fairfield: Ye Galleon Press, 1984.

——. "Ledyard and Laperouse: A Contrast in Northwestern Exploration," *Western Historical Quarterly* 9 (October 1978): 495–508.

——, ed. *Letters of the Lewis and Clark Expedition with Related Documents, 1783–1854*, 2d ed. Urbana: University of Illinois Press, 1978.

——. *Thomas Jefferson and the Stony Mountains: Exploring the West from Monticello*. Urbana: University of Illinois Press, 1981.

Jewitt, John R. *The Adventures and Sufferings of John R. Jewitt, Captive of Maquinna*, annotated and illustrated by Hilary Stewart. Seattle: University of Washington Press, 1987.

Kendrick, John, trans. *The Voyage of the* Sutil *and* Mexicana, *1792: The Last Spanish Exploration of the Northwest Coast of America*. Spokane: Arthur H. Clark, 1991.

Lamb, W. Kaye, ed. *The Journals and Letters of Sir Alexander Mackenzie*. Cambridge: The Hakluyt Society, 1970.

——, ed. *Simon Fraser: Letters and Journals, 1806–1808*. Toronto, Macmillan of Canada, 1960.

Lavender, David. *The Way to the Western Sea: Lewis and Clark Across the Continent*. New York: Harper & Row, 1988.

Lower, J. Arthur. *Ocean of Destiny: A Concise History of the North*

Pacific, 1500–1978. Vancouver: University of British Columbia Press, 1978.

Mackay, David. *In the Wake of Cook: Exploration, Science & Empire, 1780–1801*. London: Croom Helm, 1985.

Mackenzie, Alexander. *Voyages from Montreal on the River St. Lawrence, Through the Continent of North America, to the Frozen and Pacific Oceans; in the Years 1789 and 1793*. New York: Citadel Press, 1967, repr. of 1801 ed.

Meares, John. *Voyages Made in the Years 1788 and 1789, from China to the North West Coast of America*. London: Logographic Press, 1790.

Meinig, D. W. *The Great Columbia Plain: A Historical Geography, 1805–1910*. Seattle: University of Washington Press, 1968.

Merk, Frederick. "Snake Country Expedition, 1824–25: An Episode of Fur Trade and Empire," *Mississippi Valley Historical Review* 21 (June 1934): 49–62.

———, ed. *Fur Trade and Empire: George Simpson's Journal*, rev. ed. Cambridge: Harvard University Press, 1968.

Miller, David E. "Peter Skene Ogden's Trek into Utah, 1828–1829," *Pacific Northwest Quarterly* 51 (January 1960): 16–25,

Montgomery, Richard G. *White-Headed Eagle, John McLoughlin, Builder of an Empire*. New York: Macmillan, 1934.

Morgan, Dale L. *Jedediah Smith and the Opening of the West*. Lincoln: University of Nebraska Press, 1964, repr. of 1953 ed.

———. *The West of William Ashley; the International Struggle for the Fur Trade of the Missouri, the Rocky Mountains, and the Columbia, with Explorations beyond the Continental Divide, Recorded in the Diaries and Letters of William H. Ashley and his Contemporaries, 1822–1838*. Denver: Old West Publishing Co., 1964.

Morrison, Dorothy, and Jean Morrison. "John McLoughlin, Reluctant Fur Trader," *Oregon Historical Quarterly* 81 (Winter 1980): 377–89.

Moulton, Gary E., ed. *The Journals of the Lewis and Clark Expedition*, 8 vols. to date. Lincoln: University of Nebraska Press, 1983–.

———, ed. *Atlas of the Lewis and Clark Expedition*. Lincoln: University of Nebraska Press, 1983.

Moziño, José Mariano. *Noticias de Nutka: An Account of Nootka Sound in 1792*, trans. and ed. by Iris Higbie Wilson. Seattle: University of Washington Press, 1970.

Mullan, John. *Report of Lieutenant Mullan, in charge of the Construction of the Military Road from Fort Benton to Fort Walla-Walla*. 36th Cong., 2d sess. H. Ex. Doc. 44. Washington, D.C., 1863.

Munford, James Kenneth. *John Ledyard's Journal of Captain Cook's Last Voyage*. Corvallis, Oregon State University, 1963.

Murray, Keith A. "The Rule of the Hudson's Bay Company in Pacific Northwest History," *Pacific Northwest Quarterly* 31 (January 1961): 24–31.

Nielsen, Jean C. "Donald McKenzie in the Snake Country Fur Trade, 1816–1821," *Pacific Northwest Quarterly* 31 (April 1940): 161–80.

Nokes, J. Richard. *Columbia's River: The Voyages of Robert Gray, 1787–1793*. Tacoma: Washington State Historical Society, 1991.

Norris, John. "The Strait of Anian and British Northwest America: Cook's Third Voyage in Perspective," *B. C. Studies* 36 (Winter 1977–78): 3–22.

Northwest Coast of America. Second Report. 19th Cong., 1st sess. H. Report 213. Washington, D.C., 1826.

Oglesby, Richard Edward. *Manuel Lisa and the Opening of the Missouri Fur Trade*. Norman: University of Oklahoma Press, 1963.

Parker, Samuel. *Journal of an Exploring Tour Beyond the Rocky Mountains*. Minneapolis: Ross & Haines, 1967, repr. of 1838 ed.

Pearsall, Marion. "Contributions of Early Explorers and Traders to the Ethnography of the Northwest," *Pacific Northwest Quarterly* 40 (October 1949): 316–26.

Peebles, John J. "On the Lolo Trail: Route and Campsites of Lewis and Clark," *Idaho Yesterdays* 9 (Winter 1965–66): 2–15.

———. "The Return of Lewis and Clark," *Idaho Yesterdays* 10 (Summer 1966): 16–27.

———. "Rugged Waters: Trails and Campsites of Lewis and Clark in the Salmon River Country," *Idaho Yesterdays* 8 (Summer 1964): 2–17.

Pethick, Derek. *First Approaches to the Northwest Coast*. Vancouver: J. J. Douglas, 1976.

———. *The Nootka Connection: Europe and the Northwest Coast, 1790–1795*. Vancouver: Douglas and McIntyre, 1980.

Porter, Kenneth W. *John Jacob Astor, Business Man*, 2 vols. Cambridge: Harvard University Press, 1931.

Pumpelly, Raphael. *Northern Transcontinental Survey: First Annual Report of Raphael Pumpelly, Director of the Survey, September, 1882*. New York, 1882.

Rees, John. "The Shoshoni Contribution to Lewis and Clark," *Idaho Yesterdays* 2 (Summer 1958): 2–13.

Rich, E. E. *The History of the Hudson's Bay Company, 1670–1870*, 2 vols. London: Hudson's Bay Record Society, 1958–59.

———, ed., assisted by A. N. Johnson. *Peter Skene Ogden's Snake Country Journals, 1824 and 1825–26*. London: Publications of the Hudson's Bay Record Society, 1950.

Richards, Kent D. *Isaac I. Stevens: Young Man in a Hurry*. Provo: Brigham Young University Press, 1979.

Rolle, Andrew. *John Charles Frémont: Character as Destiny*. Norman: University of Oklahoma Press, 1991.

Ronda, James P. *The Exploration of North America*. Washington, D.C.: American Historical Association, 1992.

——. *Lewis and Clark among the Indians*. Lincoln: University of Nebraska Press, 1984.

——. *Astoria and Empire*. Lincoln: University of Nebraska Press, 1990.

Ross, Alexander. *Adventures of the First Settlers on the Oregon or Columbia River, 1810–1813*. Lincoln: University of Nebraska Press, 1986, repr. of 1849 ed.

Schafer, Joseph, ed. "Documents Relative to Warre and Vavasour's Military Reconnaissance in Oregon, 1845–46," *Oregon Historical Quarterly* 10 (March, 1909): 1–99.

Shane, Ralph M. "Early Explorers Through Warm Springs Reservation Area," *Oregon Historical Quarterly* 51 (December 1950): 273–309.

Smith, Barbara Sweetland, and Redmond J. Barnett. *Russian America: The Forgotten Frontier*. Tacoma: Washington State Historical Society, 1990.

Spaulding, Kenneth A., ed. *On the Oregon Trail: Robert Stuart's Journey of Discovery, 1812–1813*. Norman: University of Oklahoma Press, 1953.

Stanley, George F. G., ed. *Mapping the Frontier: Charles Wilson's Diary of the Survey of the 49th Parallel, 1858–1862, While Secretary of the British Boundary Commission*. Seattle: University of Washington Press, 1970.

Stanton, William. *The Great United States Exploring Expedition of 1838–1842*. Berkeley: University of California Press, 1975.

Steffen, Jerome O. *William Clark: Jeffersonian Man on the Frontier*. Norman: University of Oklahoma Press, 1977.

Stevens, Isaac I. *Report of Explorations for a Route for the Pacific Railroad near the Forty-seventh and Forty-ninth Parallels of North Latitude from St. Paul to Puget Sound*. Pacific Railroad Surveys, Vol I. 33d Cong., 2d sess. S. Ex. Doc. 78. Washington, D.C., 1860.

——. *Narrative and Final Report of Explorations . . . .* Pacific Railroad Surveys, Vol. XII. 36th Cong., 1st sess. S. Ex. Doc. 78. Washington, D.C., 1860.

Swagerty, William R. "Marriage and Settlement Patterns of Rocky Mountain Trappers and Traders," *Western Historical Quarterly* 11 (January 1980): 159–80.

Thompson, A. W. "New Light on Donald Mackenzie's Post on the Clearwater, 1812–1813," *Idaho Yesterdays* 18 (Fall 1974): 22–32.

Tikhmenev, P. A. *A History of the Russian-American Company*. Trans.

and ed. by Richard A. Pierce and Alton S. Donnelly. Seattle: University of Washington Press, 1978.

Tippett, Maria, and Douglas Cole. *From Desolation to Splendour: Changing Perceptions of the British Columbia Landscape*. Toronto/Vancouver: Clarke, Irwin & Co., 1977.

Townsend, John K. *Narrative of a Journey Across the Rocky Mountains, to the Columbia River, and a Visit to the Sandwich Islands, Chili, &c., with a Scientific Appendix*. Philadelphia, 1839. Repr. in Reuben Gold Thwaites, ed., *Early Western Travels*, vol. 21. Cleveland: A. H. Clark Co., 1905: 107–369.

Tyrrell, J. B., ed. *David Thompson's Narrative of His Explorations in Western America, 1784–1812*. Toronto: Champlain Society, 1962.

Vancouver, George. *A Voyage of Discovery to the North Pacific Ocean and Round the World*, 4 vols. W. Kaye Lamb, ed. London: The Hakluyt Society, 1984.

Van Orman, Richard A. *The Explorers: Nineteenth Century Expeditions in Africa and the American West*. Albuquerque: University of New Mexico Press, 1984.

Vaughan, Thomas. *Soft Gold: The Fur Trade and Cultural Exchange on the Northwest Coast of America*. Portland: Oregon Historical Society, 1982.

Villiers, Alan. *Captain James Cook*. New York: Charles Scribner's Sons, 1967.

Viola, Herman J. *Exploring the West*. Washington, D.C.: Smithsonian Books, 1987.

Walker, Alexander. *An Account of a Voyage to the Northwest Coast of America in 1785 and 1786 by Alexander Walker*. Robin Fisher and J. M. Bumsted, eds. Seattle: University of Washington Press, 1982.

Warre, Henry J. *Sketches in North America and the Oregon Territory*. Barre, Mass.: Imprint Society, 1970.

Wells, Merle W. "'A House for Trading': David Thompson on Pend d'Oreille Lake," *Idaho Yesterdays* 3 (Fall 1959): 22–26.

Wheat, Carl I. *Mapping the Transmississippi West*, 5 vols. San Francisco: Institute of Historical Cartography, 1957–63.

White, M. Catherine, ed. *David Thompson's Journals Relating to Montana and Adjacent Regions, 1808–1812*. Missoula: Montana State University Press, 1950.

Wilkes, Charles. *Narrative of the United States Exploring Expedition During the Years 1838, 1839, 1840, 1841, 1842*, 5 vols. Philadelphia: Lea and Blanchard, 1845.

———. *Western America, Including California and Oregon with Maps of those Regions and of the Sacramento Valley*. Philadelphia: Lee & Blanchard, 1849.

Williams, Glyndwr. *The British Search for the Northwest Passage in the Eighteenth Century*. London: Longman's, 1962.

Withey, Lynne. *Voyages of Discovery: Captain Cook and the Exploration of the Pacific*. New York: William Morrow, 1987.

Contributors

Richard Maxwell Brown was Beekman Professor of History at the University of Oregon. Among his best-known books are *Strain of Violence: Historical Studies of American Violence and Vigilantism* (1975) and *No Duty to Retreat: Violence and Values in American History and Society* (1991).

Robert Carriker, professor of history at Gonzaga University, has authored several studies of Native Americans in the American West and Pacific Northwest. He is currently writing a biography of the nineteenth-century missionary Pierre-Jean DeSmet.

Douglas Cole, a specialist in Canadian history, teaches at Simon Fraser University. Among his publications is *Captured Heritage: The Scramble for Northwest Coast Artifacts* (1985). He is now writing a biography of anthropologist Franz Boas.

Iris H. W. Engstrand, is professor of history at the University of San Diego. A specialist in Latin American history, she has written a number of books and articles including *Spanish Scientists in the New World: The Eighteenth-Century Expeditions* (1981).

William H. Goetzmann holds the Jack S. Blanton, Sr., Chair in History and American Studies at the University of Texas, Austin. He is the author of numerous books on the exploration of the American West, including *Exploration and Empire: The Explorer and the Scientist in the Winning of the American West* (1966), which won the Pulitzer Prize in history.

Stephen Haycox, professor of history at the University of Alaska, Anchorage, is a specialist in the history of Alaska. He writes a history column for the *Anchorage Times*, and among his publications is *A Warm Past: Travels in Alaska History* (1988).

Patricia Knapp, former acquisitions editor at the University of Nebraska Press, is now an attorney specializing in environmental law.

William L. Lang is former editor of *Montana, the Magazine of Western History* and co-author of *Montana: A History of Two Centuries* (1991). He is currently the director of the new Center for Columbia River History in Vancouver.

Gary E. Moulton, who has authored books on cartography and Native Americans of the Great Plains, is best known as the editor of a definitive new edition of the Lewis and Clark journals. He is also professor of history at the University of Nebraska.

David Nicandri is director of the Washington State Historical Society. He has long had an interest in the history of the Pacific Northwest, a field in which he published several books including *Northwest Chiefs: Gustav Sohon's View of the 1855 Stevens Treaty Councils* (1986). He is executive editor of *Columbia: The Magazine of Northwest History.*

Martin Ridge is Senior Research Associate at the Huntington Library. In addition to writing several books on the American West, he is the coauthor, with Ray Allen Billington, of the best-selling text *Westward Expansion: A History of the American Frontier* (1982).

James P. Ronda is the H. G. Bernard Professor of American History at the University of Tulsa. He holds a Ph.D. in Early American History from the University of Nebraska and he is best known for his extensive writing on the American West, including *Lewis and Clark Among the Indians* (1984) and *Astor and Empire* (1990).

Carlos A. Schwantes is professor of history at the University of Idaho and director of the Institute for Pacific Northwest Studies. He is the author of several books including *The Pacific Northwest: An Interpretive History* (1989).

Mary Lee Spence is professor emerita at the University of Illinois at Urbana-Champaign. A specialist in the history of the American West, she is currently working on a biography of Jessie Benton Frémont. With Donald Jackson she edited a multi-volume account of Frémont's expeditions (1970–84).

Index

Art and Artists. *See* Exploration, Art
Arteaga, Ignacio de, 11
Astor, John Jacob, 71, 82
Astorians. *See* Fur Trade, Astorians

Bancroft, Hubert Howe, 38, 43, 44
Banks, Joseph, 75, 81
Baranov, Aleksandr, 10
Barkley, Charles, 12
Benton, Thomas Hart, 17, 18, 117, 126
Bering, Vitus, 39, 42, 45
Boas, Franz, 31, 91–96 *passim*; 156–59
   passim
Bodega y Quadra, Juan Francisco de
   la, 11, 63, 65
Bodmer, Karl, 30, 178
Bonneville, Benjamin Louis Eulalie
   de, 17
Broughton, William, 5
Bureau of American Ethnology, 30,
   159

Cardero, José, 60, 65, 68
Carr, Emily, 89, 93, 94
Carver, Jonathan, 74, 75
Catesby, Mark, 176, 178
Catlin, George, 25, 30, 133, 178
China, 11, 12, 16, 77, 82
Chinook Jargon, 86–97 *passim*
Chirikov, Aleksei, 10
Church, Frederick Edwin, 181
Columbia River, 3, 5, 7, 14, 16, 75, 127
Cook, James, 9, 11, 12, 39, 58, 60, 74,
   81

Dall, W. H., 152
Dezhnev, Semen, 38, 39, 42, 44
Douglas, David, 90, 91, 94
Duncan, Johnson K., 143, 144

Echeverría y Godoy, Atanásio, 63, 65,
   68
Eells, Myron, 154
Exploration: anthropology, 37, 47,
   149–63 *passim*; art, 20, 30, 33, 60,
   61, 65, 123, 124, 133–48 *passim*, 181;
   cartography, 28, 30, 76, 77, 125;
   commerce, 11–12, 26, 28, 29; and

discovery, 165–88 *passim*; folklore,
   161, 162; imagination, 26, 28, 32, 80,
   170–73; language, 86, 87, 91, 151,
   160, 161; missionaries, 170–73;
   modern interest in, 3–7, 21,
   199–206 *passim*; moral questions,
   24–25; naming the land, 6, 7;
   national rivalries, 9–12, 13, 14, 83;
   naturalists, 175–76; science, 14, 20,
   27, 30, 58. *See also* Fur Trade; Native Americans; names of individual
   nations and explorers

Fort Hall, 18, 112, 114
Fort Vancouver, 119, 136, 144
Forty-Ninth Parallel Survey, 155
France, 168, 169, 171
Fraser, Simon, 83
Frémont, John C., 17, 18, 30, 112–29
   passim; personnnel of expeditions,
   122–23
Fur Trade, 11, 12, 14, 72, 133;
   Astorians, 16, 83; Hudson's Bay
   Company, 16, 17, 82, 90, 136, 143,
   150; North West Company of
   Montreal, 15, 16, 73, 76, 78, 82, 83

Gilpin, William, 114
Golder, F. A., 38, 40, 43
Gray, Robert, 5, 11, 13
Great Britain, 11, 13, 14, 15, 58
Great Reconnaissance, 9, 17, 20, 134

Hale, Horatio, 32, 91, 92, 150, 151, 156,
   157
Hayden, Ferdinand V., 18, 29, 155
Henry, Alexander, the Elder, 72, 75
Hezeta, Bruno de, 11
Horetzky, Charles, 88, 94
Hudson's Bay Company. *See* Fur
   Trade, Hudson's Bay Company
Humboldt, Alexander von, 167, 179

Jefferson, Thomas, 83, 103
Kamiakin, 140
Kane, Paul, 93, 134, 148
Kern, Edward, 123
King, Clarence, 18, 155, 181

219